Towards Independence

For Laura

Towards Independence

Essays on Scotland

Paul H. Scott

Polygon
EDINBURGH

© This collection Paul H. Scott 1991

Published by Polygon,
22 George Square,
Edinburgh.

Typeset in Linotron Sabon
by Koinonia Limited, Bury
Printed and bound by
Redwood Press Ltd,
Melksham, Wiltshire

British Library Cataloguing
   in Publication Data
Scott, Paul Henderson
   Towards Independence: essays on Scotland
   I. Title
   824.914

ISBN 0 7486 6104 2

Contents

Series Preface

CAIRNS CRAIG

Scotland's history is often presented as punctuated by disasters which overwhelm the nation, break its continuity and produce a fragmented culture. Many felt that 1979, and the failure of the Devolution Referendum, represented such a disaster: that the energetic culture of the 1960s and 1970s would wither into the silence of a political wasteland in which Scotland would be no more than a barely distinguishable province of the United Kingdom.

Instead, the 1980s proved to be one of the most productive and creative decades in Scotland this century – as though the energy that had failed to be harnessed by the politicians flowed into other channels. In literature, in thought, in history, creative and scholarly work went hand in hand to redraw the map of Scotland's past and realign the perspectives of its future.

In place of the few standard conceptions of Scotland's identity that had often been in the past the tokens of thought about the country's culture, a new and vigorous debate was opened up about the nature of Scottish experience, about the real social and economic structures of the nation, and about the ways in which the Scottish situation related to that of other similar cultures throughout the world.

It is from our determination to maintain a continuous forum for such debate that *Determinations* takes its title. The series will provide a context for sustained dialogue about culture and politics in Scotland, and about those international issues which directly affect Scottish experience.

Too often, in Scotland, a particular way of seeing our culture, of representing ourselves, has come to dominate our perceptions because it has gone unchallenged – worse, unexamined. The vitality of the culture should be measured by the intensity of debate which it generates rather than the security of ideas on which it rests. And should be measured by the extent to which creative, philosophical, theological, critical and political ideas confront each other.

If the determinations which shape our experience are to come from within rather than from without, they have to be explored and evaluated and acted upon. Each volume in this series will seek to be a contribution to that *self*-determination and each volume, we trust, will require a response, contributing in turn to the ongoing dynamic that is Scotland's culture.

Introduction

The papers collected in this volume are a selection of articles, essays, lectures, book reviews and the like which I have written during the last dozen or so years on one central theme, the condition of Scotland and its future potential. This is a matter which has concerned me for as long as I can remember. In his Introduction to the *Penguin Book of Scottish Verse* Tom Scott says: 'to MacDiarmid the English Ascendancy was a historical iniquity with no right but might behind it, and therefore to be overthrown by all good men and true'. I share that view. It seems to me that the denial of our right to control our own affairs has frustrated and distorted our national life and led to an enormous waste of human energy and ability. Not only Scotland, but the rest of Europe and the world at large are the poorer for it.

Since these papers have been written over more than a decade, they reflect different stages in an evolving process which I hope will soon lead to the recovery of our independence. I have corrected some printing errors and made some other minor changes, including some of the titles, but substantially I have left the texts as they first appeared. This inevitably means that there is some repetition which it is impossible to remove without the distortion of major surgery. The date of first publication appears with the title of each paper. They are not arranged in order of publication, but in accordance with the development of related ideas. I hope that this means that what follows can be read as a book, not as a collection of miscellaneous pieces.

I am grateful to the editors of *The Scotsman*, the *Glasgow Herald*, *Blackwood's Magazine*, *The Scots Magazine*, *Books in Scotland*, *Radical Scotland*, and *The Story of Scotland* for their permission to reprint articles which first appeared in their pages and to the Saltire Society for their permission to reprint the pamphlet *In Bed with an Elephant*.

Edinburgh   P. H. S.
March 1991

I

Autobiographical notes

Return to Scotland

(*Scottish Review*, May 1981)

I have never had any doubt that Scotland, and Edinburgh in particular, was where I wanted to live, even if I have had to spend my whole professional life in other places. It is not that I have disliked any of these other countries. I have enjoyed them all, especially France, Canada, Austria and Italy. But I have always come back to Scotland at least once a year and I have carried Scottish books, pictures and music with me everywhere. When I was asked where I was going to live when I retired – a common subject of conversation among diplomats, who are obligatorily nomadic and teased with the idea that they will eventually be able to decide this for themselves – I have never hesitated. Edinburgh, for me, was the self-evident answer. I see the charms of the Laurentians, Venice, Florence, the Tuscany hills, the Alps or the Mediterranean; but, I agree with Lewis Spence, Edinburgh dings them a'.

I do not suppose that this is something which needs any argument or justification. As David Murison argued persuasively in *The Scottish Review* No. 20, it is natural and proper for people to be drawn back to their place of origin. For him, it is Fraserburgh; for me, it is Edinburgh. We could put it down to an instinctive urge and leave it at that. Possibly that is the real reason and the explanations are only rationalisations, but I still have my explanations even so.

Sydney Smith, one of the founders of *The Edinburgh Review*, listed some of the advantages in 1798:

> I like this place extremely and cannot help thinking that for a literary man, by which term I mean a man who is fond of letters, it is the most eligible situation in the island. It unites good libraries liberally managed, learned men without any other system than that of pursuing truth; very good general society; large healthy virgins, with mild pleasing countenances, and white swelling breasts; shores washed by the sea; the romantic grandeur of ancient, and the beautiful regularity of modern buildings, and boundless floods of oxygen.

Whether or not Edinburgh still has many large-breasted virgins, in other respects this list is still precise. Consider, for instance, his point about libraries. Other places have rich libraries which are generously administered. McGill in Montreal has a fine Scottish collection and gives you free access to the shelves; the Reading Room of the British Museum is, to my mind, the best thing in London. None, in my experience, are so friendly, welcoming and helpful as those of Edinburgh, and there are four great ones a few minutes walk apart. As Bruce Lenman said in the Preface to his recent book on the Jacobite Rising, 'Edinburgh must be one of the pleasantest centres for the historical researcher in the world'. These libraries are important to me, but the kindliness is not confined to them. It is one of the most conspicuous of Scottish characteristics, even if it is only the visitor, or the returning wanderer, who is aware of it. The contrast with every other country I know is very striking. Elsewhere isolated acts of kindness to the stranger certainly occur but Scotland is the only country I know where it is the norm. Where else do shopkeepers warn you against buying something from them, if they think you are about to make a bad bargain?

For me too, it has to be Scotland because it is the heartland of my interests, the place where my responses are most acute and immediate. I enjoy other literatures, especially English and French, and some Italian, German and Spanish, but it is Scottish writing that means most to me. I understand these languages, but no tongue can stir me like Scots. Again there is a rational and an instinctive explanation. With the infinite multiplicity of the world, one has to select one's own particular corner. We all have to find our speciality and Scottish literature and history happens to be mine. It is therefore in Scotland alone that every turn awakes another association. James Boswell had a house where my flat now stands. Walter Scott's town house is a stone's throw away. Any day I choose I can go to the Portrait Gallery and see the likeness of all the people I read about. The National Library and the Record Office have inexhaustible resources of books and manuscripts. All this is rational enough and a sufficient reason in itself, but I admit that my need to be here is not merely rational. The best description I know of this state of mind is at the end of Maurice Lindsay's book, *By Yon Bonnie Banks*, even if he puts it in the past tense:

> So for me the love affair is over. The fervour, the obsession with Scottishness for its own sake, the strongly emotional response to whatever carried even the faintest Scottish overtone, all these things have faded to a gentle but regretful affection: an affection, however, which, I fancy, will persist to the end of my days.

For me, the love affair is not over, and I fancy never will be. 'So much for my Scottish feelings,' as Walter Scott put it, 'prejudices, if you will; but which were born, and will die with me.'

This attitude to Scotland does not imply contentment with the deplorable state into which the country has sunk. How could it when we are surrounded with blatant evidence of decline and decay, when Scotland compares so unfavourably with our European neighbours in almost every comparable statistic: disease, crime, poverty, unemployment and the consumption of the palliatives of sugar, tobacco and drink; when the contrast between the potential and the performance is so pitiful? Of course, world recession, abetted by the policies of Westminster, is making everything worse; but we are suffering from the accumulation of years of government which is irresponsible in every sense of the term. The more one cares about Scotland, the more these things are painful and impossible to accept. I think that Eric Linklater was right when he said in *The Lion and the Unicorn* in 1935, 'I believe people degenerate when they lose control of their own affairs'. That degeneration has blighted Scotland since Westminster assumed control of almost every aspect of life in Scotland, beginning gently in the nineteenth century and reaching a drastic degree from about the time of the First World War. The Union of 1707 prepared the way for this, of course; but its full effects were delayed for about 200 years. For that period, the Church, education, the law and local administration, all of which the Union left largely in Scottish hands, had more direct effect than central government on people's lives. The degeneration, and the resistance to it, began when that ceased to be true. It leads inevitably to a debilitating sense of inferiority.

It is for this reason that the Referendum of March 1979 was such a sorry business, which might eventually rank with Darien as a national disaster. If we do not make a quick recovery, it could even be the terminal disaster. It was disastrous not only because the hopes and aspirations of 100 years were once again frustrated but in the method of the frustration. The 'No' side so conducted their campaign that it became an exercise in mass manipulation, one of the worse aspects of contemporary life, by deliberately playing on the degenerate feeling of inferiority spawned by decades of dependence. They rigged the rules by the 40% requirement, an innovation in British politics where every issue, even the gravest, has always before been settled by simple majority. They avoided rational debate by preventing the distribution of an explanatory leaflet, by obtaining a ban on party political broadcasts and even suppressing a statement by the Church of Scotland of the position affirmed many times by the General Assembly. Instead they used advertising techniques to exploit the instinctive dislike of all government which at that time, after a miserable winter of strikes, was particularly strong. They were ingenious in their confusion of the issues. They claimed, as in Lord

Hume's broadcast and in the official leaflets of the Conservative Party, to be in favour of more effective devolution, and conveniently forgot about this immediately afterwards. Drucker and Brown in their recent book, *The Politics of Nationalism and Devolution*, said that the 'No' side 'won the argument'. That is precisely what they did not do; but they played with some success on the national inferiority complex, by advertising techniques. Now they try to make us forget that there was after all a majority for 'Yes'.

In May 1977, about two years after the Referendum, I published an essay about one of the Scottish contradictions: 'The Scot has a high opinion of himself, but he expects to fail, at least collectively, because of a long historical experience of failure'. It ended with this paragraph:

> The question now is – and this is where the other side of the equation asserts itself – have the Scots been so defeated by their past that they no longer have the confidence to resume control, entirely or in part, over their own affairs? To the optimists, this would offer release from the malaise of dependence, an invigorating challenge, an opportunity for talent and energy to find a corporate purpose. It might even finally dispose of the collective inferiority complex. But will the Scottish voters take fright at the last moment? Will they be like the football supporters who expect the team to play well but not to win? Certainly, the opponents of devolution represent, and appeal to, the inferiority complex. They expect the worst to happen, if the protecting hand of Westminster is relaxed. Many of their arguments suggest that they regard their countrymen as uniquely incompetent and untrustworthy. (Is there any other country that is likely to be told that it cannot be trusted to run its own universities?) So what we are witnessing is a trial of strength between the two aspects of the national character. Which will predominate, the self-confidence or the resigned despair?

I do not claim credit for prescience because when I wrote that, I did not expect the worst to happen. We seemed then to be on the edge of a breakthrough at last and all Scotland was striving with a new sense of optimism and hope. I did not expect the quick bright things to come so quickly to confusion.

When this 'occasional series' began with Donald MacKinnon's admirable essay in 1978, I think that he was reflecting this optimism. It was a time, so recent but apparently now so distant, when it was natural for people to return to Scotland to share in the new future that seemed to be in the making. I have dwelt on the Referendum and its aftermath because this (and Thatcherism) has changed the whole atmosphere. My return comes at a more dismal and discouraging time.

But personally I am not discouraged. Coming back to live perma-
nently in Scotland after nearly forty years, inevitably I make comparisons with the past. Certainly not all change has been for the better,
but I think that we are now closer than we were to achieving the
Scotland of our aspirations. Edinburgh is still a very agreeable and
civilised place, warm in humanity, if not in temperature, and far less
sunk in complacent acceptance of a decline to provinciality and
insignificance. Far more people are now provided with more than an
adequate income, and that is still true in spite of the current
deterioration. We have lived through a social revolution which has
been almost imperceptible in its gradualness. When Edwin Muir
wrote his *Scottish Journey* in 1935 he said this:

> There are streets in Edinburgh which correspond exactly to the
> drawing-room and the servant's hall. The people one meets in
> the first are quite different from the people one meets in the
> second. The crowds that walk along Princes Street, for instance,
> are a different race, different in their manners, their ideas, their
> feelings, their language, from the one in the Canongate. The
> distance between the two streets is trifling; the difference
> between the crowds enormous. And it is a constant and
> permanent difference. You never by chance find the Princes
> Street crowd in the Canongate, or the Canongate crowd in
> Princes Street; and without a revolution such universal American
> Post is inconceivable.

Now Muir is not the most reliable of witnesses in matters of plain
fact because he was preoccupied with his private vision of hell and
redemption, but there was a strong element of truth in this. Look at
Princes Street now. It is no longer 'quiet and genteel', as Muir
describes it, but crowded with the masses, spending money in the
shops like sailors on a spree. It is a pity that this has meant that the
sober Scottish shops selling goods of solid quality have been replaced
by English chain-stores selling mostly trash; but at least access to this
limited idea of the good life is more widely spread.

In the more important things which constitute civilisation the
progress in the last forty years or so has been immensurable. If anyone
doubts this, they have only to read one of the many books published
in the Twenties on the state of Scotland, like G. M. Thomson's
Caledonia or the Future of the Scots, for example. They will find there
a lamentable account of a society in the last stages of disintegration:
no art, no literature, no theatre, no intellectual life of any kind. 'Not
once', says Thomson, 'has there appeared in a Scottish newspaper an
article devoted to an intelligent scrutiny and investigation of a
Scottish problem. It is in such ways that the people have grown up in
incredible ignorance of their own country's state, ... and in the

illusion that their problems and difficulties were identical with those of England.' No-one could say any of that now. Thomson and the others did not know that MacDiarmid and the Scottish Renaissance were about to burst on the scene with all the consequences that have flowed from them. The Scottish theatre, as good a barometer as any of the state of intellectual health, has never been more vigorous. Scottish publishing has not been so active since the days of Constable. There is no lack of intelligent scrutiny of Scottish affairs. Historical scholarship is in a flourishing state of renaissance. More original works of sound historical scholarship have been published in the last five years or so that in any previous fifty, and this is of particular value because no people has been so misled as the Scots by false ideas of their own past.

So I am happy to be back in the Scotland of the Eighties. It is a society beset with problems but still alive, carrying the wounds of the past, but with great intellectual and material potential. It is exciting and challenging to be part of it. The apparent docility with which Scotland accepted the swindle of the Referendum is, I think, illusory. The efforts of the last 100 years have not been wasted; we are merely taking breath before the next surge forward.

Switzerland: The Scotland of the Alps

(*Glasgow Herald*, 13 December 1986)

For the last 30 years or so, I have spent part of nearly every winter in Switzerland, usually in Klosters. Partly, this is because it has the best skiing in the world but there is also something especially congenial about the place. When I first went there, Klosters was a small village with so few cars that you could ski down the main road. Now it has grown and sprawled and, like most places, suffers badly from cars and even buses. Somehow it still manages to look like a village and survive the pressures and vulgarities of the tourist industry. There is also something about Switzerland as a whole which I find very attractive. This is a tantalising and stimulating mixture of similarities and opposites to Scotland. It is not very obvious at first, but the longer you stay the more you notice the parallels and contrasts.

At first sight, the differences are more obvious than the similarities. Nowadays when you go from this country to almost any other in Western Europe, you notice at once how far we have declined in comparative standard of living. You see it in clothes, in the quality of the shops and restaurants, and in the state of public buildings such as airports and railway stations. You have the feeling that most things in this country are shabby and third rate and are steadily getting worse. Switzerland is at the opposite extreme. Everything seems to be of higher quality than usual. To arrive in Zurich by air is to arrive suddenly in a different world where a benevolent intelligence has been at work, not official or private vandalism. All is spacious, comfortable, well-designed and in good order. Even the railway platforms are carpeted in deep rubber.

In nothing is the contrast between Scotland and Switzerland more obvious than in the matter of nuclear defence. Switzerland has no nuclear weapons and is therefore unlikely to be a target for nuclear attack. Scotland has a denser concentration of nuclear bases than any other country in Europe, if not the world. It is therefore bound to be one of the first targets in any nuclear exchange. We have no nuclear shelters (except, I suppose for the top brass). Switzerland has them for everybody and no new building is put up without one. Perhaps shelters would only prolong the agony, but they show the concern of the Swiss Government for the ordinary Swiss citizen. At least, the shelters will do no harm. They will not provoke an attack, which is more than you can say for our so-called deterrent.

The contrast between the two countries is obvious from every statistic. In Switzerland the GNP per head is about £10,000; in Scotland, it is less than half of that, just over £4,000. The unemployment rate in Switzerland in the last two years was about 1%; in Scotland, it was 15%. One of the most significant statistics of all is that the population of Switzerland increases year by year. In Scotland, with people forced to emigrate in search of work, it is actually in decline.

The difference is not only in affluence but in morale. The Swiss have a national pride in their tradition and achievements which is not assertive but is visible in everything they do. They are very responsive to new technology but they keep it in its place. New buildings harmonise with their surroundings. They have not destroyed their railway system but improved it. They cherish and encourage their own languages. Swiss German, for example (which bears the same sort of relationship to standard German as Scots does to English), is widely used by all kinds of people and on radio and television. You have the feeling that people are content not just because they are well fed and have money in their pockets, but because they live in a community that respects itself and the individuals who comprise it. They are not alienated by a remote authority with a different voice, different standards and different attitudes.

Superficially then, prosperous and contented Switzerland could hardly be more different from declining, exploited and impoverished Scotland. The strange thing is that the more you get to know Switzerland, the more you realise that beneath the surface there is a very strong affinity with Scotland. Admittedly, I am speaking mainly about the German-speaking part of the country, which is the only part that I know well. Here I have been going back to the same house year after year. I speak the languages and hardly feel like a visitor at all. I am no longer surprised to notice how frequently the reactions and instincts of the Swiss seem natural and predictable to me but not to my English acquaintances. The truth is that Swiss habits of thought are in many ways remarkably Scottish. I suppose that is why I feel more at home in Klosters than London.

To begin with, we are both small countries. Our populations are about the same although Scotland is nearly twice as large in area. A large part of both is mountainous. The Swiss mountains are much higher, but they are so much further south that the general climate is kinder. Vines grow plentifully in the glens and straths of Switzerland. The country is, of course, land-locked. The Swiss do not have the good fortune to be surrounded, as we are, by seas full of oil and fish.

In fact, apart from agriculture, which is possible in only about a quarter of the country, they have no natural resources at all. They have no coal, no other minerals and no oil. They have more snow in winter and more sun in summer which is good for the tourist trade. Otherwise, they have none of our natural advantages at all. This makes it very strange that they should be so much more prosperous. (What on earth would they be like if they had oil?) It suggests that either Switzerland is singularly fortunate in its government or that there is something fundamentally wrong in our system.

There are many echoes and parallels in the history of the two countries. Swiss independence was largely established by the Battle of Morgarten in 1315, just one year after Bannockburn did the same for Scotland. Throughout the Middle Ages, the survival of both countries depended on infantry using the Bannockburn formation, the *schiltrom* of spearmen. The reason was the same in both cases. Both were countries defended by the ordinary people against the aristocratic, heavily armed knights of a wealthy aggressor. Consequently, both countries from early times developed egalitarian instincts. The Reformation brought us even more closely together. Zwingli in Zurich was similar to Knox in his thoroughgoing denunciation of the old system. Above all, the influence of Calvin in Geneva, with his explicit and logical doctrine and emphasis on education, was decisive for the Kirk in Scotland, as it was for the whole of the Protestant part of Switzerland.

In fact, I suspect that the affinities between Swiss and Scottish habits of thought are probably due more to our common religious background than to any other single factor. For most of this century, it has been fashionable to criticize Calvinism as a malignant force which tended to discourage the arts and make life gloomier that it had to be. This overlooks the positive side which introduced a respect for education and for logic and encouraged certain attitudes to life – a belief in work and the virtues of self-control, a disapproval of extravagance, waste, ostentation and self-indulgence. It might all be summed up, as R. H. Barrow said of the Romans, 'in *severitas*, which means being stern with oneself'. I think that it was these qualities which lay behind the achievements of Scotland in the age of the Enlightenment. The same qualities have enabled Switzerland to build prosperity in a country without resources. In both countries the influence of the Church is now a mere shadow of what it used to be, but I think that there is still a lingering respect for the standards and qualities it encouraged. We may all be atheists nowadays, but some of us are Calvinist atheists. At least, we recognize and sympathize with these attitudes when we find them, and we find them very often in both Scotland and Switzerland. For all their wealth, the Swiss still disapprove of ostentation or waste and have a due respect for the intellect. The intelligence and width of interest of the *Neue Zurcher Zeitung* reminds me of the great days of the *Edinburgh Review*.

The main difference between Switzerland and Scotland is that the Swiss have succeeded in holding on to their hard-won independence, but that we succumbed to 400 years of pressure. They had three aggressors to contend with, from France, Italy and Germany; but perhaps it suited all three to be separated by a neutral buffer. It is easier to balance and play off against one another a number of diverse influences than to resist one neighbour ten times your own size. At all events, the Swiss, unlike the Scots, have always had a government of their own to safeguard their interests. It is a highly democratic and decentralized system. Switzerland is divided in to 22 Cantons, each of which has more power than it was proposed to restore to Scotland under the Scotland Act. Within them, the units of local government, the communes, have real power and autonomy. Throughout the system, there is provision for the decision of controversial issues by referendum. Voting is, of course, by proportional representation. It is all very different from the system which condemns us to control by a remote and centralized government repeatedly rejected by the great majority of Scottish voters.

Everyone concerned with the future of Scotland should take a close look at the Swiss example. It is a country with which we have a great deal in common. In the past it has not achieved as much as Scotland, but it is now a country which is not only wealthier but offers a quality of life which is superior in almost every way. This is true of all the small independent countries of Europe. Among them, Switzerland in particular is an object lesson in the virtues of independence.

Scotland and the Union

(The Story of Scotland, no. 21, June 1988)

Maurice Lindsay once wrote about his love affair with Scotland, 'a strongly emotional response to whatever carried even the faintest Scottish overtone'. I know what he means for I have felt like that for as long as I can remember. It is not the sort of love which blinds you to blemishes. In fact, it makes you more acutely aware of them and of the great gap between the potential of Scotland and the present sorry reality. It also makes you desperately anxious to try to do something about it.

By a series of accidents, resulting directly or indirectly from the last War, I have spent much of my life abroad. I never lost touch with Scotland. I had family and friends there and I came back nearly every year for at least a week or two. Wherever I went I carried quite a lot of Scotland with me, not only in my head but in Scottish books, paintings and recordings of music. Almost since I could read at all, I have been reading systematically through Scottish history and litera-ture. I make occasional digressions into other literatures, but I always come back to Scottish books with the greatest pleasure and response.

I do not know how this started, because of course there are more forces in Scotland which blind people to their own past than make them aware of it. Certainly, I was fortunate in my school, the Royal High School of Edinburgh. Almost unconsciously we absorbed a feeling of continuity with the long history of the school and with the extraordinary contribution which it has made to Scottish achievement. One of my schoolmasters was Alexander Law, learned in the Scottish eighteenth century. I first discovered MacDiarmid in the school library.

In some ways I regret the years which I spent abroad, because I think that I might have become more involved in Scottish affairs and made more of a contribution if I had been able to stay. On the other hand, as a diplomat, I had a front-line seat to observe other countries at close quarters. This gives you a certain detachment and perspec-tive. Perhaps it helps you to understand your own country better. It certainly made me painfully conscious of how much we had lost in Scotland when we lost our independence.

Not that this was an entirely new discovery for me. I had long been convinced that Scotland desperately needed independence, not only for her own sake, but also for the sake of the contribution which Scotland could again make to the rest of the world. I joined the SNP when I was at school in the 1930s, and I agreed then, as I do now, with points made by Eric Linklater in a book called *The Lion and the Unicorn* which was published in 1935: 'People degenerate when they lose control of their own affairs ... To any nation the essential vitamin is responsibility ... By reason of its association with England, Scotland became insular. Its political frontier was broken down, and its mind was walled up'.

When I was in the diplomatic service, I made no secret of my opinions on these matters. Most of my Scottish colleagues agreed with me. The English, as always when Scotland is in question, regarded the whole matter with polite indifference; as something of supreme unimportance. The more I saw of the rest of the world, the more I understood how seriously Scotland was harmed by having no control over her own affairs and no voice in international organisations. The world is increasingly interdependent, but the component units are nations with governments. Without your own government, you simply do not exist and your interests can be disregarded – and they always are.

There are some countries in Europe of similar size to Scotland, or smaller, which I know well. Take Switzerland, for example. Even more of its territory is mountainous than ours. It has no access to the sea and few natural resources, no oil, no coal, no fish. In spite of all these disadvantages, Swiss standing in the world is incomparably higher than ours and so is their standard of living. The small independent countries of Europe are among the most prosperous in the world. There is no reason why an independent Scotland should not be as prosperous as any of them.

Independence has social, cultural and psychological consequences which are even more important than economics. It has been said of the novelist, Neil Gunn, that he found in Scotland 'the sense of weariness, the absence of hope, and the lacerating self-contempt which are marked components in the psyche of colonised peoples'. The denial of responsibility for our own affairs destroys self-confidence and encourages a feeling of helplessness and despair. We are powerless to defend either our economy or our culture against take-overs from the outside. The independent countries of Europe have a self-assurance and a confidence in their own identity which it is hard to find in Scotland.

Unionists used to argue that the Scots went into the Union of 1707 because they thought that it would bring economic advantages.

Recently even the official historian of the Tory party in Scotland has admitted that it was a sordid transaction imposed on Scotland for the advantage of England. The economic arguments were advanced most persistently by the English spy and propagandist, Daniel Defoe. He admitted when he toured Scotland 20 years after the Union that he had been wrong. Scotland's traditional trade with France and Holland was destroyed by the association with England. After 1707, Scottish manufacturing was swamped by the flood of English goods which poured into Scotland. 'The common people all over the country', Defoe wrote in 1727, 'not only are poor, but look poor; they appear dejected and discouraged.' Certainly, the Glasgow tobacco merchants benefited when the Union allowed them to trade legally with the English colonies in America, but this lasted only for a short time. After the Declaration of Independence, trade with America was no longer a British privilege.

For most of the eighteenth century, the British government hardly intervened in Scotland at all. The exception was the suppression of the Jacobite rising of 1745, carried out so ruthlessly that it destroyed the whole Highland way of life. Apart from that, Scotland was left, in Sir Walter Scott's words, 'under the guardianship of her own institutions, to win her silent way to national wealth and consequence'. These institutions included the church, the law and the schools and universities which had survived the Union intact and which were far more important for the life of the country than the distant and indifferent government. Scotland, left to her own devices, not only prospered but became in the age of the Enlightenment and the age of Scott, a major source of intellectual and cultural influence.

The interference of the British government in Scottish affairs began with a vengeance after the Napoleonic wars. Britain, more honestly called England, was now the strongest power in the world. England, in this mood of overweening self-confidence, began, as Sir Walter Scott complained in the *Malachi* letters: 'a gradual and progressive system of assuming the management of affairs entirely and exclusively proper to Scotland, as if we were totally unworthy of having the management of our own concerns. All must centre in London.' At the same time, and perhaps in consequence of it, Scottish self-confidence collapsed; in George Davie's phrase, there was a 'loss of intellectual nerve'. The country which had reached such heights of achievement in the preceeding hundred years, descended for a time after the 1830s into provincial mediocrity.

Part of the reason for this may well have been the absorption of Scottish energies in the development of the British Empire. One of the main consequences of the Union for Scotland was the opportunities it provided for Scots for careers all over the Empire as administrators, explorers, politicians, doctors, engineers, teachers and soldiers. Many Scots felt that they were equal partners with England in a great enterprise, to which they could always turn if they could not find employment at home. The talents and energies which benefited Canada, India or Australia were lost to Scotland itself. The process was described by Edwin Muir: 'Scotland is gradually being emptied of its population, its spirit, its wealth, industry, art, intellect, and innate character.' The territories overseas developed towards self-government; Scotland itself was left behind.

It is now time that we caught up. In the past, it used to be argued that the Union at least brought to Scotland the advantages of a wider market. This was always a very dubious argument; it is not necessary to be absorbed politically into another country in order to be able to sell into it. While the Empire lasted, some industries may have benefited from privileged trade with it; but these days have long gone. Now that we are about to enter a single Europe, the United Kingdom market will be absorbed within it. But it becomes increasingly urgent that we have our own voice at the Council of the EEC, and to achieve that we have to be independent.

In the past, the Union has done more harm than good to Scotland. There is no doubt that it is now an intolerable impediment to our progress. I began by speaking about the gap between our present condition and our potential. We can only hope to realise that potential if we take responsibility for our own affairs, assert our independence, and rejoin the world by becoming again a full and equal partner in it.

II

The Scottish Character

Severitas: The Romano-Scottish Ideal

(*Blackwood's Magazine*, November 1976)

R. H. Barrow, in his book *The Romans*, has a long catalogue of the Roman virtues, the qualities which the Romans admired and liked to think they possessed: *pietas, gravitas* ('a sense of the importance of the matters in hand'), *constantia, firmitas, disciplina, industria* ('hard work'), *virtus* ('manliness or energy'), and *frugalitas* ('simple tastes'). 'It might all be summed up,' Barrow says, 'in *severitas,* which means being stern with oneself.' This homogeneous and severe mixture is tempered by two softer qualities: *comitas,* which means 'the relief given to overseriousness by ease of manner and humour', and *clementia,* 'the willingness to forgo one's rights'.

With the possible exception of the relieving *comitas* and *clementia,* why does this list sound so familiar? I think it is because we have been brought up in Scotland to admire, and aspire to, the very same qualities, at least since the days of John Knox. Some of us have succeeded, and some even too well. Whenever anyone tries to define the Scottish character – and I shall quote a few examples – he ends up with a list very similar to Barrow's. According to Knox himself, Queen Mary was one of the first to comment on Scottish *gravitas*. He says of her, in his *History of the Reformation*, 'Her common talk was that she saw nothing in Scotland but gravity, which repugned to her nature, for she was brought up in joyousitie.' Knox disapproved of joyousitie, and we have had a bad conscience about it ever since.

Few people, and certainly no other Scotsman, has given us such a full and frank account of their internal struggles as James Boswell. Naturally enough, therefore, his diaries contain the most explicit statement, as far as my knowledge goes, of the pursuit of the Roman ideal. We all know, because he has taken pains to tell us, that Boswell was just as vain, lecherous and self-indulgent as the rest of us, and just as ready to abandon *severitas*; but he struggled to a deliberate plan to return to the Roman path. When he was in Holland, just before his twenty-third birthday, he drew up an 'Inviolable Plan' as a guide to life, which, he instructed himself, was 'to be read over frequently':

> You are to attain habits of study ... You must avoid affectation ... Remember religion and morality ... Remember the dignity

of human nature. Remember everything may be endured ...
Have constant command of yourself. Restrain ludicrous talents
... Be firm, and persist ... Never indulge your appetite without
restraint.

Barrow might have been cataloguing the aspirations, not of the
Romans, but of James Boswell. But there is one difference. Barrow
says there is nothing in his list to suggest that the Romans thought of
intellectual power as a high ideal; Boswell made study his first point.
Concern for education is firmly established as part of the accepted
view of the Scottish character, and much evidence could be produced
to suggest that it may be true. It is on everyone's list. I promised some
examples, and I avoid the more obvious. J. F. Murray, writing in
Blackwood's in December 1841, spoke of 'a hardy race, inured to
labour, and no way fastidious in his living...But it is to his education
that he owes everything'. Grace Fletcher is quoted by the Carswells:
'Virtues peculiarly Scotch – of self-denial, submission to severe
hardship without repining, education and refinement much beyond
their condition, with considerable ambition and aspiring thoughts'.
Sydney Smith wrote to Jeffrey in 1819: 'You must consider that
Edinburgh is a very grave place and that you live with Philosophers,
who are very intolerant of nonsense'.

So a rather flattering picture emerges of a people possessing the
Roman virtues, plus a respect for the intellect. The Romans were
severe with themselves for military and imperial purposes. The Scots,
we like to think, practised the same self-denial in the interests of the
mind to promote learning in a sparse economy, where there were few
resources to spare for anything that was not essential. *Tenui musam
meditamur avena* – we cultivate literature upon a little oatmeal – was
the motto Sydney Smith proposed for the *Edinburgh Review*.

Before we congratulate ourselves, let us remember that these
qualities, even when attained, have their limitations. They are noble
qualities, but they emphasise endurance more than inspiration; they
tend more to prudence than to excitement and discovery. In *The Letters
of Malachi Malagrowther*, Walter Scott said that when a Scotsman
went among the English, 'his national character ... is supposed to
imply the desirable qualities of information, prudence, steadiness,
moral and religious feeling'. (Once again, the Roman virtues, plus
education.) But he went on to say that these were admirable,
qualifications for jobs as 'confidential clerks, land-stewards, head-
gardeners ... or any similar situation in which the quality of trust-
worthiness is demanded'. Maurice Lindsay made much the same
point more than a hundred years later when he wrote of Scottish
bankers, businessmen and 'heids o depairtments' as 'grave, worthy
and wise; men of pomp, few words, and less imagination'. The

Romano-Scottish qualities, if unrelieved, can make good, but ponderous, subordinates. If that were all, it would be a poor result for so much effort. Fortunately, they are seldom unrelieved. The conflicting and contradictory impulses, which Gregory Smith called the Caledonian Antisyzygy, enliven and confuse the outcome. Instincts rebel against *gravitas*, individuality against *disciplina*, and emotion against all attempts at control. But even when we reject, or fail to achieve, the Roman virtues, we are still affected by them. They set the standards by which we are judged, whether we like it or not.

It is paradoxical that a part of Europe which defied Roman annexation should have cultivated Roman qualities with more perseverance than countries subjected to the direct influence of the Empire. Is Roman law part of the explanation? At the very least, and in the words of Professor T. B. Smith, 'the law of Rome – or possibly what Scottish lawyers *thought* was the law of Rome – had been a factor of major importance at a formative period of Scots law'. This was something which Scotland shared with much of Europe, with England as the insular exception. Scotsmen in their thousands went to France and, after the Reformation, to Holland to study Roman law and contribute to a common European experience, which cannot, therefore, explain a Scottish peculiarity. If there was a difference in Scotland, it was in the unusually high prestige of the lawyers, who became an intellectual élite, as conspicuous for literature, philosophy and history as for law. By these means, something of the spirit of the Roman lawyer, or the civilian, became part of the general Scottish intellectual tradition. But the qualities we are discussing, *severitas* and the rest, are inherent and personal or they are nothing; they cannot be imposed by authority or law – nor are they the subject-matter of the law.

The *severitas* in question is *severitas* towards oneself. This is a theme, I suppose, of Stevenson's *Weir of Hermiston*. In one sense it is a study of the conflict between the Roman *severitas* of Hermiston and the emotional indulgence, the splairging, of Archie – between the Roman and the Romantic, if you like. (How curious that these two qualities which we see as opposites should both be described by variations of the same word; Roman influence is multifarious.) But Stevenson describes Archie, too, as having 'a Roman sense of duty'. The whole novel is a commentary on the Romano-Scottish ideal. The conflict between the judge and his son, it seems to me, is not over law, although it arose in a legal context, but over personal attitudes, over degrees of *severitas*. We are in the province of conscience and feeling, not of law.

If not Roman law, what about classical education? Certainly, for some hundreds of years, Scottish education was obsessed with Latin. The burgh high schools taught very little else, and even the village dominie aspired to instil at least the elements of the grammar. Of course, Latin was predominant in the schools of the whole of Europe; but education was more widespread in Scotland and so therefore was the Roman influence. Even if Caesar, Cicero and Virgil were not deliberately used to point a moral, some of their ideas were likely to be absorbed with the syntax.

The supremacy of Latin died hard. In the late nineteenth century, the High School of Edinburgh moved with the times and accepted mathematics, science, modern languages and other such frivolities; but when I was there we still spent more time on Latin than on anything else. I remember the Rector, King Gillies, saying publicly, and without attracting either surprise or opposition, that the only subjects worth teaching to those who were worth the effort were the classics and (he conceded so far) mathematics; a mind so trained could easily absorb anything else at leisure. But this was educational doctrine, not a moral philosophy. As far as I can remember, the Roman writers were left to speak for themselves. I once asked James Allan Ford (with whom I sat on the High School benches), whether he thought there had been any conscious attempt to indoctrinate us. He is a good witness to the point because he is so conscious of the classical background that he divides his novels in his own mind into the Greek and the Roman. 'It was inescapable,' he said. 'King Gillies was the reincarnation of a Roman Emperor.' This was true. He even looked like Caesar, and was clearly intended by nature to rule an empire, not a petty republic of schoolboys. Perhaps the influence was more pervasive than we realised at the time.

I suspect, however, that the influence of Latin was no more than ancillary, if only because its effects were quite different elsewhere. Take the example of England, just as classical at the same period, but in quite a different spirit. If the Romano-Scottish ideal can be summarised in *severitas*, the English equivalent is the idea of the gentleman, even if the word sounds unfashionable. Of course, it is a word which has been used in Scotland too in its day. You find it, for example, in the Waverley Novels, where it seems usually to mean little more than that the man is reasonably respectable, at least moderately prosperous and tolerably well-dressed.

In traditional English usage it has included all this, but it has meant much more: a judgement of character and morals, for example. This is all so contrary to the prevailing mood of happy-go-lucky egalitarianism that you would hardly expect to find an example in a book which has just been published, even if it has been kept for some years in cold storage. From *Churchill and Morton*, letters exchanged between Desmond Morton and R. W. Thompson about Winston Churchill, we learn that in his youth, Churchill was rejected by his English officer contemporaries because he was not a gentleman according to their standards. 'Nothing to do with sex or money, and certainly nothing whatever to do with birth. To them, a gentleman was not self-centred and not a go-getter in a vulgar way ... It is a question of general conduct and behaviour. What one does and does *not* do, and how one does certain things. What one says, how one says it and what one does *not* say.' Morton tells us that an Etonian marquis might not be a gentleman, and that a dustman from Borstal might be; but we are left with the impression that both would be exceptional. There is much that is ridiculous about all this and much that is admirable too; but it is a world apart from the Romano-Scottish.

Levitas, a quality which, Barrow tells us, the Romans despised, is the opposite of *gravitas*; it means 'trifling when you should be serious'. The English gentlemanly code, in its original and extreme form, makes a virtue of precisely this quality. Even when something is serious, you must pretend to take it lightly; even if you have to struggle and try hard, you must conceal it. The whole idea is effortless superiority, and the effortlessness is as important as the superiority. You should be wealthy, but you must not work. Some education is desirable, provided it is acquired without taking pains, and is not too specialised, pedantic or assertive. Nothing could be further from *gravitas* and *industria*, but it has a classical basis as well. In the eighteenth century, when the English gentleman was most assured, he lived in a house of classical elegance, and his library was full of Greek and Latin. His conception of society, of the acceptability of politics or the Army, but not of trade, was a reflection of the ideas of the Roman Patrician. In both cases, effortless superiority was a luxury which could be sustained only by a privileged group within a secure and prosperous society. The Patrician had wealth in land and slaves and unlimited opportunities in the Empire for political and military ambition. The English gentleman had all of these, except the slaves, and he had inherited wealth, accumulated from generation to generation with almost no taxation in a prosperous and peaceful country, which for centuries was not disturbed by invasion.

The Scottish experience was completely different. For some three hundred years, Scotland had to struggle for survival against a country with ten times the population and more than ten times the wealth; the richest part of Scotland was close to the Border and was repeatedly devastated. This long war was followed by a century of religious and dynastic struggle, while all the arts of peace continued to decay. Even without these tribulations, the climate and soil were not conducive to an easy life or the accumulation of plenty. Life was bound to be a struggle. Probably the severe Roman virtues took root in Scotland for the simple reason that survival was not possible without them. The puritan spirit of the Reformed Kirk, curiously coinciding with the ideas of pagan Rome, made a virtue of necessity.

Almost everything that has happened since the late eighteenth century has either made the Roman virtues less necessary or questioned their value. Technology, beginning with the agricultural improvements of the Enlightenment and the Industrial Revolution, has liberated us from dependence on agriculture and opened up new sources of wealth. We are surrounded by devices and machines which are supposed to make life easier and more comfortable. The State defends us against poverty and disease. Even if we have doubts about some of the consequences, we must at least admit that neither survival nor even education now demands, as it once did, rigorous self-denial. Ideas have changed along with technology. The discipline of the Kirk was relaxed by the eighteenth century moderates. The Romantic enthusiasm for spontaneous emotion attacked Roman self-control, and psychological theory has suggested that it is, in any case, only a futile attempt to control the uncontrollable. Perhaps we are no longer as confident as we were that affluence has destroyed *frugalitas* for ever; but we continue to press further the Romantic revolt against *severitas* and *disciplina*.

Has the Romano-Scottish ideal served its purpose, and has it now lost all meaning? I can judge only by my own impressions. I think that it is a little like the Scottish atheist who reserved the right to be a Presbyterian atheist. We share the current preference for self-indulgence and self-expression without rules, but we still feel the restraining tug of the old virtues. We are more comfortable even now with *gravitas* than *levitas*. We are prepared to accept many of the indulgences of the 'seventies, but we reserve the right to look at them in a Roman spirit.

The Discouraged Optimists

(*Blackwood's Magazine*, May 1977)

Once before in *Blackwood's* ('*Severitas:* The Romano-Scottish Ideal', November 1976), I mentioned Gregory Smith's 'Caledonian antisyzygy', the theory that Scottish thought and literature are divided between two opposing tendencies: one rational, realistic, cautious, precise; the other, extravagant, grotesque, exuberant, uncanny. No doubt Gregory Smith had a fair point, but there is another Scottish contradiction which has an even stronger and more baleful grip. It is seldom discussed, perhaps because we are reluctant to admit that it exists, but it is easy to produce evidence to show that it has been with us for a very long time. It is an oscillation between optimism and despair, between too much and too little self-confidence, between a 'guid conceit o' onesel' and a massive inferiority complex. In a letter written in July 1757, David Hume provides an illustration in one sentence: 'Is it not strange that, at a time when we have lost our Princes, our Parliaments, our independent Government, even the Presence of our chief Nobility, are unhappy in our Accent and Pronunciation, speak a very corrupt Dialect of the Tongue which we make use of; is it not strange, I say, that, in these Circumstances, we should really be the People most distinguished for literature in Europe?'

The American historian, Wallace Notestein, attempted to analyse the Scottish character in his book *The Scot in History: A Study of the Interplay of Character and History*. In his introduction, he speaks of the Scottish experience of 'lost battles and lost causes ... defeat and disaster'. He goes on to say:

> The Scot expects the worst to happen. He is experienced in making his escape and coming back to fight another day. He is willing to wait for that other day and not give up even if it is lost ... Yet he thinks well of himself. In his heart he believes that no people since the Athenians have so much to their credit and he might, in a pinch, leave the Athenians out.

Unfortunately, having stated the problem, Notestein leaves it as he found it and ventures no further comment. But he has identified precisely the contradiction I mean. The Scot has a high opinion of himself, but he expects to fail, at least collectively, because of a long historical experience of failure. To my mind, this is the essential, and largely unexplored, product of the 'interplay of character and history', as far as Scotland is concerned. It has long been at the heart of Scottish politics, and still is.

Scottish history is certainly full of defeat and disaster. Pierre Trudeau has said that, for the Canadians, living next door to the Americans is like being in bed with an elephant. But it is a more docile elephant than the one with which Scotland has had to contend. For centuries, Scotland was adjacent to a self-assured and expansive England with ten times the population, many more times the wealth, and no inhibitions about the naked use of superior force. Scotland was consolidated by one great victory at Bannockburn, and then fought a desperate holding action against hopeless odds for the next 300 years. To survive was remarkable enough, but it was at the cost of repeated devastation and humiliation. In 1703, when the English administration was urging the Scots to accept Union, the Lord Treasurer, Godolphin, sent a letter of polite threat to Seafield, the Lord Chancellor of Scotland. He mentioned the prospect of war, and said that 'if the Scots were to consult history, they will not find the advantage of those breaches has often been on the side of Scotland'. This was not an empty boast but a statement of fact, and an inevitable consequence of the discrepancy in size and power.

Some of the defeats were catastrophic. Early in the sixteenth century, Scotland had achieved something of Renaissance splendour. It was the golden age of her poetry; learning, naval power and diplomatic influence were expanding. All was lost on the battlefield of Flodden – an overwhelming defeat, from which, in many ways, Scotland has never fully recovered. Three hundred years later, Walter Scott said that the battle could still not be mentioned 'without a sensation of terror and sorrow'.

Failure was not only military. At the end of the seventeenth century, Scotland decided that the solution of her economic problems was to be found by forming a company for overseas trade. National fervour was so aroused that an amount equal to two-thirds of all the coin in circulation in the country – several times the annual public revenue – was subscribed. Everything was invested in a colony at Darien; perhaps no other country has ever staked so large a proportion of her resources on one throw. 'Our hopes of ever being any other than a poor and inconsiderable people are embarked with them,' Andrew Fletcher wrote of the colonists in 1698. Less than two years later, the colony, the ships and the investment were lost and most of the men were dead from disease. The great venture was reduced to a few pitiful ships, crammed with starving and dying men who were refused help when they sought refuge in the English colony of Jamaica. Once again, humiliation was complete.

There have been many other instances. The English historian, Henry Hallam, wrote of the Union: 'From its own nature, not more than from the gross prostitution with which a majority had sold themselves in the surrender of their legislative existence, it was long odious to both parties in Scotland'. The Scots, in Hume Brown's phrase, 'averted their gaze' from so painful a subject, and we might say they did the same at the time of Culloden and the Clearances. That many of the disasters were more the fault of the Scots themselves than of anyone else only increased the damage to national self-confidence. 'The Scots expect the worst to happen' simply because it has in fact happened with such dismal frequency.

If one is tempted to think that all this is in the past and can no longer have any effect, an apt example was cited in the October 1976 issue of *Blackwood's*. This was in a short review of a new book on Scottish football, which, as the writer remarked, was revealing on more than sport. 'It is important to take part in the big game and to play well, but not to win it (Scottish Nationalists, please note). For the Scots, Culloden is the daily round; Bannockburn is a flash in the pan.'

But what of the brighter, optimistic side of the contradiction, the unabashed self-confidence in spite of eveything? Paradoxically enough, this also is firmly based on historical evidence; it is not simply a refusal to face facts. It rests on the achievements of individual Scotsmen in diverse activities and in many countries. The point has been made many times, but one of the earliest examples I have come across is in a travel book, *A Journey Through Scotland,* which John Macky wrote in about 1720: 'The Scots have made a greater Figure Abroad, than any other Nation in Europe; this hath been generally ascribed to the Bareness of their Country, as not being able to maintain its inhabitants. But this is a vulgar Error, for it's entirely owing to the Fineness of their Education'. He then went on to give many examples of the prominent part played by Scotsmen all over Europe – Scottish generals and twenty-two colonels in the army of Gustavus Adolphus, many Marshals of France, the Garde Ecossaise of the French kings, and so on.

The acceptability of Scotsmen for positions of the highest trust in so many countries is indeed very remarkable. Take the case of the two brothers, George and James Keith, who left Scotland because they were Jacobites. James became a Russian general, of whom the

Tsarina said, 'I had sooner lose 10,000 of my best soldiers than Keith.' Later James served as Governor of the Ukraine, and then as a Prussian field-marshal and right hand of Frederick the Great. His brother George was Prussian Ambassador to France and then to Spain. When the Union cut Scotland off from Europe, energies like these went into the development of countries such as Canada and India. At home in Scotland, Scottish philosophers were making a decisive contribution to a whole range of intellectual disciplines – history, economics, sociology, chemistry, geology and medicine. All of this encouragd the Scots to form a high opinion of their own abilities. It explains too why Horace Walpole said that they were 'the most accomplished nation in Europe; the nation to which, if any country is endowed with a superior partition of sense, I should be inclined to give the preference'. Most Scots would accept this as a fair statement of fact – of one side of the dichotomy. Many people have compared the Scots to the Greeks and the Jews as nations which have made a contribution to the world out of all proportion to their numbers.

J. K. Galbraith made the same point recently in the first programme of his television series: 'But no one can question the eminence of the Scotch.' (He was talking specifically about economists, but the application can be extended.) 'The only really dangerous competition to the Scots is, in fact, from the Jews.' The comparison with the Jews recurs. Apart from the high incidence of talent, there are other analogies. Both Scots and Jews are spread over the world in a great diaspora; both have had a tormented history. In spite of, or because of these facts, both have clung to a strong sense of identity. Also, again because of their history, both have a sense of insecurity, of incompleteness, of the need to recover something that has been lost. Of course, this is a comparison that should not be pushed too far. The traumatic experiences of the Scots are less dreadful in degree and more distant in time. Unlike the Jews, they have never completely lost their national homeland, but only independence and the corporate identity of statehood. Even so, many feel the need to restore, to use Edwin Muir's phrase, 'the broken image of the lost Kingdom'. It is this which gives emotional force to Scottish nationalism.

The question now is – and this is where the other side of the equation asserts itself – have the Scots been so defeated by their past that they no longer have the confidence to resume control, entirely or in part, over their own affairs? To the optimists, this would offer release from the malaise of dependence, an invigorating challenge, an opportunity for talent and energy to find a corporate purpose. It might even finally dispose of the collective inferiority complex. But will the Scottish voters take fright at the last moment? Will they be like the football supporters who expect the team to play well but not to win? Certainly, the opponents of devolution represent, and appeal to, the inferiority complex. They expect the worst to happen, if the protecting hand of Westminster is relaxed. Many of their arguments suggest that they regard their countrymen as uniquely incompetent and untrustworthy. (Is there any other country that is likely to be told that it cannot be trusted to run its own universities?) So what we are witnessing is a trial of strength between the two aspects of the national character. Which will predominate, the self-confidence or the resigned despair?

'That Extreme Nationality'

(*Blackwood's Magazine*, September 1977)

I recently had another look at a slender book which has been hidden away on my shelves since 1947, *The Illusion of National Character* by Hamilton Fyfe. It was first published at the beginning of the Second World War, a fact which explains many of its preoccupations. At the time, it was highly praised by Bernard Shaw, who described it as 'a righteous piece of work', and by H. G. Wells, who said that it was a 'cool, clear, cleansing book'. Fyfe said that his purpose was to prove that the idea of national character was an illusion, which had done great harm: 'Soon it will be numbered among the popular errors and superstitions that have confused and injured mankind.'

Twice before in *Blackwood's* ('*Severitas*: The Romano-Scottish Ideal', November 1976; 'The Discouraged Optimists', May 1977) I have discussed some ideas about what I supposed to be the national character of the Scots. Have I then been guilty of propagating dangerous illusions? I was fortified by recalling that no less formidable an Edinburgh sceptic than David Hume had written an essay 'Of National Characters'. It is true that he says: 'The Vulgar are very apt to carry all *national Characters* to extremes; and having once establish'd it as a Principle, that any People are knavish, or cowardly, or ignorant, they will admit of no Exception'; but he goes on to say: 'Men of Sense condemn these indistinguish'd Judgements; tho' at the same time, they allow, that each Nation has a peculiar Set of Manners, and that some particular Qualities are more frequently to be met with among one People than among their Neighbours.' That is as good a definition as we are likely to find. It is exactly such 'particular qualities' that I have attempted to analyse in the case of the Scots. That such peculiarities do exist is a matter of common observation; but it is easy to exaggerate them and treat them as though they were inevitable and invariable. At best, anything that one can say on this subject is no more than a generalisation, admitting doubt and confusion, and wide open to exceptions. It is a handy rule of thumb, not a precise measurement.

When it comes to the point, Hamilton Fyfe takes the same attitude himself. He argues convincingly enough that national character is not immutable, that there are always exceptions, that it probably owes more to environment than inheritance, that it does not necessarily condemn one people to be hostile to another. Even in stating his case like this he is conceding the existence of national character in Hume's definition. As he develops the argument, he assumes that differences exist between one people and another of the kind which in the early part of the book he seemed set to deny: '… there were also seen the beginnings of the South American nations. Spaniards interbred with Indians. The resulting strains were neither Spanish nor Indian. All can perceive that the Argentines, Chileans, Bolivians, Uruguayans are different from both'. If it is an illusion that such differences exist, it is one which Hamilton Fyfe shares with the rest of us.

As if to illustrate the persistence of such ideas, and their liability to error, Miles Kington has just compiled an anthology from the pages of *Punch* – *Punch on Scotland*. I am not sure if this tells us very much about Scotland, but it certainly suggests that the English have very definite ideas about the Scottish character. They include that most persistent of foreign notions about the Scots, that they are mean and penny-pinching. When the world at large thinks about the Scots, if it does at all, it does not think of Hume, the Adam brothers, Walter Scott or Hugh MacDiarmid, but of the mythical Aberdonian. Miles Kington mentions a theory that it was all started by Charles Keene's 'Bang went Saxpence' in *Punch* itself. I suspect that it goes back much farther, to English contempt for a people much poorer than themselves, of which there is an extensive literature, exhausting the vocabulary of zoological abuse. In 1704 Andrew Fletcher published *An Account of a Conversation*, where there is an example: 'Sir Edwrd [Sir Edward Seymour], all in a flame, cries out, What a pother is here about an union with Scotland, of which all the advantage we shall have, will be no more than what a man gets by marrying a beggar, a louse for her portion?'

Even in *Punch*, we come back to the 'antisyzygy', the contradictions, without which no discussion of the Scottish character seems to be possible. In the cartoonist's view of the matter, it veers between strenuous seriousness (*severitas*, if you like) and a weakness for whisky. Between: '"The bairn ought to be at his books. Ye'll destroy his mind wi' yer freevolous goin's-on"' (it is nothing more frivolous than chess), and '"Does Mr MacMurdoch live here?" – "Aye; carry him in!".' There is nothing frivolous about Hamilton Fyfe but he discusses the problem in terms of the same contradiction. He sees the division as one between the Highlanders and the Lowlanders because of the effects of their different systems of land tenure and agricultural methods, which seems to be a desperate attempt to find a simple economic explanation for something infinitely more complicated and obscure. At all events, he argues that it was only in the Lowlands that people were 'trained in habits of frugality, foresight, assiduous labour, strict attention to the matter in hand'. In precise contradiction to the usual assumption, he believes that this is something which only happened when the Scots were liberated from the tyranny of a 'gloomy irrational religion'.

The classical statement of this view of the Scottish Kirk is in Henry Thomas Buckle's *On Scotland and the Scotch Intellect*, one of the few completed volumes of his *History of Civilisation*. Bernard Shaw placed Buckle, along with Marx, as among the very few writers 'that make any permanent mark on the minds of those who read them'. The book is an elaborate, solid and sustained attempt to explain the Scottish intellect. He was puzzled by two things, the gulf between the Scottish and English outlook, and the contradiction, as he saw it, between the superstition of Scots towards religion and their scepticism towards everything else:

> The essential antagonism which still exists between the Scotch and English minds; an antagonism extremely remarkable, when found among nations, both of whom, besides being contiguous, and constantly mixing together, speak the same language, read the same books, belong to the same empire, and possess the same interests, and yet are, in many important respects, as different, as if there had never been any means of their influencing each other, and as if they had never had anything in common ...
>
> The two-fold paradox, which forms the prominent peculiarity of the history of Scotland ... first, that the same people have long been liberal in politics, and illiberal in religion; and, secondly, that the brilliant, inquisitive, and sceptical literature, which they produced in the 18th Century, was unable to weaken their superstition.

But how tenable is this view of the Scottish Kirk? In *Scotland's Relations with England: A Survey to 1707*, William Ferguson has reminded us that 'the rule of the high theocratic party, far from being a constant theme of post-Reformation Scottish history, endured, and even then only intermittently, only for three brief troubled years – from 1648 to 1651'. H. G. Graham, in his *Social Life of Scotland in the 18th Century*, one of the earliest of social histories, reached the opposite conclusion from Buckle:

> It is not uncommon to speak of the Scots as a 'priest-ridden people', as entirely under the domination of their ministers, who terrorised them by discipline in this world and by threats

of the next. It is in this light that Buckle especially has represented the Scottish populace. The reverse is far nearer the truth, and the ministers may rather be called a 'people-ridden clergy'.

The structure of the Scottish Church was democratic before Parliament ever was, and the ministers themselves were chosen by their congregations. In its origin, the Reformation in Scotland was encouraged by a grasping nobility anxious to follow the English example and get its hands on the wealth of the Church, but it quickly became a popular mass movement, hostile to royal or aristocratic control. The Kirk could not have resisted interference by absentee kings and then by absentee governments if it had not been sustained by genuine popular enthusiasm.

Buckle and Hamilton Fyfe are by no means alone in denouncing the Scottish Church. It has been blamed for everything unlovely, joyless and harsh. The Scottish revival in this century began as a literary movement, of which one aspect was a revolt against Calvinism and John Knox. MacDiarmid's demand that Scottish poetry should return to William Dunbar was partly a search for the linguistic richness and homogeneity of the fifteenth century poets, but it also meant an escape from the Reformation. If less has been heard about this more recently, perhaps it is because the Kirk has itself changed. Who can accuse the Kirk of hostility to the arts, when the *Three Estaits*, the greatest achievement of the Scottish theatre, is performed in the Hall of the Church Assembly, and the audiences pass to their seats under the uplifted arm of the bronze statue of John Knox himself?

No doubt the Kirk has been intellectual rather than emotional and has distrusted ornament and music as seductive and misleading beguilements. This is the obverse of its great strength, the appeal to reason and the encouragement of education. The Scottish school system is the creation of the Kirk, which as early as 1560 set out in pursuit of the ideal of a school in every parish. Even if this was only imperfectly achieved, it was centuries in advance of other countries, and it is probably the main reason why the Scots have made an impact on the world out of all proportion to their numbers. R. G. Cant wrote of the Scottish Church in the seventeenth century that it 'had a more democratic constitution sustained by a more literate society than could be found almost anywhere else in Europe'. T. B. Macaulay said of the period a generation or two later: 'It began to be evident that the common people of Scotland were superior in intelligence to the common people of any other country in Europe ... This ... is to be attributed, not indeed solely, but principally, to the national system of education.'

In this respect, Scotland had the advantage of an early start. Other countries have caught up, and perhaps surpassed, Scottish standards of education; schools for all are now a commonplace. No longer can it be said that 'England has two universities – and so has Aberdeen'. But respect for education and the application of reason are still Scottish predilections. Charles Ritchie, a Canadian diplomat who was in London during the last war, remarked in his diary, *The Siren Years:* 'Just as whenever in England you meet with a genuine interest in the arts you may suspect Jewish blood, so whenever you meet with respect for the human intelligence you may guess that there is a Lowland Scot about'. It is a characteristic which, like all others, has disadvantages. The argumentativeness which Walter Scott called the Edinburgh *pruritus disputandi,* is one result. It means too that the Scots do not have the English genius for compromise, which depends on an ability to drop the argument and agree to differ. Like the Scottish Army before Cromwell at Dunbar, we are still inclined to engage in an endless debate instead of getting on with the business in hand.

The concern of the Kirk with education had a religious purpose; it wanted everyone to be able to read the Bible and grasp the metaphysics of its theology. But the control of the Kirk by the members at large and not by remote authority meant that any objective persistently pursued over a long period had to reflect popular desire. There is no doubt that this was true of education; generations of Scotsmen have endured privation for the sake of learning. It is part of the same attitude to life as the cultivation of the Roman qualities of frugality, seriousness of purpose and the rest. I suggested in '*Severitas*' that this was a response to the challenge of the difficulties of living in a harsh, embattled, northern country. Effort was the price of survival. Of course, it has often been remarked (it is the most obvious expression of the 'antisyzygy') that the stern qualities go hand in hand with the opposite. The *Punch* anthology is a case in point. In an essay about Balliol College in *My Oxford,* Sir John Betjeman has put it succinctly: 'The whole tone of the college was Scottish and frugal, but like all things Scottish, it had a side of unbridled exuberance.' The Scottish football supporters after the defeat of England in May this year were unbridled enough.

Even if we do not accept Hamilton Fyfe's ideas about the effects of land tenure, it is tempting to look for an explanation of this contradiction in the different traditions on the two sides of the Highland Line. A love of panache, music, dance, colour and exuberance in everything from dress to emotional response is more obvious in the Highlands, and restraint and distrust of display in the Lowlands. Perhaps the people of Scotland are torn between two traditions interacting within a small country. Not that the differences are as fundamental as they sometimes appear. Gaelic was once spoken over nearly the whole of Scotland, and the structure of Border society was recognisably similar to the clan structure of the Highlands. The distinctions may be more of time-scale than of kind. The mountains of the north were difficult to penetrate, and successive governments in Edinburgh found that it was a far cry to Loch Awe. New influences of all kinds were later and weaker, and this applied to the Reformed Kirk and the educational system that it brought about.

From whatever angle one looks at the Scottish character, one tends to return to religious influence, now weaker certainly but not insignificant. While I was writing this, I came across this passage in the 4th June issue of *The Economist*:

> The Scottish Kirk exerts a uniquely powerful influence over young minds. In their different ways, Andrew Carnegie, John Buchan and Lord Reith all bore through the rest of their lives the marks of their early Presbyterian upbringing. So did Thomas Carlyle. He never lost the terrifying vision of eternity and the overwhelming sense of duty which had been instilled into him as a boy by the "hoary old heads" of the minister and elders at Ecclefechan.
>
> Carlyle never really abandoned his childhood faith. Like those other eminent Victorian agnostics, George Eliot and Leslie Stephen, he spent most of his life searching for a substitute for it. For them scepticism and moral equivocation were more deadly sins than they were for many professing Christians ... It was through the Calvinist gospel of hard work and strict duty that Carlyle ultimately worked out his own salvation.

Think too, we might add, of the preoccupation of James Bridie's plays with the ideas of the Devil and sin. Think of the fundamentally religious attitude of a theoretical atheist like MacDiarmid. The Presbyterian atheist is very much with us still.

One reason for the endurance of the Scottish sense of identity is that the Kirk survived the Union intact. Union would not have been possible on any other terms. Religion, Defoe wrote at the time, was 'the most dangerous rock ... on which this Union could split'. The people were reluctant enough to surrender their Parliament but they would not surrender their Church – more genuinely representative of them than Parliament at that time – on any terms whatever. It was only when the Court hit upon the device of incorporating in the settlement an Act guaranteeing for all time the independence of the Church of Scotland and the universities, that the Union became a practical possibility. Then, and for long afterwards, the Church, and the educational and welfare systems which depended on it, had much more effect on people's lives than the inactive Government, of which they saw and heard little.

For all that, the loss of political independence was traumatic, and we have not yet recovered from the shock. As David Daiches remarks in *Scotland and the Union*, we can study the immediate effects in the voluminous and frank self-analysis of James Boswell (see '*Severitas*'). Boswell detested, as he often confided to his diary, 'Our cursed Union'. 'You undid yourselves then,' Rousseau said to him, and he agreed at once. He gloried in his 'true patriotic soul of an old Scotsman', and proposed to help to preserve Lowland Scots by writing a dictionary of it. In other moods, he aspired to be accepted by the English almost as one of themselves. He quoted with satisfaction a verse by Courtenay:

  Amid these names can Boswell be forgot,
  Scarce by North Britons now esteem'd a Scot?

He wanted to escape from 'Scotch sarcastic jocularity' and 'shocking familiarity'. He thought that English speech was 'much more agreeable than Scots', and approved of efforts by a Scotsman to be 'rid of the coarse part of his Scotch accent, retaining only as much of the "native wood-note wild" as to mark his country; which, if any Scotchman should affect to forget, I should heartily despise him'. In brief, he was in such a state of confusion between fidelity to Scotland and to the new entity, Britain, that he did not know what he was or what he wanted to be. It is a confusion which continues among us to this day.

David Daiches mentions two of the Scottish responses to the humiliation of the Union, a 'patriotic nostalgia' and a determination to show that North Britain can 'beat the English at their own game'. The first of these accounts for the preoccupation of the Scots and their literature with the past, often to an unhealthy extent, distracting from the problems of the present, but irresistible because it is only in the past that an independent Scotland existed. The same spirit pervades the Scottish attitude to the monarchy, which, despite all discouragements, is seen as a link with the lost Kingdom. The second response is often said to be one of the impulses behind the Scottish Enlightenment, although that was probably a natural consequence of the superiority of Scottish education, at a time when Oxford was, in Gibbon's words, 'steeped in port and prejudice'. This explanation of the Enlightenment is really a self-justifying attempt to find some good consequences for the Union.

There were other effects which were psychologically more destructive. The loss of political identity undermined personal identity and self-confidence. In compensation, it produced a prickliness, an insistence on nationality, a cliquishness, all intended to assert and preserve the national identity threatened by the Union. According to Courtenay, it was this which provoked Samuel Johnson's prejudice against the Scots. He complained to Boswell of 'that extreme nationality which we find in the Scotch. I will do you, Boswell, the justice to say, that you are the most *unscottified* of your countrymen. You are almost the only instance of a Scotchman that I have known, who did not at every other sentence bring in some other Scotchman'. To this day, it is a charge to which we have to plead guilty. Walter Scott put a brave face on it in *The Heart of Midlothian*:

> The eagerness with which Scottish people meet, communicate and, to the extent of their power, assist each other, although it is often objected to us as a prejudice and narrowness of sentiment, seems on the contrary, to arise from a most justifiable and honourable feeling of patriotism, combined with a conviction, which, if undeserved, would long since have been confuted by experience, that the habits and principles of the nation are a sort of guarantee for the character of the individual.

I hope that this is true, and I think that to an extent it is. For all that, it is a symptom of insecurity. It is seen too in an over-defensiveness which destroys critical judgement. 'The love affair', Maurice Lindsay calls it, 'The fervour, the obsession with Scottishness for its own sake, the strongly emotional response to whatever carried even the faintest Scottish overtone.' 'A Scotchman must be a very sturdy moralist', said Johnson more succinctly and robustly, 'who does not love Scotland better than the truth.'

The erosion of the two Scottish languages, Gaelic and Scots, not entirely but largely a consequence of the Union, is a major cause of the confusion and self-doubt. Alexander Carlyle long ago said that it was no wonder that the English thought that the Scots were lacking in humour and verbal sparkle because they could not reproduce in English the vivacity of their own native speech. More recently, Edwin Muir argued that the Scots could not see life as a whole because they thought in one language and felt in another. 'The ballads', he wrote elsewhere, 'enshrine the very essence of the Scottish spirit, and they could have been written only in the Scottish tongue.' If that is so, it means that without the language we are deprived of the means of self-expression altogether. Generations of Scottish schoolchildren have been condemned to clumsy inarticulacy by being forced to use a language which did not come naturally to them. The process is so far advanced that we are threatened with an inability to understand our own literature.

Is it any wonder, then, that the Scottish character is so divided that

it can only be described in terms of contradiction? It has been pulled
in two directions, the Scottish and the British – which really means
English – to the extent that everywhere in the world, except Scotland,
the terms are interchangeable. It has been trying to ride, in James VI's
analogy, both the Scottish 'wild unruly colt' and the English 'towardly
riding horse', and they are two horses with different ideas on where
they want to go. Two recent writers on Scottish themes, Karl Miller
(in *Cockburn's Millenium*) and Christopher Harvie (in *Scotland and
Nationalism*), have both reached the conclusion that Scotland is
schizophrenic and can best be explained by Stevenson's allegory of
Dr Jekyll and Mr Hyde.

Is this exaggerated? In a sense it is because most of us get on with
the business of living in spite of it. Even so, no one can explore the
Scottish scene very far without feeling that many Scots will not be able
to live at peace with themselves and overcome a sense of deprivation,
almost of mutilation, until they can reassert control over their own
affairs. It is not a matter of economic or administrative convenience
but an emotional need. Of all people, the English should be able to
understand; they have encountered and accepted it in so many other
places. It is strange and alarming that they seem to have a blind spot
so close to home.

Postscript – which should have been a preface

Collections of short autobiographical sketches by people sharing a
common background seem to be fashionable. After *My Oxford* and
My Cambridge, we now have *Jock Tamson's Bairns* edited by Trevor
Royle. Twelve men and women educated in Scotland in the 1950s tell
us about the experience. Not all of them are Scottish, but none has any
doubt that Scotland and Scottish education are distinctive, with
tensions, confusions, strengths and weaknesses peculiar to themselves. The book might almost be a set of case histories to illustrate
'*Severitas*', 'The Discouraged Optimists' and 'That Extreme Nationality'. Writer after writer remarks on the arduous and serious purpose
of Scottish education, vulgarised as 'getting on', but meaning an
acceptance that life is a struggle demanding effort and self-discipline
as the price of survival. The miners in Newarthill, Liz Lochhead tells
us, chose as their Gala Queen, not the prettiest or most popular girl,
but the Dux of the school: 'The miners respected education above all'.
Although some of the writers are Roman Catholic, and others assert
with suspicious emphasis that the Church meant nothing to them ('It
did not matter a damn,' says Alan Bold), you are left with the feeling
that Allan Massie is right: 'I feel Scotland is properly a Calvinist
country and there is dignity and beauty in the Scots Kirk, however far

I've travelled from it'. The Kirk and *severitas* are akin – 'stern and upright and grim', in Alan Spence's words. There is plenty of discouraged optimism. 'Willing to accept second place too often, expecting to lose,' says Bill Bryden. And Giles Gordon: 'It seemed that the point about Scottish history was that everyone came to a sticky end, and that for the Scot everything went wrong sooner rather than later'. The 'antisyzygy' raises its head, of course. 'The divided-self triumphs,' says Giles Gordon again, 'moral ambiguity rules, Hogg's Justified Sinner, Deacon Brodie, Jekyll and Hyde, and R. D. Laing are the touchstones.' So does the Boswellian confusion between Scottish, British and English. An example from Alan Spence: 'I was Scottish. ... Sometimes being Scottish meant being British; sometimes British just meant English.' Trevor Royle, who is English, makes the point about the Union: 'The Union of 1707 had been an awkward way of doing things and many Scots still smarted with shame at the nature of the joining together of the two very different peoples.'

So, is it all familiar territory, illustrating the points I have been trying to make, and with no surprises? To me there are two points which are not exactly surprising in themselves, but in the emphasis they are given. The first is violence. You have the impression that Scottish schoolchildren are perpetually thrashing one another when they are not being thrashed by their teachers – even more, it seems (and this, I suspect, is the opposite from England), in the State schools than in the minority institutions, for which the authors unblushingly use the English euphemism, 'public school'. Their evidence is so unanimous that I suppose it must be accepted. I can only say, as one who went through the process in earlier and presumably rougher times, that either they have got it out of proportion or things have grown worse. The other point – and here I think they hardly exaggerate – is the constant complaint that Scottish history and literature are neglected in Scottish schools. 'Of Scotland's real past we knew little.' 'I was, and long remained, quite ignorant of Scotland.' Such remarks run through the book like a refrain. It seems that the boys of the Edinburgh Academy cannot even understand Burns. In this respect, it is better now, one hears. But it shows just how strong 'that extreme nationality' was to survive generations of brainwashing like this.

Then there is class. We like to think in Scotland that our tradition is egalitarian. The High School of Edinburgh, 'the most important in Scotland, and intimately connected with the literature and progress of the Kingdom', was, according to Lord Brougham, 'invaluable ... because men of the highest and lowest rank of society sent their children to be educated together'. The tradition was eroded by the aping of English ways in the nineteenth century; but petty snobberies in Scotland are only skin deep and easily vulnerable to the national habit of derision of any such absurdity.

But there is a grimmer reality, and it is brutally expressed in Alan Bold's essay, which for this reason is the most telling in the whole book. 'The educational system – at least as it existed then – did nothing to liberate the unprivileged child but rather reinforced his limitations ... For them the occasional explosion of violence will have to compensate for the lack of conversational equipment...The typically anti-social, anticultural working class environment is an oppressive prison ...' Of course, his own example shows that escape is possible, and always many have escaped. It is the hardened cases, happy in brutish indifference, who are the problem, and, on the evidence around us, increased opportunity does not seem to have reduced their number – anywhere in the world and not only among the least privileged. Trevor Royle says in his preface that Scotland has a 'legacy of an impressive belief in learning for its own sake, a foundation for scholarship added to a strong vein of scepticism and a necessity for an ordered framework to life itself'. That is what we have been aiming at since the sixteenth century. Alan Bold reminds us that we have not succeeded yet.

Another thing which most of these essays have in common is a curious kind of reticence. They are of two kinds. Some are impressionistic, random reminiscence without comment; others have reflection without much raw material of fact. In both cases, you have the feeling that, although honest as far as they go, the picture is incomplete. Perhaps Edwin Muir was right about the Scottish separation of heart and head. Certainly they seem to be kept in separate compartments among Trevor Royle's contributors.

It is a pity too that he did not throw the net wider. The contributors are not only of the same generation, but all are professional writers, either in fact or in aspiration. Maybe 'the chief glory of every people arises from its authors', as Dr Johnson said, but they are not typical. And perhaps writers in their thirties are too far away from their schooldays to remember very vividly, but not far enough to recollect in perspective.

The Scottish Malaise

(July, 1979)

In an article in *Blackwood's* of May 1977, 'The Discouraged Optimists', I made some comments on the Scottish tendency to veer between moods of unabashed self-confidence and resigned acceptance of defeat or disaster. '"The Scots expect the worst to happen" simply because it has in fact happened with such dismal frequency.' This article ended with a paragraph which was a comment in advance of the Referendum which was held nearly two years later, on 1st March 1979:

> The question now is – and this is where the other side of the equation asserts itself – have the Scots been so defeated by their past that they no longer have the confidence to resume control, entirely or in part, over their own affairs? To the optimists, this would offer release from the malaise of dependence, an invigorating challenge, an opportunity for talent and energy to find a corporate purpose. It might even finally dispose of the collective inferiority complex. But will the Scottish voters take fright at the last moment? Will they be like the football supporters who expect the team to play well but not to win? Certainly, the opponents of devolution represent, and appeal to, the inferiority complex. They expect the worst to happen, if the protecting hand of Westminster is relaxed. Many of their arguments suggest that they regard their countrymen as uniquely incompetent and untrustworthy. (Is there any other country that is likely to be told that it cannot be trusted to run its own universities?) So what we are witnessing is a trial of strength between the two aspects of the national character. Which will predominate, the self-confidence or the resigned despair?

I take no credit for foresight because when I wrote that I did not, in fact, expect the worst to happen this time. Effort and thought had been devoted to the issue of Scottish autonomy for nearly a hundred years; public opinion polls for decades had shown a steady and overwhelming majority in favour; so many hopes and aspirations were bound up in it; even the Government was so confident that it had spent a lot of public money to make sure that the debating chamber would be ready in time. At last, some autonomy, admittedly modest in degree, but real, was within grasp. Surely the Scottish people would not fall at the last fence.

Well, the opponents did play on the collective inferiority complex with skill and determination. They frightened enough people into either voting 'no' or staying away from the polls, that the majority in favour was so small that it has given the Conservative Government an excuse to repeal the Act. Of course, on every other issue, a majority is a majority; but that is another story. Scotland is often said to be the only country which agreed voluntarily to relinquish its independence (in fact, it was not as voluntary as all that); it is certainly the first to fluff a chance like this to recover at least part of it.

No doubt, there were many extraneous factors which confused the issue. How many people were voting not against autonomy as such, but – as the 'no' campaign assured them – against this particular Act? How many believed Lord Hume that a vote against was the best way to get a stronger Assembly with proportional representation and revenue-raising powers? The fact remains that the collective inferiority complex has never been more blatant. I think that we have to accept that this is a malaise which exists. We have to try to understand it and overcome it, if we are to recover a healthy, constructive and reasonably optimistic state of mind.

The malaise is as old as the Union. The English historian, P. W. J. Riley in his recent book *The Union of England and Scotland,* says that it was difficult for Scottish supporters of the Union in the years before 1707 to find respectable arguments for it. He continues: 'Some were driven to seek justification within an already well established Scottish tradition of national self-denigration, sombrely indicating what they took to be serious defects in the Scottish character. According to Baillie, "... considering the temper of this people, how unfit to govern ourselves ... I must be convinced that union is our only game".' (He is quoting from a letter which Baillie of Jerviswood, a prominent Scottish politician of the period, sent to the Earl of Roxburgh on 3rd January 1705/6.) Baillie has his successors. Tam Dalyell, a Labour MP who has been one of the most obsessive opponents of Scottish autonomy, published a book in 1977 as a contribution to the 'no' campaign, *Devolution: The End of Britain?* In this, there is one supremely revealing, giveaway, sentence. He describes a conversation with Crowther Hunt who told him not to worry; all would be well after Devolution. Dalyell's comment is: 'He neither knows us Scots, nor our history of faction.' The inferiority complex is so extreme that we are asked to believe that the Scottish people have such defects of character that they are incapable of governing themselves.

This is an astounding assertion when one considers the facts. In the

British Commonwealth alone, over 750 million people have been given independence since the Second World War. In Western Europe in this century, Norway, Iceland and the Irish Republic have achieved independence and made a notable success of it. Most of these new countries had no previous experience of Statehood, only very rudimentary institutions and few educated people. Scotland is one of the oldest nation states in Europe. It has never lost its own Church and legal and educational systems; it has all the attributes of a State except a Parliament. Education has been widespread throughout the whole population for much longer than anywhere else in the world. In Europe before the Union, and in the Empire and Commonwealth since then, Scots have made an extraordinary contribution to the government and development of other countries. They are widely regarded as pre-eminently dependable, hard-working, rational, open-minded and adaptable. The assertions of the Baillies and the Dalyells are not only monstrous effrontery, they are completely opposed to all common sense.

This massive inferiority complex is active and outspoken only among a minority of people like the 'no' campaigners, but it is latent in many people. The main cause is the Union itself. 'With the loss of nationhood we lost our nerve', as J. B. Caird wrote recently. Not only the loss but the shameful method of the loss was a humiliation that shattered self-confidence. One possible compensation was to try to identify with the winning side, which meant accepting their traditions and denying one's own. This tendency was encouraged by the wealth of England and all the power and fashion which naturally gravitated to the centre of power in London. Everything in Scotland seemed in comparison, and perhaps still seems, smaller, more impoverished and more old-fashioned. The response of a certain minority in Scotland was to grow ashamed of their origins and ape the wealthier people across the Border, trying to adopt their speech, their habits and standards of value. It is a habit which has persisted even when the English are no longer conspicuously successful and when their economy is largely dependent on Scottish assets. H. J. Paton, who was Professor of Moral Philosophy at Oxford, wrote a book *The Claim of Scotland*, in 1968 which is still very topical. At one point he describes people of this kind: 'They echo English clichés about Scottish traditions and ideals and practices. Some of them – though this, I am sorry to say, is found more often in women – become almost venomous in their contempt for Scotland's past and present.' I have come across this attitude in some women myself; I have no idea why it seems to affect them more than men.

In passing, I might mention two events shortly before the Referendum which I think encouraged the loss of confidence. The first, trivial and irrelevant as it might seem, was the fiasco of the Scottish football team in the World Cup. If it is absurd to regard the fortunes of a football team as a barometer of national prowess, it is an absurdity by no means confined to Scotland, but a nation deprived of the normal symbols of Statehood clings to such symbols as it can find. The other was the new BBC programme, Radio Scotland. The BBC, I think, made a mistake in aiming at wide popularity, when there are already many programmes of that kind, and in doing so it removed most of the serious and intelligent content. The Scottish Press was deluged with indignant letters. Many people were made to feel that a country which could not run a football team or a radio programme, could not be trusted to run anything else.

But these were minor and ephemeral depressants, the main encouragement of the feeling of inferiority is more persuasive and continuous. Above all it is in the schools and universities. As *The Scotsman* remarked last February, 'In every country except Scotland, it is taken for granted that national history and literature should be well taught in the schools.' In fact, the schools have been in the forefront of the Scottish attempt to play the Union game according to the letter of the Treaty. In the interests of assimilation, they have discouraged Scottish speech and largely disregarded Scottish history and literature. It is possible for a child to go through the Scottish school system and know virtually nothing about the Scottish contribution to literature, the arts, philosophy and the sciences. In the process, he has been made to feel ashamed of his own speech and deprived of all confidence in it. After the schools, the media continues the same pressures. It might almost be deliberate brainwashing to create a feeling of inferiority, although it has all been done in good   faith   and with good intentions. The Scottish Universities, despite their great achievements have also been subjected to anglicisation, as G. E. Davie has described in his remarkable book *The Democratic Intellect*, one of the most important books written in Scotland in this century. There have, of course, been improvements in the schools and universities, but we have still a long way to go.

A great deal of thought has been directed to Scottish problems in the last 40 years. There is a very substantial and lively literature. There is no shortage of analyses, of ideas, of blueprints and proposals. But somehow this has not penetrated to the people at large. An enlightened minority has been conducting an internal debate. Much of it has been hidden away in small magazines of limited circulation. We thought that the Scottish malaise had been cured, or was about to be, in this new atmosphere of concern, optimism and constructive thought; but the malaise is still there. This malaise is not good for anyone, not for Scotland, not for England, not for Europe. It means a great waste of intellectual and material potential. We are no longer starting from the beginning. The work of the last 40 years is there, but the need now is for communication.

III

In Bed with an Elephant

1. The Three Hundred Years' War

(Saltire Society pamphlet, 1985)

It was Pierre Trudeau, I believe, who said that for Canada to share a continent with the United States was like a man having to share a bed with an elephant. It is an experience which can be dangerous or very uncomfortable and lead to pressures which are difficult to avoid or resist. The elephant can use its sheer bulk and weight to flatten resistance altogether. This can happen even by accident without any malicious intention. If there is a conflict of interests or of tastes, weight is liable to predominate. This sort of experience is common whenever a country has a neighbour much larger and wealthier than itself. The world is full of examples, but one which has a longer history than most, some 700 years at least, is the case of Scotland and England. I should like to look at this example, which affects almost every aspect of our lives. It is a long and continuing story and, to understand it at all, it is necessary to begin with a little history.

The relationship between Scotland and England is the oldest of its kind in Europe, because they were the first countries to consolidate within very much the same borders as still exist. You could trace this border back to the time of the Roman Empire because it closely coincides with Hadrian's Wall. At all events, by the end of the thirteenth century both Scotland and England were relatively consolidated and prosperous states, living in relative peace and harmony with one another. This was an era which came to an abrupt end with the accidental death of King Alexander III of Scotland in 1286. The oldest surviving Scottish poem looks back to his reign as a lost Golden Age, because Edward I of England seized the opportunity of the disputed succession to attempt to take over Scotland, first by diplomatic manipulation and then, when that failed, by force. It was a pattern that was to be repeated frequently for the next 300 years, with the slaughter and destruction renewed in each attack.

The destructive effects of this prolonged attempt to conquer or subvert Scotland are beyond calculation; it was the longest war in European history. English historians, to their credit, have written some of the strongest condemnations of it. Henry Thomas Buckle, for example:

> The darling object of the English, was to subjugate the Scotch; and if anything could increase the disgrace of so base an

enterprise, it would have been that, having undertaken it, they ignominiously failed.[1]

Or James Anthony Froude:

The English hated Scotland because Scotland had successfully defied them: the Scots hated England as an enemy on the watch to make them slaves. The hereditary hostility strengthened with time, and each generation added fresh injuries to the accumulation of bitterness. [2]

It was the misfortune of Scotland to have on her border a country which was not only larger, and therefore more powerful, but which was, for centuries, particularly aggressive and expansionist. Scotland, Wales, Ireland and France were all exposed to repeated English efforts to subjugate them, with varying degrees of success. Every country within reach was fair game. Scotland had the further misfortune that the richest part of the country in the south was the most exposed to English attack and was frequently laid waste.

The national consciousness of Scotland, tempered in the crucible of this long struggle, found early expression in three notable documents. The first of these, the *Declaration of Arbroath of* 1320, was a diplomatic despatch in Latin. It was outstanding among such documents for its eloquence and passion but also for the startling originality, at such an early date, of its political ideas. The orthodox view among modern historians is that the idea of national self-determination evolved at about the time of the French Revolution with Rousseau's doctrine that sovereignty resides in the people and not the ruler. About 400 years before Rousseau, the same fundamental philosophy is expressed clearly and powerfully in this Declaration. Scotland is the oldest nation in Europe because it was the first to evolve two related ideas: that the distinctiveness of a national community is worth defending for its own sake, and that rulers exist to serve the community and not the reverse. There is a paragraph in the Declaration where these two ideas are combined. The previous passage refers to the appointment of Robert as King 'with the due consent and assent of us all'. It then continues:

Yet if he should give up what he has begun, and agree to make us or our kingdom subject to the King of England or the English, we should exert ourselves at once to drive him out as our enemy and a subverter of his own rights and ours, and make some other man who was well able to defend us our King; for, as long as but a hundred of us remain alive, never will we on any conditions be brought under English rule. It is in truth not for glory, nor riches, nor honours that we are fighting, but for freedom – for that alone, which no honest man gives up but with life itself.[3]

The constitutional principles of the Declaration of Arbroath have never ceased to strike echoes in Scotland. Let me give only one example. In his novel *Ringan Gilhaize,* John Galt is concerned to justify the resort by the Covenanters to 'the divine right of resistance' against established authority. He recalls the Declaration in support and, to make sure that the reader does not miss the point, prints the whole text as an appendix. Scottish constitutional theory has always tended to reject the notions that sovereignty resided with a King or with Parliament or with any institution other than the whole community. It follows from this that there is a manifest right to resist injustice from whatever source it comes. Another implication is the egalitarian view that all men have equal rights. This is another assumption which from these early times has strongly influenced Scottish attitudes to politics and religion.

The other two documents which emerged from the struggle for independence are works of a very different character from the Declaration, but they are imbued with the same spirit, the two long narrative or epic poems, Barbour's *Brus* and Hary's *Wallace*. They are two of the earliest surviving works of Scottish literature. So it is a literature which began with the celebration of the two national heroes of the War of Independence and with the assertion and elaboration of the ideas of the *Declaration of Arbroath*. The two poems have had a long-continuing influence, directly and indirectly. Until about the end of the eighteenth century, versions of them were among the most widely read books in Scotland. They in turn influenced other writers who continued to be read long after Barbour and Hary themselves had been relegated to the specialists. Robert Burns, for example, in his famous autobiographical letter to John Moore said: 'the story of Wallace poured a Scottish prejudice in my veins which will boil along there till the flood-gates of life shut in eternal rest'.[4] Many other people have said much the same. It is by such means as these that the epic Scottish struggle for independence has passed into legend or folk memory and helped to shape instinctive attitudes and responses.

One of the consequences of the long war of resistance against England was that Scotland was encouraged to seek markets, allies and cultural and intellectual exchange with continental Europe. For centuries, Scottish merchants, soldiers and scholars travelled everywhere, from Scandinavia to Italy, from Portugal to Russia. Many established themselves in country after country as generals, ambassadors, architects or professors. The contribution which many of these men made to the development of other countries in Europe is very remarkable. Take, for example, James Keith, exiled from Scotland by his Jacobitism. In Russia, he became a general at the age of 32, then Ambassador to Sweden and Governor of the Ukraine. He left the Russian service to become the right-hand man and Field Marshal of Frederick the Great. His brother, George, Earl Marischall of Scotland, was the Prussian Ambassador to Spain, Governor of Neuchatel and the only man to win the unqualified approval of Rousseau. Patrick Gordon, another native of Buchan, also became a Russian General and he was a key figure in the transformation of Russia under Peter the Great. After the Czar himself, John Hill Burton wrote, 'it may be questioned if any other man did so much for the early consolidation of the Russian empire'.[5] John Law of Lauriston shaped French financial policy and founded the Bank of France. George Buchanan, who wrote in Latin (one of the four languages of Scottish literature) was regarded as the leading poet in Europe, 'poetarum nostri saeculi facile princeps'. He was not only Principal of St Leonard's College in St Andrews, but at various times an intellectual force in the universities of Paris, Bordeaux and Coimbra in Portugal. These are only a few random examples from different countries and periods of the intimate Scottish relationship with Europe. Above all we had a close alliance with France for over 300 years, so close that the two countries exchanged citizenship and Scots formed the guard of the French Kings. We were actively and consciously European centuries before the EEC.

This Scottish involvement with the rest of Europe was so different from the much more insular and self-sufficient attitude of England that it alone accounts for many of the radical differences between the Scottish and English traditions. The Scottish interchange with other countries in Europe brought foreign influence at its most stimulating and beneficial. It was diverse and accepted on its merits, not monolithic and imposed; it was quite different from suffocation by elephantine weight. Every aspect of life in Scotland from music and dance to architecture and law was affected by this European influence. In particular, the universities from the fifteenth century onwards developed in close touch with intellectual movements in the rest of Europe. Scottish scholars went, as a matter of course, to study and teach in the universities of France, Italy, Germany and the Low Countries. Many of them brought back new ideas to Scotland. Dugald Stewart, the first historian of the Scottish Enlightenment, had no doubt that its origins were to be found, at least partly, in this 'constant influx of information and of liberality from abroad'[6] during the previous centuries. The Enlightenment was the culmination of a long process, not a sudden and mysterious apparition.

In spite of the constant devastation and wastage of the long war with England, the achievements of the medieval Scottish kingdom were considerable. They reached their highest point towards the end of the fifteenth century during the reign of James IV, a true Renaissance prince. It was the age of Henryson, Dunbar and Douglas, whose poetry was among the most impressive written in Europe in that century. Their language was Middle Scots, a rich and expressive tongue, used for all purposes and at all social levels. It was an age also of intellectual and artistic innovation in many diverse directions and of active involvement in European diplomacy. The demands of the French alliance led to the campaign which ended disastrously at the Battle of Flodden in 1513. So ended, abruptly, the bright hopes of the fifteenth century Renaissance. Indeed it is possible that Scotland never fully recovered from that disaster. It was, wrote Francis Jeffrey, 'the day that broke for ever the pride and splendour of the country'.[7] In the present century, the film director John Grierson said: 'We were driven into the wilderness of national poverty at Flodden by the English and the English have never let us out of it to this day'.[8]

The sorry record of destruction continued long after Flodden. In 1544, for example, Henry VIII sent the English fleet under the Earl of Hertford to sack and burn Leith, Edinburgh, Holyrood and all the towns and villages between them and Dunbar. In the following year, the same Earl of Hertford crossed the Border by land and destroyed 5 market towns, 243 villages, 16 fortified places, hundreds of churches and the Abbeys of Kelso, Melrose, Dryburgh and Roxburgh. The ruins of these Abbeys remain to this day, giving us some idea of how much was lost. But Henry VIII's intervention in Scotland was not confined to marauding armies. Like other English rulers before and since, he used both the stick and the carrot, or, to be more precise, the sword and the bribe. He continued the traditional English policy of seeking out disaffected, greedy or ambitious Scots who could be bribed to serve English interests. There was often, therefore, a faction in Scotland who were secretly in the pay of England. This became a particularly tempting policy to England at the time of the Reformation when the spread of the new religious ideas offered the prospect of breaking Scotland's historical alliance with France. Then, as later, it was not easy to unravel the complex interplay of self-interest and ideological conviction.

2. From the Reformation to the Enlightenment

The Reformation led to a fundamental change in Scotland's international alliances and in the relationship with England. To Protestant

Scotland the continuation of the alliance with Catholic France became untenable. For the first time in more than 300 years, an element of mutual interest affected relations between England and Scotland and pressure towards co-operation instead of conflict began to be felt. So drastic a change did not come easily, but only after some two centuries of travail which culminated with the defeat of the Jacobites at Culloden in 1746. The sixteenth century, when this process began, was a time of quite extraordinary self-confidence in England, which was rationalised and encouraged by theological writers like John Foxe and John Aylmer. They interpreted the Book of Revelation to prove, to their own satisfaction, that Elizabeth was a latter-day Constantine, destined as a Godly Prince to defeat the Anti-Christ and save and lead the world. Aylmer even proclaimed that 'God is English'. Scottish reformers taking refuge in England, and in particular John Knox, came under the influence of these curious ideas, in spite of the destruction of what passed as argument by Napier of Merchiston. The acceptance by the Kirk in Scotland of the Authorised Version of the Bible in 1611 reflected a new attitude to England. To generations of Scots it carried the implication that whether or not God was English, he certainly spoke in English, and that it was the proper tongue for serious and weighty matters. Nothing could have done more to undermine the status of the Scots language at the time when it was beginning to evolve a prose to match its high achievement in verse.

In recent years, the Scottish Reformation has, on the whole, had a bad press, mainly because of its tendency to regard music, dance and the drama as frivolous distractions from the serious matter of man's relations with God. On the other hand, the Kirk has been a beneficial force in more than one direction. It embodies the Scottish egalitarian instinct and distrust of ranks and hierarchy in its representative structure of Kirk Sessions, Presbyteries, Synods and General Assembly. This was the first attempt in these islands to create democratic representation, open to all classes of the community, some 300 years before it was attempted in Parliament. Secondly, from the sixteenth century onwards, it placed high value on education and set about the task of establishing a free school in every parish. By the end of the following century, this policy had been so successful that the great historian, T. B. Macaulay, believed that it had made the common people in Scotland the most intelligent in Europe. 'Scotland made such progress', he wrote, 'in all that constitutes civilisation, as the old world had never seen equalled, and as even the new world has scarcely seen surpassed ... This wonderful change is to be attributed, not indeed solely, but principally, to the national system of education.'[9]

From its beginning, Calvinism has been an intellectual religion, elaborating its doctrines by a process of rigorous logic. This approach was followed not only by the theological writers but by every service in the Kirk. The emphasis was on a closely argued sermon, which the congregation were expected both to follow and to subject to a critical analysis. In his novel *Rob Roy*, Walter Scott describes such a service in Glasgow Cathedral and he concludes:

> The Scotch, it is well known, are more remarkable for the exercise of their intellectual powers, than for the keenness of their feelings; they are, therefore, more moved by logic than by rhetoric, and more attracted by acute and argumentative reasoning on doctrinal points, than influenced by the enthusiastic appeals to the heart and to the passions, by which popular preachers in other countries win the favour of their hearers.[10]

Whether the Kirk created or responded to this national addiction to metaphysical speculation and logical argument, the fact is that for a long period most of the population were exposed to this sort of intellectual exercise every Sunday of their lives.

The parish schools produced a high level of literacy, probably higher than any other country in Europe for about 300 years. The universities were in touch with the movements of European thought. The whole people were trained in 'acute and argumentative reasoning' by the services of the Kirk. All these influences together prepared the way for the intellectual and artistic explosion of the eighteenth century. As John MacQueen has said, 'The Scottish Enlightenment was the natural, almost the inevitable, outcome of several centuries of Scottish and European intellectual history.'[11]

The change which the Reformation brought to the relationship with England was reinforced by a dynastic accident, the succession of a Scottish King, James VI, to the English throne in 1603. This was a consequence of the marriage of the daughter of Henry VII of England to James IV of Scotland. When it was under discussion in the English Court, some of Henry's advisers pointed to the risk that it might bring England under the rule of a Scottish prince. Henry told them not to worry. If that happened, it would mean the accession, not of England to Scotland, but of Scotland to England, since 'the greater would always draw the less, as England had drawn Normandy under her sway'.[12] He was right. The transfer of the Royal Court to London deprived Scotland at a stroke of the control of the Executive, of State appointments and of the conduct of foreign policy. Royal patronage of the arts disappeared with the King. Scots was no longer the language of a royal Court and inevitably began to lose the status of a national speech. In the words of Hume Brown, Scotland had become 'a severed and a withered branch and her people knew it'.

By the beginning of the eighteenth century, this position had become intolerable. The Monarch was still much more than a constitutional myth, and in fact the effective head of executive government. Scotland was nominally independent, but was subject to a Monarch who was under the strong influence of English ministers. Matters came to a head over the Darien Scheme, approved by William as King of Scotland, but undermined by him as King of England. The Scottish Parliament of 1703, largely under the inspiration of Andrew Fletcher of Saltoun, decided that it must either free policy and its execution from royal control or choose a separate successor to the throne of Scotland. The English response was to press for an incorporating union which would absorb the Scottish Parliament in the same way as the Scottish monarchy had been absorbed. This was achieved in 1707, in defiance of the wishes of the people of Scotland at large, by a mixture of bribery, propaganda and military intimidation.[13]

The Jacobite risings were in part an expression of hostility to the Union, but the issue was not simple and clear-cut. Part of the price which England had been prepared to pay for the Union was the acceptance, and indeed guarantee, of the Presbyterian Kirk in Scotland. A restoration of the Stuarts implied the revival of the French alliance and a threat to Presbyterianism. This was a dilemma which meant a painful choice between unpalatable alternatives. Scots might opt, in all conscience, for either side. There were therefore Scots in Cumberland's army at Culloden and some were involved in the barbarous oppression which he carried out in the Highlands after the battle. This, the first exercise of English power in Scotland after the Union, was an act of genocide, the deliberate suppression of a people, a way of life, a culture and a language.

From the earliest times, Scotland has been a multiracial and a multilingual community. We have literatures in four languages, Gaelic, Latin, Scots and English. At the time of Culloden, Gaelic was spoken in more than half of the country and by about a third of the people. As a direct consequence of the policies imposed after Culloden, which made the Clearances possible, most of the Highlands are now largely uninhabited, and Gaelic has been driven to its last stronghold in the Western Isles. Perthshire, for instance, had a rich oral literature in poetry and story. With the loss of the language, the curtain falls and only scraps of the literature remain. In the words which Tacitus attributed to Galgacus, 'They made a desert and they called it peace'.

It was against this discouraging background that occurred the great effloresence of the Scottish eighteenth century, a period of achievement in literature, science and the arts, for which you can find a parallel in a small country only in Periclean Athens or Renaissance

Florence. Certainly, it was the culmination of a long process; so rich a growth can only spring from deep roots. Perhaps also, in a paradoxical way, the immediate political circumstances were a spur to effort. The humiliation of 1707 had threatened the extinction of Scotland. Now the intellect and the arts were being called in evidence to show that Scotland was not to be ignored. One aspect of this was a determination to find new life in the old literary roots. This was explicit in the anthologies of the older poetry, such as John Watson's *Choice Collection* of 1706 and Allan Ramsay's *The Ever Green* of 1724, which were among the first signs of revival. Like MacDiarmid in the present century, they went back to Dunbar as a preparation for a new advance. Burns collected songs and Scott the ballads in the same spirit of resistance to cultural assimilation. Ramsay, Fergusson and Burns wrote poetry in Scots with this conscious purpose, and all three strongly condemned the Union. Both Scott and Galt were anxious to record a Scottish way of life that was being eroded under pressure, and they used Scots as a necessary part of this. At the same time, and in the same spirit, there was a rich flowering of Gaelic poetry in the work of Alasdair Mac Mhaighstir Alasdair, Donnchadh Bàn, Rob Donn and Uilleam Ros.

On the other hand, the philosophers, historians, economists and sociologists, Hume, Robertson, Smith, Adam Ferguson and the others, took pains to write in English but it was not the language which they spoke. An English visitor, Edward Topham, said of them: 'They appear to me, from their conversation, to write English as a foreign tongue; their mode of talking, phrase and expression, but little resembling the language of their works'.[14] They wrote English partly for the same reason that George Buchanan wrote Latin, to reach a wider audience. Also, they were faced with a difficult choice. As Ramsay of Ochtertyre explained it at the time, the events of the seventeenth century had frustrated the development of a Scots prose. In the following century, the literati had either to undertake what Ramsay called the 'Herculean labour' of creating a prose suitable for their purposes or the only slightly less difficult task of learning to write English. 'In this generous but unpromising attempt our countrymen at length succeeded, to the conviction of all the world.'[15] To some extent, Ramsay was looking for an excuse. The need to find a workable prose does not explain the neurotic anxiety with which the literati excised every Scots word or turn of phrase and which provoked the old joke that Hume died confessing not his sins but his Scotticisms.

There was a parallel in the content of their writing. They were preoccupied with the evolution of human society. This was forced on their attention because they were living in Scotland at a time of particularly rapid and violent change, following the loss of independence, the destruction of Highland society after the '45 and the beginning of the industrial revolution. But if their ideas evolved from their Scottish experience, there is remarkably little sign of it in their writing. Take the case of Adam Ferguson. He was a Gaelic-speaking Highlander, born in Logierait in Perthshire in 1724, and he spent nine years as chaplain to the Highland regiment, the Black Watch, immediately after Culloden. In one of his surviving letters, he makes it plain how much he admired the Highland way of life that was being destroyed in his own lifetime. But when he wrote about social change, and speculated about its causes and effects, he drew his examples from ancient Greece and Rome, or the Red Indians of North America, or almost anywhere but Scotland. The same is true of most of his fellow literati. Perhaps the reality of the Scottish situation after the Union and Culloden was so painful that they had to disguise their thought in generalities.

Certainly, there were many other contributory factors. Everywhere in Europe education was still preoccupied with Latin, and to a lesser extent with Greek. It was natural to look to Greece and Rome because their literature and history were more familiar to the educated than those of their own time and country. Sweeping generality was the fashion of the age. There were strong pressures on conformity with the ruling establishment because of their monopoly of patronage. The weight of the London market was already making itself felt. Both Hume and Smith found their publisher there, even if he was Scottish.

Also, there was another attitude which was more openly acknowledged in the second half of the eighteenth century than at any time before or since. Certain people in certain moods felt that they should make the best of a bad job and accept the political implications of the Union by resigning themselves to assimilation. It was a mood, especially acute after Culloden, of let us forget the past and try to be English. No doubt, there have been Scots then and subsequently who have followed this policy in practice, if not always in theory. They have always been a minority, although sometimes an influential one. They have remained a minority partly because of the resilience of the Scottish sense of identity and partly because of the attitude of the English themselves. There is a well-known letter in which David Hume (who was British Chargé d'Affaires in Paris at the time) replies to a suggestion of this sort. 'Can you seriously talk of my continuing an Englishman? Am I, or are you, an Englishman? Will they allow us to be so? Do they not treat with Derision our Pretensions to that Name, and with Hatred our just Pretensions to surpass and to govern them?'[16]

Hume was more than half serious in talking about these pretensions. His letters are full of condemnation of the people whom he called 'the Barbarians who inhabit the Banks of the Thames'. 'John Bull's prejudices are ridiculous', he remarked, 'as his Insolence is intolerable.' He wrote to Edward Gibbon to express polite surprise that an Englishman in that age could write a book of the quality of his *Decline and Fall of the Roman Empire*. The most frequently quoted passage of all from his letters is one where he salutes the achievements of the Scottish Enlightenment: 'Really it is admirable how many Men of Genius this country produces at present. Is it not strange that, at a time when we have lost our Princes, our Parliaments, our independent Government, even the Presence of our chief Nobility, are unhappy in our Accent and Pronunciation, speak a very corrupt Dialect of the Tongue which we make use of; is it not strange, I say, that, in these Circumstances, we shou'd really be the People most distinguis'd for Literature in Europe?'[17] Adam Smith takes a similar position in his explanation of the reasons for the superiority of the Scottish universities over the English.[18] There is a significant remark in Adam Ferguson's *Essay on the History of Civil Society*. The whole book is an argument in favour of the social advantages of life in a community, and he says: 'We need not enlarge our communities, in order to enjoy these advantages. We frequently obtain them in the most remarkable degree where nations remain independent, and are of small extent.'[19] Whatever the reason for the flight of the Scottish Enlightenment literati into generality, it was not due to an inferiority complex or a lack of concern for the interest, standing and reputation of Scotland.

It remains true that the literati in most of their public utterances moved in a disembodied world of pure intellect. One of the first to criticise them for this was John Gibson Lockhart in his book *Peter's Letters to His Kinsfolk*, published in 1819. He discusses the whole question in a letter about a visit to Walter Scott at Abbotsford. The literati of the previous century, he says, had displayed a force of intellect as applied to matters of reasoning, but had largely neglected both feeling and the resources of Scottish history and literature. 'The folly of slighting and concealing what remains concealed within herself, is one of the worst and most pernicious that can beset a country, in the situation wherein Scotland stands.' Scott, he added, was the great genius who had shown Scotland 'her own national character as a mine of intellectual wealth, which remains in a great measure unexplored'.[20]

No one who reads much of Scott can fail to see that one of the mainsprings of his being was a deep concern about the erosion of the Scottish identity and a determination to resist it by drawing on the resources of Scottish history and literature. You can see it in the Introduction to his first substantial work, *The Minstrelsy of the Scottish Border* (1802):

By such efforts, feeble as they are, I may contribute something to the history of my native country, the peculiar features of whose manners and character are daily melting and dissolving into those of her sister and ally. And, trivial as may appear such an offering to the Manes of a Kingdom, once proud and independent, I hang it upon her altar with a mixture of feeling which I shall not attempt to describe.

'There is no mistaking', as Edwin Muir said, 'the emotion in these words.'[21] You can see it again in an episode, which Lockhart recounts in his *Life,* after a meeting of the Faculty of Advocates in Edinburgh in 1806. They had been discussing proposals to bring the administration of justice in Scotland closer to English practice. Lockhart tells us that Scott opposed them with 'a flow and energy of eloquence for which all those who knew him best had been quite unprepared'. He continues:

> ... when the meeting broke up, he walked across the Mound, on his way to Castle Street, between Mr Jeffrey and another of his reforming friends, who complimented him on the rhetorical powers he had been displaying, and would willingly have treated the subject-matter of the discussion playfully. But his feeling had been moved to an extent far beyond their apprehension: he exclaimed, 'No, no – 'tis no laughing matter; little by little, whatever your wishes may be, you will destroy and undermine, until nothing of what makes Scotland Scotland shall remain.' And so saying, he turned round to conceal his agitation – but not until Mr Jeffrey saw tears gushing down his cheek – resting his head until he recovered himself on the wall of the Mound. Seldom, if ever, in his more advanced age, did any feelings obtain such mastery.[22]

These examples are from the beginning of Scott's career. The fullest statement of his feelings and opinions on these matters appeared towards the end of it in *The Letters of Malachi Malagrowther* of 1826. 'I will sleep quieter in my grave', he told James Ballantyne, 'for having so fair an opportunity of speaking my mind.'[23] These letters make a powerful case for the ideas that diversity is preferable to uniformity and centralisation; that Scottish characteristics are valuable for their own sake and should not be abandoned without good reason; that government should be responsive to local needs and wishes; that the overburdened government machine in London should refrain from interference in Scottish affairs.[24] 'There has been in England a gradual and progressive system of assuming the management of affairs entirely and exclusively proper to Scotland, as if we were totally unworthy of having the management of our own concerns.'[25] Scott's position on this matter is very close to views which are widely held in Scotland today; we have still not found a remedy to the problem which disturbed him so deeply. MacDiarmid has pointed out that the line of Scott's thought 'leads naturally on to the separatist position'.[26] Indeed, when it comes to the question of Scotland, there is much in common between Scott, the professed Tory, and MacDiarmid, the professed Communist.

One might ask why this issue came to a head more than a hundred years after the Union. Scott's answer, and modern scholarship has confirmed that he was right, is that English interference began seriously only in the early nineteenth century. Before that, Scotland had been left to sink or swim by her own devices, with the disastrous exception of the suppression of the Highlands after the '45. When James Stuart Mackenzie was appointed in 1761 as the Minister responsible for Scotland, he was surprised to find no papers in his office and no sign that any business was being carried on.[27] Of course, at that time, and for long afterwards, the role of government was very limited. Education and such social services as existed were the concern not of the State, but of the Kirk and the burghs. The Union had left the Scottish legal system, the church and local government intact. They continued to function in their separate ways, although deprived of a Parliament to explore abuses and seek reforms. In Scott's words, Scotland had been left 'under the guardianship of her own institutions, to win her silent way to national wealth and consequence ... But neglected as she was, and perhaps *because* she was neglected, Scotland, reckoning her progress during the space from the close of the American war to the present day, has increased her prosperity in a ratio more than five times greater than that of her more fortunate and richer sister. She is now worth the attention of the learned faculty, and God knows she has plenty of it ... A spirit of proselytism has of late shown itself in England for extending the benefits of their system, in all its strength and weakness, to a country, which has been hitherto flourishing and contented under its own. They adopted the conclusion, that all English enactments are right; but the system of municipal law in Scotland is not English, therefore it is wrong.'[28]

3. The Nineteenth Century Decline

Scotland in the early nineteenth century, when the Elephant began to assert itself, was 'flourishing and contented' in more than a material sense. Her universities were still a major source of stimulation and new ideas for the whole world. The ministers of the Kirk had produced in the *Statistical Account* the first attempt anywhere to study conditions of a country in depth as a rational basis for future policy, even if Scotland had no parliament to give legislative effect to the ideas. Literature was more flourishing in Scotland than almost anywhere else. Scott was the dominant figure internationally, but he was not alone. Both Galt and Hogg were innovative but rooted in the Scottish tradition. *Blackwood's Magazine* and the *Edinburgh Review* were among the most influential periodicals in the world. The Edinburgh of the time was described by John Buchan in these words:

> Many of the great academic figures had gone, but Dugald Stewart and John Playfair were alive; there was a national school of science and philosophy as well as of letters, and there were scholarly country gentlemen, like Clerk of Eldin and Sir William Forbes, to make a bridge between learning and society. Edinburgh was a true capital, a clearing house for the world's culture and a jealous repository of Scottish tradition.[29]

Lord Cockburn, the most perceptive observer of the contemporary scene, described this period as 'the last purely Scotch age that Scotland was destined to see'. 'According to the modern rate of travelling,' he continued (he was writing in 1852), 'the capitals of Scotland and of England were then about 2400 miles asunder. Edinburgh was still more distant in its style and habits. It had then its own independent tastes, and ideas, and pursuits.'[30]

Already by 1852, Cockburn remarked on a sudden and drastic change. The whole country had begun to be 'absorbed in the ocean of London'. Edinburgh, to some extent, resisted. 'This city has advantages, including its being the capital of Scotland, its old reputation, and its external beauties which have enabled it, in a certain degree, to resist the centralising tendency, and have hitherto always supplied it with a succession of eminent men. But, now that London is at our door, how precarious is our hold of them, and how many have we lost.'[31] In his *Journal*, some twenty years earlier, Scott had already remarked on the beginning of the same process: 'In London, there is a rapid increase of business and its opportunities. Thus London licks the butter off our bread by opening a better market for ambition. Were it not for the difference of the religion and laws, poor Scotland could hardly keep a man that is worth having.'[32] 'Triumphant and eclipsing England', wrote Lockhart, 'like an immense magnet, absolutely draws the needles from the smaller ones.'[33]

We might take Carlyle's departure for London in 1834 as the symbolic date of this abrupt and astonishing loss of self-confidence and achievement. For about 100 years Scotland, and Edinburgh in particular, had been in a ferment of artistic and intellectual activity. It was a veritable renaissance which had profound effects on the evolution of the modern world. Both in its sources and its consequences it was international, but it was sustained by Scottish tradition and it was not dominated by any one external influence. A generation earlier, it would have been natural for Carlyle to stay in Scotland and participate in the intellectual excitement. By 1834, the interference of London in Scottish affairs, aided by the improved communications with railways and steamships, made it equally natural for him and countless others to succumb to the pull of the 'immense magnet'. 'The operation of the commercial principle which tempts all superiority to try its fortune in the greatest accessible market, is perhaps irresistible', wrote Cockburn, 'but anything is surely to be lamented which annihilates local intellect, and degrades the provincial spheres which intellect and its consequences can alone adorn.'[34] This is precisely what happened. Scott, writing in 1826, had described the English pressure as beginning in 'the last fifteen or twenty years, and more especially the last ten'.[35] Within two or three decades, the pull and the pressure (for it worked both ways) threatened to reduce Scotland to provincial mediocrity.

The effect was most obvious in literature, which is, I suppose, as good an indication as any of the cultural health of a society. After the brilliance of Scott, Galt and Hogg, all of whom died in the 1830s, there is a melancholy hiatus for the next fifty years. Scotland, which had shown the way at the beginning, failed to continue the development of the realistic novel which distinguished the literatures of England, France and Russia in the mid-nineteenth century. There was, to use a phrase of George Davie's, a sorry 'failure of intellectual nerve'.[36] William Power's explanation is that Scottish writers had 'lost the native tradition, the literary sense of Scottishness. They floundered about in the English scheme of things, and never caught on to anything vital'.[37] Gaelic poetry suffered a similar decline. The sensitivity, intelligence and virtuosity of the eighteenth century was followed by a collapse into triviality in the nineteenth. In one of his letters, Scott said: 'If you *unscotch* us, you will make us damned mischievous Englishmen.'[38] Not so much mischievous, perhaps, as inadequate and second-rate.

An even more astonishing, and, one might think, impertinent campaign of anglicisation was directed against the most successful of Scottish institutions, the universities. They were, after all, the powerhouse of new ideas and of trained minds which had made the Scottish Enlightenment. They were respected, admired and imitated throughout the civilised world, except perhaps in England with its customary attitude of complacent insularity. At the same period, the

two universities in England itself were sunk in lethargy, 'steeped in
port and prejudice', as Edward Gibbon expressed it.[39] Yet, from early
in the nineteenth century, there was a determined and ultimately
largely successful campaign to subordinate the Scottish universities
to English standards. This whole subject is the theme of George
Davie's classic book, *The Democratic Intellect,* one of the most important written in Scotland in this century. It was, he wrote, 'the
tortuous, dark revolution whereby a nation noted educationally both
for social mobility and for fixity of first principles gradually recon-
ciled itself to an alien system in which principles traditionally did not
matter and a rigid social immobilism was the accepted thing'. The
intention was 'to prepare the way for the cultural subordination of
Scotland to England parallel to its political subordination'.[40] Sig-
nificantly, the first move in this campaign was in 1826, the year in
which Scott wrote *The Letters of Malachi Malagrowther.*

Shortly after the publication of George Davie's book in 1961,
C. P. Snow, who wrote one of the enthusiastic reviews of it, made a
speech in Edinburgh. He summed up the matter in these words:

> 150 years ago Edinburgh had probably the best University in
> the world, with a deep and serious intellectual tradition, which
> still exists in this country. I could wish that Scottish education
> had remained a little more different from English rather than
> the reverse, because the Scots have always believed in democratic
> education and in the generalised intellect in a way that my more
> empirical countrymen have never quite believed.[41]

Another distinguished Englishman, V. H. Galbraith, was for many
years Professor of British History in Edinburgh. When he left in 1944,
he drew conclusions from his experiences in Scotland: 'I am perfectly
sure that the future of Scotland lies in a tremendous development of
its own affairs, and having the power to do that. No proposal with
regard to education which comes up here from England is worth a
damn to you'.[42] Unfortunately, this was not the view which had
prevailed during the previous 100 years.

A similar process applied to the schools, again in spite of their
acknowledged achievement. As in the universities, the school system
was distorted in the course of the nineteenth century by the imposition
of incompatible English ideas. One of the qualities of Scottish
education from the sixteenth century was its accessibility to the whole
population without distinction of social class. Take, for example, the
High School of Edinburgh, described by James Grant as 'the most
important in Scotland and intimately connected with the literature
and progress of the Kingdom'.[43] In a speech in 1825 Lord Brougham

said this about it: 'A school like the old High School of Edinburgh is invaluable, and for what is this so? It is because men of the highest and lowest rank of society, send their children to be educated together'.[44] Yet at about the time he was saying this, it was becoming increasingly common for the aristocracy and the more socially ambitious of the middle class to send their sons to the so-called public schools in England which were run on the opposite principle of social exclusivity. For those who wanted to compromise, or who could not afford Eton or the rest, a number of schools on the English model began to be established in Scotland beginning with the Edinburgh Academy in 1824. Apart from the social implications, there was a fundamental divergence in intellectual approach because the English, or imitation-English, schools believed in early specialisation in place of the Scottish principle of a general, broadly based education. The effect of all of this was socially divisive and it tended to create an influential class whose education, and therefore attitudes and allegiance, were more English than Scottish. They were predisposed to form an internal lobby favourably inclined towards anglicisation.

Even so, it is puzzling that the country succumbed so easily when it had such solid achievement behind it and such a history of determined resistance. There were a number of reasons, some peculiar to the period and some which have persisted. In the first place, the assertion of English influence in the early nineteenth century was contemporary with the victory over Napoleon. It was the beginning of a period, which lasted about 100 years, when Britain (which means predominantly England) was the richest and most successful of World Powers. It was the zenith of the British Empire which coloured a large part of the map of the world in red. England was in a triumphant and assertive mood and more than usually difficult to resist. The Napoleonic Wars had direct effects on Scotland. They caused the Establishment, either reacting in panic or seizing an opportunity, to suppress radicalism and curb the free expression of political ideas. At the same time, they encouraged a spirit of British patriotism which tended to displace or conceal traditional Scottish attitudes.

The development of the Empire was to a disproportionate extent the work of Scots who were active everywhere as explorers, administrators, engineers, soldiers, doctors, missionaries and teachers. This preoccupation with careers in the Empire strongly contributed to the distortion of Scottish education. When entrance examinations for the overseas services were introduced, they were based on the English educational system and the Scottish schools and universities had to adjust accordingly if their candidates were to have a fair chance. This helped to establish a habit of concentration on English

history and literature to the exclusion of the Scottish which still
persists, much to the detriment of Scottish self-knowledge and self-
confidence. It may well be true, as Elizabeth Hay wrote recently, that
'the Scots participated in the Empire as Scots. They did not feel it was
England's Empire ... They thought of themselves as Scottish first and
then British'.[45] Even so, the energy which the Scots expended in India,
Canada, Australia, New Zealand and Africa was lost to Scotland.
The one benefit, if it was a benefit, which the Union brought to
Scotland was access to careers in the Empire while it lasted. In any
case, it was benefit to individuals, not to Scotland as a whole. When
this loss of population is added to the wholesale clearance of the
Highlands and the emigration compelled by the neglect of Scotland
itself, it amounts to a massive haemorrhage of talent, energy and skill.
This has been on a scale which threatens the very survival of Scotland;
but Scotland had no Parliament even to discuss the matter and no
government to take action. The haemorrhage has continued. Writing
in 1935 Edwin Muir drew the obvious conclusion:

> Scotland is gradually being emptied of its population, its spirit,
> its wealth, industry, art, intellect, and innate character... If a
> country exports its most enterprising spirits and best minds
> year after year, for fifty or a hundred or two hundred years,
> some result will inevitably follow ... [Scotland is] a country
> which is becoming lost to history.[46]

In the early nineteenth century the people of Scotland were even more
defenceless than they are today. Not only was there no Scottish
Parliament, but only an insignificant part of the population had the
right to vote for the small minority of Scottish members in the British
House of Commons. Parliamentary Reform began in 1832, but it was
not until the Third Reform Act of 1884 that most adult men, but still
no women, had the vote. It was only then that there began to be any
real opportunity for the people at large to have any influence on
events. It is probably not coincidental that it was at about the same
time, as we shall see, that some restraint began to be applied to the
nineteenth century decline.

On the other hand, if Scotland had no Parliament, it did have the
long-established democratic structure of the Church of Scotland,
several centuries in advance of Parliament in accepting the democratic
ideal of equality. Although the General Assembly did not have the
political power of a Legislature, the Church was a great cohesive force
in Scottish society. It had far more impact on the lives of the people
than the remote Government in London, especially as it was largely
responsible for the social services. In Scott's phrase, it was one of the

'institutions' which carried on the life of the country after it was deprived of its Parliament in 1707. As it happened, the Church was incapacitated by an internal crisis precisely at the time when English interference began to assert itself and at the same time as the existing social structure was under strain because of the effects of the new industrialisation. The crisis was a consequence of the imposition of the system of patronage on the Church by Parliament, although this violated guarantees contained in the Union settlement itself. By 1843, this led to the remarkable event of the Disruption, when 450 ministers of the Church, more than a third of the total, gave up their churches, homes and incomes for the sake of their conscience. It was, Cockburn wrote, 'as extraordinary, and in its consequences will probably prove as permanent as any single transaction in the history of Scotland, the Union alone excepted ... It is one of the rarest occurrences in moral history. I know of no parallel to it'.[47] Eventually the Church for the most part reunited, but it never regained the pivotal position which it had held in the life of the country before the Disruption. Nothing has, so far, taken its place. Scotland as never before was left, in Edwin Muir's phrase, with 'no centre, no heart radiating a living influence'.[48] It is a vacuum which in modern conditions only a Parliament can fill.

For all these reasons, Scotland was particularly vulnerable to anglicisation when the process began effectively in the early nineteenth century. The most systematic study of it so far has been one by an American sociologist, Michael Hechter, in his book *Internal Colonialism,* first published in 1975. He identifies three characteristics:

1. 'A defining characteristic of imperial expansion is that the centre must disparage the indigenous culture of peripheral groups.'

2. 'One of the consequences of this denigration of indigenous culture is to undermine the native's will to resist the colonial regime.' (I might remark in passing that one of the commonest forms of this denigration is to describe anything Scottish as 'parochial' or 'narrowly Nationalist', and this is usually said by someone who is himself particularly parochial and chauvinist.)

3. 'Political incorporation also had a decisive effect on the progress of anglicisation, which proceeded not only by government fiat, but through the voluntary assimilation of peripheral élites.'[49]

The implications of Hechter's analysis is that this process, which also applied to Wales and Ireland, was the result of a deliberate and sustained government policy. At least as far as Scotland is concerned, I do not think that this is normally true. English policy in this respect has usually been unconscious, except in moments of panic, as in 1745 and the 1970s. It has been the result more of ignorance and indifference over Scottish interests and aspirations than of a conscious plan to thwart them. In R. L. Stevenson's words, 'The egoism of the Englishman is self-contained. He does not seek to proselytise. He takes no interest in Scotland or the Scots, and, what is the unkindest cut of all, he does not care to justify his indifference.'[50] The sheer elephantine weight of greater numbers and wealth, and a majority of about ten to one in Parliament, has applied itself without conscious effort. The assumption, as Scott said in the *Malachi* letters, has always been that what is English is right and what is not English is therefore wrong.

On the other hand, the efforts of those that Hechter calls the 'peripheral élite', the internal anglicisers, have often been deliberate and even painstaking. In Hechter's words, 'The conscious rationale behind anglicisation among the peripheral élite was to dissociate themselves as much as possible from the mass of their countrymen, who were so strongly deprecated by the English culture. Thus, they eagerly learned to speak English in the home, to emulate English manners and attitudes, to style their very lives on the English model. In effect, this was a voluntary renunciation of their national origins.'[51] This is a phenomenon which began with a small minority as long ago as the Union of the Crowns in 1603. When the King and Court moved to London, the politically and socially ambitious inevitably followed and had to adopt English speech and fashions if they were to be found acceptable. After 1707, Scottish members of Parliament had to do the same to avoid the mockery of the House of Commons. Careers in government service had the same effect. We have already noted the influence of this on the Scottish educational system which in consequence itself tended to become an instrument of anglicisation. To this were added in more recent times the forces of the London press and, even more powerfully, of radio and television. By these means, and once again largely unconsciously on their part, generations of Scots have been brought up to regard English traditions and habits of thought and expression as the norm and to be left almost entirely in ignorance of their own. It is easy to see why Muir felt that Scotland was 'a country which is becoming lost to history'.

4. Does It Matter?

Are we then an endangered species, about to become in fact, as some people already regard us, no more than the inhabitants of a region of England? If so, does it matter? Should we perhaps yield to superior force and give up the struggle? I think that the answer to all of these questions depends on whether there is anything of value in the Scottish tradition which is worth an effort to preserve.

There is first of all the consideration that diversity has a value in itself and is to be preferred to uniformity, especially when it is imposed by external circumstances. This is a proposition to which most people would, I suppose, subscribe. A world reduced to uniformity would not only be dull, but also sterile; inventiveness and the arts would be stifled. Most of us would, as it were, be thinking in translation and trying to adopt attitudes which are not natural to us. Imitation is always likely to be inferior to the spontaneous. As Scott said in the *Malachi* letters:

> For God's sake, Sir, let us remain as Nature made us, English-men, Irishmen, and Scotchmen, with something like the impress of our several countries upon each! We would not become better subjects, or more valuable members of the common empire, if we all resembled each other like so many smooth shillings. Let us love and cherish each other's virtues – bear with each other's failings – be tender to each other's prejudices – be scrupulously regardful of each other's rights. Lastly, let us borrow each other's improvements, but never before they are needed and demanded. The degree of national diversity between different countries, is but an instance of that general variety which Nature seems to have adopted as a principle through all her works, as anxious, apparently, to avoid, as modern statesmen to enforce, anything like an approach to absolute uniformity.[52]

T. S. Eliot, consciously or unconsciously echoing Scott, argued, 'It is to the advantage of England that the Welsh should be Welsh, the Scots Scots and the Irish Irish ... It is an essential part of my case, that if the other cultures of the British Isles were wholly superseded by English culture, English culture would disappear too.'[53] And the principle, of course, has a much wider application than to the British Isles alone.

The world as a whole has never had more need to defend its diversity than today. The forces working towards a monotonous uniformity have never been stronger from the power of mass consumerism, mass advertising and mass entertainment. The rich diversity of human cultures is threatened by a stifling overlay of a meretricious appeal to the lowest common denominator. Pop music is its most obvious and appropriate symbol with its monotonous repetition and trite lyrics expressed in mock American speech, regardless of the natural language of the singer or his audience. It is in the interests of mankind as a whole that each of us should preserve our identity from the flood which threatens to engulf all of us. The Scottish struggle is part of a world struggle.

In Scotland we have had long experience of the consequences of the imposition through the schools and social pressures of external cultural standards. For over 200 years our schools have tried to suppress natural speech, Gaelic or Scots, and make their pupils ape the English. They have diverted attention from our own history, literature and achievement to those of England. The consequence has been a loss of articulacy, spontaneity and self-confidence. If a child is taught to be ashamed of his natural speech, he tends to lose all confidence in self-expression. If he is made to believe that everything of importance happened somewhere else, he is led towards an inferiority complex and a feeling of hopelessness and despair. It is a recipe for an unhealthy society, conditioned to failure, where the only hope is the escape of emigration.

That anything like this should happen in Scotland is particularly remarkable and outrageous in view of the extraordinary record of Scottish achievement. In the words of an American, Harold Orel: 'The record is rich, when seen as an entirety, almost unbelievably so. No nation of its size has contributed as much to world culture.'[54] Another American, H. W. Thompson, in discussing the Scotland of the Enlightenment in the lifetime of Henry Mackenzie, concluded: 'To discover comparable achievements by so small a nation in so short a time we should need to go back from the Age of Mackenzie to the Age of Pericles'.[55] Yet another American, J. K. Galbraith, said that 'the only serious rivals to the Scots were the Jews'.[56] These comparisons are not exaggerated. 'The peculiar history of the Scots', wrote Christopher Harvie, 'has meant that, man for man, they have probably done more to create the modern world than any other nation.'[57] Watt's improvements of the steam engine created the first Industrial Revolution. Clerk Maxwell's discoveries ushered in the new revolution of electronics. The modern approach to such diverse matters as history, economics, sociology, geology, chemistry, medicine and banking were all fundamentally affected by the Scottish Enlightenment. We have produced a notable literature in four languages, including much of the greatest poetry of the late Middle Ages. Our traditional song, poetry and dance are among the most vigorous to be found anywhere. Scots have made a remarkable contribution to many European countries as well as to those of the former British Empire all over the world. You would expect us all to agree with the judgement of the English historian, J. A. Froude: 'No nation in Europe can look with more just pride on their past than the Scots, and no young Scotchman [and I would add woman, of course] ought to grow up in ignorance of what that past has been'.[58] The anglicisation of our education has decreed otherwise. Ironically, at the same time, there is increasing appreciation of the Scottish contribution to our common civilisation in other countries from America to Japan.

It would be a particular loss of a component of human diversity if the Scottish approach to life were supplanted by the English because they are so fundamentally different, socially and intellectually. We share with the French, and perhaps this is the reason for the remarkable persistence of the spirit of the Auld Alliance, a fondness for first principles and an appreciation of precision and logic. The English distrust these things and make a virtue of acting by instinct without a rigorous, and perhaps inhibiting, intellectual analysis. The formidable English historian, H. T. Buckle, one of the great Victorians, made a deep study of this question as part of his preparation for his *History of Civilisation*. His conclusion was that there was:

> An essential antagonism which still exists between the Scotch and English minds; an antagonism extremely remarkable, when found among nations, both of whom, besides being contiguous, and constantly mixing together, speak the same language, read the same books, belong to the same empire, and possess the same interests, and yet are, in many important respects, as different, as if there had never been any means of their influencing each other, and as if they had never had anything in common. [59]

It is not, of course, a question of the superiority of one national tradition over another. All have their strengths and weaknesses; but the more diverse they are, the more likely they are to enrich our common civilisation with a wide range of achievement and offer a choice of different possible solutions to our problems. It is an impoverishment of civilisation as a whole, if a valuable national tradition is suppressed or supplanted by another. At the same time, the cross-fertilisation of ideas and influence is a fruitful source of stimulation, provided the recipient is free to take, in Scott's words, what is 'needed and demanded', and to reject what is not suitable for his purposes. This is something which is quite different from the stifling imposition by force or elephantine weight of different standards, attitudes and values from one particular source. The great medieval poetry of Scotland and the Scottish Enlightenment are examples of the benefits of wide international influence. The collapse of confidence and achievement after about 1830 is an example of the consequences of elephantine pressure.

Eric Linklater in his book *The Lion and the Unicorn,* of 1935, summed up the effects of the substitution of English culture for 'that diversity of cultures with which, in earlier times, Scotland had always been in contact':

> By reason of its association with England, Scotland became insular. Its political frontier was broken down and its mind was walled up. Geographical or political enlargement, beyond

certain limits, is nearly always accompanied by intellectual shrinkage.[60]

5. Revival

In *The Democratic Intellect* George Davie says that in the Scotland of the nineteenth century, 'the old confident grip on the situation was noticeably slackening. Instead of the steady rhythm of independent institutional life, a new pattern emerged of alternation between catastrophe and renaissance, in which the distinctive national inheritance was more than once brought to the very brink of ruin only to be saved at the last minute by a sudden burst of reviving energy.'[61] In the mid-nineteenth century, Scotland seemed about to decline into passive acceptance of provincial mediocrity, into what C. J. Watson has described as 'the sense of weariness, of the absence of hope, and lacerating self-contempt which is a marked component in the psyche of colonised peoples'.[62]

Even so, the decline was only in comparison to the generation before. There was strong resilience in the Scottish spirit in spite of the conformity on the surface. In Scotland, oral and traditional literature has always nourished and been nourished by literature of the more formal kind, as in the revival introduced by Watson and Ramsay in the eighteenth century. These traditions remained vigorously alive. In the mid-century, J. F. Campbell collected four volumes of Gaelic traditional stories. Towards the end of the century, Gavin Greig and the Rev. James Duncan found about 3,000 Scots songs alive in folk tradition in Buchan alone. William MacTaggart was painting from about the middle of the century. Brewster, Kelvin and Clerk Maxwell continued the scientific traditions of the Enlightenment, although they were no longer sustained by the 'independent institutional life' which had encouraged the achievements of the previous century.

The first coherent 'burst of reviving energy' came in the 1880s and 1890s. In this, as subsequently, political developments and the formation of new institutions coincided with a resurgence of literature and the other arts. It seems that a quickening of one aspect of Scottish life stimulates the others. In the 1880s, for instance, the Scottish Home Rule Association was formed and the conference of the Scottish Liberal Party adopted for the first time the policy of Home Rule for Scotland. Parliament passed an Act to re-establish the office of Secretary of State. The National Portrait Gallery, the Scottish Text Society and the Scottish History Society were formed.

Stevenson wrote *Kidnapped* and *The Master of Ballantrae.* By 1895, Sir Patrick Geddes was able to write in his periodical, *Evergreen,* of a Scots Renaissance, long before the term was applied to the movement associated with Hugh MacDiarmid. Geddes was himself a leader in this revival devoted to the cause of escaping from the 'intellectual thraldom of London' and restoring the old sympathies between Scotland and the Continent.[63] In the same spirit, he tried to found a College des Ecossais in Montpellier as a revival of the Scots College in Paris, established in 1326 as the first Scottish institution of higher learning.

The First World War intervened, with the destructive effects on Scottish communities chronicled by Lewis Grassic Gibbon in *Sunset Song.* Like the Napoleonic Wars, it diverted attention away from Scotland's own concerns. On the other hand, it purported to be a war fought for the right of self-determination and it did lead to the restoration of several small nations to the map of Europe. These ideas contributed to a second wave of 'reviving energy' in the 1920s and 30s. This is associated particularly with Hugh MacDiarmid who campaigned throughout his life for Scottish independence and for a revival, not only of Scots and Gaelic, but of Scottish culture in the widest sense, far-ranging both in intellectual content and in its international ramifications. His work resumes and restates many of the constant themes of Scottish writing. In resisting anglicisation, he was echoing Scott; in returning to Dunbar for inspiration and example, he was following the lead of Ramsay; in extending the use of Scots, he was building on the foundation of Fergusson and Burns; in responding to the latest tendencies in international thought, and regarding all knowledge as an interlocking whole, he was in the tradition of the Scottish Enlightenment; in his radical politics he was extending a tradition that goes back through MacLean, Muir of Huntershill, the Covenanters, the Reformation and George Buchanan to the Declaration of Arbroath. 'To MacDiarmid,' wrote Tom Scott, 'the English Ascendancy was a historical iniquity with no right but might behind it, and to be overthrown by all good men and true.'[64]

Once again, literary, political and institutional developments moved forward together. MacDiarmid published *A Drunk Man Looks at the Thistle* in 1926. He became the centre of a very lively literary life, with poets, novelists and dramatists like Sydney Goodsir Smith, Robert Garioch, Sorley MacLean, George Campbell Hay, Neil Gunn, Lewis Grassic Gibbon, Eric Linklater, Robert Kemp, Robert Maclellan and many others. The National Library of Scotland was established in 1925 on the basis of the Advocates Library, founded in 1682. (Like the National Portrait Gallery, it was made possible by private generosity.) In 1936, the Saltire Society was formed to 'work for a revival of the intellectual and artistic life of Scotland such as we experienced in the eighteenth century'. The Scottish National Party was founded in 1934 by the fusion of two older parties. In 1939, the Government moved Departments concerned with Scotland from London to Edinburgh.

Again, a World War deferred expectations and scattered the men involved in the new atmosphere of intellectual vitality. However, during the War itself, MacDiarmid and the others continued to write and plan and work for the future. Tom Johnston as Secretary of State gave an impetus to the search for Scottish solutions to Scottish problems. Scottish Convention began a campaign which led in 1949 to the collection of some two million signatures to a Covenant demanding a Scottish Parliament. In the immediate post-war period, both the political and the intellectual movements gathered momentum. The first Edinburgh International Festival was held in 1947. In the same year, the Scottish Arts Council became largely autonomous (although constitutionally still a part of the Arts Council of Great Britain). Since then it has been a valuable channel of public subsidy to the arts, and has contributed substantially to the revival of Scottish publishing and to the emergence of a diversity of literary magazines. Scottish historical scholarship in particular has acquired new vitality and challenged many accepted ideas of the Scottish past. The electoral successes of the SNP in the 1960s and 70s attracted attention as never before to Scottish issues. All political parties committed themselves to a measure of Scottish self-government. When the Scotland Act was put to the people in the Referendum of 1979, however, the Conservative Party campaigned for a 'No' vote with the promise that they would introduce an improved measure with stronger powers. They then used the small 'Yes' majority as a justification for taking no further action.

The optimism and self-confidence generated by the hopes of constitutional advance in the 1970s led to a marked quickening of the national life. There was an injection of new spirit into the Scottish theatre and a strong increase in the writing and publication of serious Scottish books. Planning for a revitalised Scotland was very active. The Saltire Society, for example, held a conference in 1977 to consider the policies necessary in an autonomous Scotland for the encouragement of artistic and intellectual life. The conference decided to consult all organisations concerned with these matters with a view to the formation of a combined think-tank. This, the Advisory Council for the Arts in Scotland, was established after wide consultation in 1981, two years after the Referendum.

This continuation of effort in spite of the setback was not untypical. There is no doubt that the muted 'Yes' majority in the

Referendum, and the confusion of the issues by the disingenuousness of the 'No' campaign, brought with it a mood of humiliation and resignation. At the same time, the forward momentum was not entirely lost, even if much of it went below the surface. All political parties, with the present exception of the Conservatives, are more fully committed than ever to self-government, and these parties had more than 70% of the Scottish vote in the last two general elections. The Campaign for a Scottish Assembly has been active in promoting co-operation between the parties and in drawing up detailed plans for a Constitutional Convention. Constitutional advance now seems only a matter of time, but there is not much time left before it is too late.

This consideration of contemporary politics is unavoidable because it is central to the issue. In Donald Dewar's words, 'There is a real connection between political power and the survival of a culture.'[65] The close association which we have noted between political and cultural confidence and activity is not accidental. They have advanced together and declined together. Scotland is threatened with extinction as an active, creative component of European civilisation because of the vacuum at its heart, the absence of any focus for the national life and the denial of responsibility for its own affairs. 'I believe', said Eric Linklater, 'people degenerate when they lose control of their own affairs, and as a corollary that resumption of control may induce regeneration. To any nation the essential vitamin is responsibility.'[66]

Scotland is now poised for a new surge of political and cultural advance. It has been a slow process, but each of the surges during the last 100 years has left us a little further up the beach. We are equipped as never before with the tools for an intelligent understanding of our position, both in the results of the new historical scholarship and in such reference works as the *Companions* of David Daiches, Derek Thomson and Trevor Royle. W. L. Lorimer's *Translation of the New Testament* has given new force to Scottish prose. *The Concise Scots Dictionary* has made widely available the great resources of *The Scottish National Dictionary* and the *Dictionary of the Older Scottish Tongue*. The Report in 1985 of the Consultative Committee on the Curriculum was a positive revolution in the thought of Scottish educationalists. Their recommendation that 'the Scottish dimension, Scottish language, literature, geography and history are not frills, but should be central to the education of the children who attend Scottish schools'[67] may seem self-evident but it is far from the practice which has prevailed up to the present. At the same time, there has probably never been a stronger political consensus on the need for constitutional change. As I write, the latest opinion poll on the subject shows a majority in favour of an independent Parliament. That is what we need. Any degree of self-government would be beneficial; but for Scotland to be free to develop and play its full part in Europe as in the past, it needs as much independence as Luxembourg or Denmark or any other member of the EEC.

Can we then be optimistic? Are we to be saved at the eleventh hour by another 'burst of reviving energy'? Only, I think, if we all make a determined effort. All the positive forces which I have mentioned are opposed, if largely unconsciously, by the forces of assimilation and they have the weight of superior numbers and wealth on their side. Our minds are flooded daily by television programmes and very few of them originate in Scotland. To the activities of the internal anglicisers, who are always with us, are added an increasing number of immigrants who actually are English. This is a new phenomenon on anything like the present scale. We welcome them, as is proper, with our traditional hospitality. Many of them take trouble to learn about us and bring with them qualities of real value. Others live in a cocoon of deliberate and complacent ignorance of the society that surrounds them. This would not matter very much, except that many of them occupy key positions in our institutions, even in those which are supposed to be the custodians of our traditions and values. This is prevalent not only in Government but in the universities, the theatre and even in local arts festivals where there is often no Scottish element at all. We are sometimes left feeling like strangers in our own country who are gradually being displaced by a colonial regime. It was such a thought as this that led James Campbell to say of the Clearances in his book *Invisible Country,* in 1984: 'Throughout the entire country there is the sense that what took place in the Highlands during the earlier part of last century is a clue to what has happened to modern Scotland'.[68]

One of the founding members of the Saltire Society, Andrew Dewar Gibb, in considering the consequences of the elephantine pressures, concluded: 'Thus have closer ties with England resulted in the debasement, if not the total destruction, of a great national possession'.[69] When you consider the facts, this is a conclusion which it is difficult to avoid. As I have said, I do not think that this effect has been deliberate or malevolent, at least since the suppression of the Highlands; but it is inherent in the present constitutional position. We want to have friendly and productive relationships with all countries, and certainly with our nearest neighbour. Not the least of the reasons why we urgently need a constitutional change is that otherwise an equitable and fair relationship with England is impossible.

IV

The Democratic Intellect

The Scottish Enlightenment

(Lecture to the Melrose Literary Society, 4 October 1983)

The William Smellie who not only printed the first edition of the *Encyclopaedia Britannica* in Edinburgh in 1771 but wrote most of it himself also wrote an account of some of the characters of Enlightenment Edinburgh, the *Literary and Characteristical Lives*. In it there is a well-known report of a conversation which describes one of the characteristics of the Edinburgh at the time:

> Mr Amyat, King's Chymist, a most sensible and agreeable English gentleman, resided in Edinburgh for a year or two. He one day surprised me with a curious remark. There is not a city in Europe, said he, that enjoys such a singular and such a noble privilege. I asked, What is that privilege? He replied, Here I stand at what is called the Cross of Edinburgh and can, in a few minutes take fifty men of genius and learning by the hand. The fact is well known; but to a native of that city, who has all his days been familiarized with it, and who has not travelled in other countries, that circumstance, though very remarkable, passed unnoticed: Upon strangers, however, it makes a deep impression. In London, in Paris, and other large cities of Europe, though they contain many literary men, the access to them is difficult; and, even after that is obtained, the conversation is, for some time, shy and constrained. In Edinburgh, the access of men of parts is not only easy, but their conversation and the communication of their knowledge are at once imparted to intelligent strangers with the utmost liberality. The philosophers of Scotland have no nostrums. They tell what they know, and deliver their sentiments without disguise or reserve.[1]

Smollett's *Humphrey Clinker* was published in the same year as the first *Encyclopaedia Britannica*. In it Matthew Bramble described Edinburgh as 'a hotbed of genius' and said that the literati were as 'agreeable in conversation as they are instructive and entertaining in their writings'. 1771 was also, as it happens, the year of Walter Scott's birth. Looking back on the age immediately before his own he said that it was a 'period when there were giants in the land' and added in *Guy Mannering* that these men were 'a circle never closed against

strangers of sense and information, and which has perhaps at no
period been equalled, considering the depth and variety of talent
which it embraced and concentrated.'

Smellie, Smollett and Scott are, of course, all talking in these
passages about what we now call the Scottish Enlightenment, which
was part, but by no means the whole, of an extraordinary explosion
of intellectual and artistic achievement. Although it has its roots deep
in the past, and the effects still reverberate, the Enlightenment
reached the highest point of its achievement in the second half of the
eighteenth century with a second peak in the age of Walter Scott. As
it happened, both of these periods fell within the lifetime of Henry
Mackenzie, who was born in the year of the last Jacobite Rising,
1745, and died in 1831, only a year before the death of Scott.

In the passage from Scott from which I have already quoted, he
noted this connection. He was writing a series of introductions for
Ballantyne's *Novelists' Library* of 1821 and said this:

> It is enough to say here, that Mr Mackenzie survives, venerable
> and venerated, as the best link of the chain which connects the
> Scottish literature of the present age with the period when there
> were giants in the land – the days of Robertson, and Hume and
> Smith, and Home and Clerk and Ferguson.

When the American, Harold Thompson, wrote a biography of
Henry Mackenzie a hundred years later in 1931 he remarked on the
great range of accomplishments by Mackenzie's Scottish contemporaries. He summarised it in these words:

> Within Mackenzie's crowded lifetime of eighty-six years (1745–
> 1831) Scotland produced the greatest of sceptical philosophers,
> David Hume; the best loved of song-poets, Robert Burns; the
> king of romancers, Sir Walter Scott; the two chief masters of
> modern biography, James Boswell and John Gibson Lockhart;
> the most virile of British architects of his century, Robert Adam.
> At the same time, the dynasty of the Doctors Monro made
> Edinburgh's Medical College the most respected in the world;
> Adam Smith founded the modern science of Political Economy,
> James Hutton did as much for Geology, and Joseph Black
> revolutionized Chemistry. Nor was this all; the world's roads
> were rebuilt according to the methods of John Loudon McAdam:
> the world's industry was remade by the steam-engine of James
> Watt ... Nearly all that makes Scotland great is of that Golden
> Age; to discover comparable achievements by so small a nation
> in so short a time we should need to go back from the Age of
> Mackenzie to the Age of Pericles.[2]

That is a formidable catalogue by any standards, but it is far from
complete. Thompson does not mention, for example, the contribu-

tions of Hume and Robertson to modern historical scholarship, the importance of Adam Ferguson for the sociologists, the great civil engineers like Telford and Rennie, the stimulation of psychological enquiry, nor the transformation of agricultural methods and even of banking practice. I do not propose to attempt to cover the whole ground. That is a subject for a book or a series of books. The fact, quite simply, is that almost every field of human effort, ideas, science and technology was fundamentally affected by this Scottish contribution. It profoundly marked the subsequent evolution of human society. My object is to try to identify some of the characteristics of the Scottish Enlightenment and to consider the historical origins of this astonishing outburst of intellectual energy.

I think, if only to keep the subject within manageable limits, that we should confine ourselves to what might be called the central themes of the Enlightenment, as distinct from all the other diverse activities that were going on at the same time. To some extent, this is an artificial distinction, even one that is alien to the spirit of the Enlightenment itself. It has, for example, been customary to differentiate sharply between Hume, Smith and Robertson, who took pains to write in English (although this was not the language they spoke) and the revival of poetry in Scots by Ramsay, Robert Fergusson and Burns. Modern scholarship, as in a recent book of Professor John MacQueen, has found a strong influence of Enlightenment ideas in the poets. Still, it is possible to look at the work of such men as Hume, Robertson, Adam Ferguson, Adam Smith and Lord Kames, as one strand, even if it is an interlocking strand, in a complex web.

Perhaps the first thing to notice about them is how closely they were interconnected. Many of them, like Hume, Ferguson and Smith, spent some time outside Scotland, often as tutors to noblemen on the grand tour; but most of their lives were spent in or around Edinburgh and Glasgow. In the intimacy of those comparatively small towns, as both were still, they met almost daily. They joined in clubs, like the Select and the Poker, to exchange ideas and they took an evident pleasure in the society of one another. A friend of Alexander Carlyle said of one of the clubs that it was 'composed, he believed, of the ablest men of Europe'. When Hugh Blair devoted one of his sermons, 'On the Happiness of a Future State', to life after death, the description sounds very much like one of these Edinburgh clubs. 'The intercourse we here maintain with one's fellows', he said, 'is a source of our chief enjoyments.' As Neil McCallum put it in his recent book, 'This momentous generation was in constant converse with itself'. 'It was', wrote Lord Cockburn, 'a discussing age.'

At a time when travel further afield was difficult, there was constant exchange between Edinburgh and Glasgow. Adam Smith lectured in Edinburgh before taking a Chair in Glasgow. The chemists Cullen and Black both moved between Chairs in Glasgow and Edinburgh. There was a third pole at Aberdeen where Thomas Reid was a regent of King's College. The great mathematician, Colin McLaurin moved from Aberdeen to join James Gregory at Edinburgh. Under them, and James Gregory at St Andrews, the Scottish universities became the first in the world to teach Newtonian mathematics.

The Enlightenment movement did not depend on the universities alone but also on two other institutions, the Church and the Law. These institutions were left unscathed by the Union of 1707. Indeed their independence was guaranteed by the Treaty, even if the Treaty was frequently disregarded by Westminster. The universities, the Church and the Law formed three overlapping circles within which the same men moved freely. William Robertson, the historian, who was a central figure in the Enlightenment, was a strong influence in both University and Kirk, Principal of Edinburgh and Moderator of the General Assembly. David Hume trained in the law at Edinburgh and was for a time Keeper of the Advocates Library. Adam Ferguson was ordained as a minister. Lord Kames was a judge.

The Law and the Church both influenced, and were influenced by, the ideas of the Enlightenment. The Law, with a philosophical jurisprudence first elaborated in Stair's *Institutions* in 1681, was (in Neil MacCormick's words) 'rationally related to general principles of right'. It therefore had a close association with the Enlightenment concern with ethics and it is not surprising that so many of the literati of the Enlightenment, like Hume, Monboddo and Kames, were lawyers either by training or in practice.

Virtually all of the thinkers of the Enlightenment had grown up in the atmosphere of the Presbyterian Kirk. The concern of the Kirk for rigorous analysis of first principles and for individual responsibility was one of the formative influences behind the Enlightenment. In the eighteenth century the 'Moderate' movement in the Kirk reacted against the religious 'enthusiasm' and preoccupation with theological controversy of the seventeenth century. At the same time, this very controversy had established a habit of speculative thought and the rigorous application of logic to questions of human belief and behaviour.

The Scottish universities, in which the literati, the ministers and the lawyers were trained, were themselves moulded on a philosophical ideal which George Davie has called the 'democratic intellect'. It was democratic in two senses. Firstly, because the universities were widely open to the population at large and not restricted to a social élite. Secondly, because they were intended to give a broad philosophical education, treating all knowledge as interrelated, to widen mental horizons, not to restrict them to one narrow specialisation.

This all-embracing approach to all learning and all human activity was reflected throughout the whole Scottish Enlightenment movement. Adam Smith wrote and lectured on jurisprudence and moral philosophy as well as economics. He intended *The Wealth of Nations* to be only part of a wide examination of all the problems of human society. Hume, too, wrote on economics as well as history and philosophy. Cullen lectured on agriculture as well as chemistry. Kames wrote on law, literary criticism, morality and religion, history and the improvement of agriculture, provoking Voltaire to the jibe that if you wanted to learn the rules of anything from epic poetry to gardening, you had to go to Scotland to learn them. James Watt's workshop was described as a 'kind of academy whither all the notabilities of Glasgow repaired to discuss the nicest questions in art, science and literature'. There were relationships of family and friendship, as well as mutual intellectual appreciation and stimulation, between the disciplines. Adam Ferguson was a cousin as well as the biographer of Joseph Black. James Hutton, the founder of modern geology, was a close friend and dining companion of both Black and Adam Smith. Joseph Black was Hume's doctor in his last illness; Adam Smith was his literary executor. The consequence of these relationships and this breadth of view was a cross-fertilisation between abstract speculation and its practical application. As usual, David Hume summed up the matter: 'The same age, which produced great philosophers, and politicians, renowned generals and poets, usually abounds with skillful weavers and ship-carpenters. We cannot reasonably expect, that a piece of woollen cloth will be brought to perfection in a nation, which is ignorant of astronomy, or where ethics are neglected'. That might well be taken as the motto of the Scottish Enlightenment.

The study of medicine in the universities encouraged research in botany and chemistry. In turn, this new knowledge not only benefited medicine but was directly applied to agricultural and industrial development. Agricultural improvement was one of the great themes of the Enlightenment. We have seen how many of the literati combined philosophy and the law with concern over crops, manure or animal husbandry. Many of them were directly involved in farming because they were lairds as well as lawyers and philosophers. The lairds as a class were caught up in the Enlightenment partly because of this urge to apply the new science to agriculture and also because they dominated the legal profession. This was a tradition with deep roots.

In 1496, an Act of James IV required the eldest sons of barons and freeholders to attend the grammar schools until they had perfect

Latin and then spend three years in the study of law. For centuries, Scottish students and professors had travelled freely between the universities of Europe. After the Reformation, they turned largely to Holland, where the religious climate was congenial and the legal system, as in Scotland, was based on Roman Law. Many students of the law in Holland were influenced as well by Dutch agricultural methods. To give only one example, Andrew Fletcher of Saltoun, who was one of the first writers to speculate on political questions in an Enlightenment spirit, was also one of the first 'improving' lairds to introduce new agricultural techniques from Holland.

The improvement of agriculture began with a series of Acts of the Scottish Parliament between 1661 and 1695, which encouraged the consolidation and enclosure of land. Farming in Scotland was gradually transformed to become a model for the rest of Europe in skill and efficiency, with radical effects on standards and habits of living. But this was only one of the changes which affected Scotland in the course of the eighteenth century. The Revolution of 1688 ended the attempts of the Crown to impose Episcopalianism by force and released the energies which had been absorbed in religious controversy and resistance. The Union of 1707 destroyed Scottish independence and was a shock to Scottish pride, but in a curious way, it also released energy. Westminster, after reducing Scotland to political impotence then lost interest and Scotland was largely left to its own devices. For example, when James Stuart Mackenzie was appointed as the Minister in charge of Scottish affairs in 1761, he was astonished to find hardly any papers in his office and no sign that any business was being carried out. Scotland became, for a time, a political vacuum; but this was also a challenge to the Scots to see what they could do for themselves to repair the damage.

The initial economic effect of the Union was to destroy Scottish industry because of the free entry of English goods. The close connection with the continent of Europe which Scotland had enjoyed for centuries was severed. On the other hand, the Union facilitated, although it did not begin, Scottish trans-Atlantic trade. This brought new wealth to Glasgow through tobacco. It also encouraged the close intellectual relationship between Scotland and America which enabled the Scottish Enlightenment to play a decisive part in both the constitutional and educational development of the United States. The exception to Westminster's indifference to Scotland was, of course, in the reaction to the '45. For a time, the Government in London was scared and it reacted with the systematic destruction of Highland society, another drastic and traumatic change.

Added to all these changes was the beginning of the industrial revolution, to which James Watt's improvement of the steam engine was crucial. All over Europe, society was in transformation; but, despite the French Revolution, perhaps nowhere so drastically as in Scotland. As Walter Scott wrote in the last chapter of *Waverley* in 1814: 'There is no European nation, which, within the course of half a century, or little more, has undergone so complete a change as this Kingdom of Scotland'. Against this background, it is not surprising that the thinkers of the Scottish Enlightenment were moved, almost inevitably, to look at the world in historical terms, to consider the nature of the historical process and its effects on man in society. Among their early achievements were the histories of Robertson and Hume which, as Bruce Lenman has said, 'represent the first emergence of recognisably modern historical scholarship'. David Hume said himself: 'I believe this is the historical Age and this the historical Nation', and added that he knew of no less than eight histories then being written in Scotland.

The Scottish Enlightenment approached history, as everything else, in a philosophical spirit. That is to say, they sought not merely to discover what had happened, but to establish a chain of cause and effect and to deduce from it the general principles of the evolution of human society. They added an historical dimension to the work of Montesquieu to show that the structure of society, its beliefs and aspirations, its form of law and government, were determined by the environment and by the stage of economic development. In making this analysis, they sought to apply to society the scientific methods which Bacon and Newton had used for the study of physical phenomena. As John Millar wrote in 1786, 'The great Montesquieu pointed out the road. He was the Lord Bacon of this branch of philosophy. Dr Smith is the Newton.' These enquiries, particularly in the work of Hume, Smith, Ferguson and Millar, laid the basis not only of the modern approach to history, and of the Marxist analysis of it, but of the whole discipline of sociology.

The Scottish Enlightenment applied the same scientific approach to the study of human nature, or, as we now say, of psychology. Hume described his *Treatise of Human Nature* as 'an attempt to introduce the experimental method of Reasoning into Moral Subjects'. One of the earliest of the literati, Francis Hutcheson, Professor of Moral Philosophy at Glasgow from 1729 to 1746, related both aesthetic and moral ideas to human sentiments. Kames similarly related law to human drives and emotions. This psychological approach to such diverse themes as aesthetics, ethics and jurisprudence is one of the ways in which the Scottish Enlightenment saw an underlying unity in apparent diversity. "Tis evident', Hume wrote in his *Treatise,* 'that all the sciences have a relation, greater or less, to human nature'.

The Scottish Enlightenment was essentially a Scottish phenomenon, the work of a group of Scots, based on Scottish institutions, with deep roots in Scottish intellectual tradition and responding to the historical situation in which Scotland found itself. Neil McCallum in his recent book put it like this: 'Hume, Smith, Watt, Cullen, Hutton and their fellows were all products of their country. They were made familiar in their youth with a habit of thought which dealt in fundamentals. Whatever individual genius each possessed, it was nourished to maturity by the country into which they had been born'. That is certainly true, but it is also true that the Enlightenment was not something which developed in isolation. In the first place, all educated men at the time were deeply steeped in the Latin classics. The High School of Edinburgh, where so many of the literati were educated, and similar schools in other burghs, offered little else. It is something which we easily forget now in an age which knows little Latin, but ancient Rome was never far from the minds of these men of the eighteenth century. Hume found the origin of many of his ideas in Cicero. Adam Ferguson was a Gaelic-speaking Highlander. When he wrote his *Essay on the History of Civil Society* in 1767, the '45 and its aftermath could not have been far from his mind, but he drew most of the examples to illustrate his arguments from classical antiquity.

Secondly, Scottish thought was very much in touch, and had been for centuries, with the literature, science and philosophy of continental Europe. Dugald Stewart succeeded Adam Ferguson in the Edinburgh Chair of Moral Philosophy in 1785 and was widely regarded in his day as the most successful teacher of philosophy to be found anywhere. In his history of European philosophy, he had this to say about this Scottish involvement in Europe:

> It deserves to be remarked, as a circumstance which throws considerable light on the literary history of Scotland during the latter half of the eighteenth century, that, from time immemorial, a continual intercourse had been kept up between Scotland and the Continent. To all who were destined for the profession of law, an education either at a Dutch or French university was considered as almost essential. The case was nearly the same in the profession of physic; and, even among the Scottish clergy, I have conversed, in my youth, with some old men who had studied theology in Holland or in Germany. Of our smaller country gentlemen, resident on their own estates, (an order of men which, from various causes, has now, alas! totally vanished,) there was scarcely one who had not enjoyed the benefit of a university education; and very few of those who could afford

the expense of foreign travel, who had not visited France and Italy. Lord Monboddo somewhere mentions, to the honour of his father, that he sold part of his estate to enable himself (his eldest son) to pursue his studies at the University of Groningen. The constant influx of information and of liberality from abroad, which was thus kept up in Scotland in consequence of the ancient habits and manners of the people, may help to account for the sudden burst of genius, which to a foreigner must seem to have sprung up in this country by a sort of enchantment, soon after the Rebellion of 1745.[3]

With the comment by Dugald Stewart (whose monument in Edinburgh, you may remember, dominates the view towards the Castle from the Calton Hill), we move from considering the nature of the Scottish Enlightenment to its historical origins.

There is one idea on this subject which can be dismissed at once because it does not stand up to serious examination. This is the notion that the Scottish Enlightenment derived in some unexplained way from the Union of 1707, as though it were possible for such a deep-rooted and wide-reaching intellectual movement to spring out of nothing in so short a time. Apart from anything else, England was in no position in the eighteenth century to provide intellectual stimulus. Oxford and Cambridge, her only universities, were, in Gibbon's phrase 'steeped in port and prejudice'. When Gibbon himself published his *History of the Decline and Fall of the Roman Empire*, Hume sent him a letter on 18th March 1776, which Gibbon printed in his *Autobiography*, where he said that it 'overpaid the labour of ten years'. After praising Gibbon's *History*, Hume continues: 'If I had not previously had the happiness of your personal acquaintance, such a performance from an Englishman in our age would have given me some surprise. You may smile at this sentiment, but, as it seems to me that your countrymen, for almost a whole generation, have given themselves up to barbarous and absurd faction, and have totally neglected all polite letters, I no longer expected any valuable production ever to come from them'. The Englishmen who had some influence on the Scottish Enlightenment, Bacon, Locke and Newton, had completed their important work in the previous century. Most of the contemporary foreign influences were French or Dutch.

T .B. Macaulay suggested that the explanation for the eighteenth century achievement was to be found in the Act of the Scottish Parliament for the Settling of Schools of 1695:

Before one generation had passed away, it began to be evident that the common people of Scotland were superior in intelligence

to the common people of any other country in Europe...
Scotland made such progress ... in all that constitutes civilisation, as the Old World had never seen equalled, and as even the
New World has scarcely seen surpassed.
    This wonderful change is to be attributed, not indeed solely,
but principally, to the national system of education.[4]
    The 1695 Act was, of course, only one in a series going right back
to the *First Book of Discipline* of 1561, which called for a school in
every parish. Even if this policy of universal, free education was only
imperfectly achieved, Scotland was well ahead of other countries in
this respect – by about three centuries. With the schools went the
libraries, many of them founded in parishes in the seventeenth
century or even earlier. In 1699, James Kirkwood published a scheme
to found and maintain a library in every parish, and an Act for the
purpose was adopted by the General Assembly in 1709. The registers
of these parish libraries show that working people in all parts of
Scotland read the historical and philosophical works of the literati.
The intellectuals were not out of touch with the mass of the people.
The English historian, T. H. Buckle, said of eighteenth century
Scotland: 'That so poor or thinly-peopled a country, should, in so
short a period, have produced so many remarkable men, is extremely
curious'. It is less curious when you consider that a much higher
proportion of the people was educated, and their minds sharpened by
theological debate, than in other countries. But the roots of the
Enlightenment go back much further still. You might say that it
reached its first flowering in the reign of James IV (1473–1513).
There was then an explosion of creative achievement especially in the
poetry of Henryson, Dunbar and Gavin Douglas. As in the eighteenth
century, there was awareness both of classical literature and of
contemporary European literature and science. James IV was a true
renaissance prince interested in, and encouraging, almost all the arts
and sciences: poetry, music, surgery, printing, even experiments in
flight more or less contemporary with Leonardo da Vinci. By the end
of the fifteenth century, Scotland had three universities.
    This first 'Golden Age' came to an abrupt end with the disaster of
Flodden, a disaster so overwhelming that we have never fully
recovered from it. There was another set-back with the removal of the
King and Court and royal patronage to London in 1603 and the civil
and religious wars that followed. These were blows to the artistic and
intellectual life of the country, but they did not destroy it. As Dugald
Stewart reminded us, Scotland kept in touch constantly with the
intellectual life of continental Europe. George Buchanan (1506–
1582), by general agreement the finest poet in Latin since classical
times, was a scholar of European reputation. So were many

others, like James Crichton – 'the Admirable' – (*c.* 1560–85), Thomas Dempster (?–1625), Arthur Johnston (1587–1641), and John Napier of Merchiston (1550–1617), the inventor of logarithms. Scottish scholars went to Europe not only to learn but to teach. In Scotland itself, the universities were responsive to new learning. The way in which they developed shows the extent to which Scotland, even after she lost her own King in 1603, remained part of a European-wide intellectual community. Let me give only a few examples: Archibald Pitcairne (1652–1713) was one of the founders of the Edinburgh Medical School. He was a student at Edinburgh, Paris and Rheims, and then, for a time, Professor of Medicine at Leyden, where he taught the celebrated Boorhaave (1668–1738). In turn, Boorhaave taught Alexander Munro (1697–1767), the first in the succession of Munros who were professors of anatomy in Edinburgh. In 1577, the University of Glasgow was remodelled in the Nova Erectio, which established the broad 'democratic intellect' pattern of the Scottish university curriculum followed for the next 300 years or so. The Principal who introduced the reform, Andrew Melville, had been a student at St Andrews, Paris and Poitiers and a professor in Geneva. In 1613, a Chair of Mathematics was established at Marischal College, Aberdeen, by means of a bequest by Duncan Liddel. He had spent 25 years studying and teaching mathematics, philosophy and medicine in universities in Germany.

In the light of this history of continuous intellectual activity, the Scottish Enlightenment ceases to be a 'sudden burst of genius ... sprung up ... by a sort of enchantment'. On the contrary, Professor John MacQueen's judgement is seen as a simple statement of fact: 'The Scottish Enlightenment was the natural, almost the inevitable, outcome of several centuries of Scottish and European intellectual history'. If you want a date for the effective beginning of the Enlightenment, I think that you would have to put it in the 1680s. That was the decade of the establishment of the Advocates' Library and of the Royal College of Physicians, of the publication by both Stair and Mackenzie of their *Institutions of the Law of Scotland*. It might be more appropriate to regard the Enlightenment as the continuation of the Renaissance which began in the fifteenth century and which was halted for a time by the catastrophe of Flodden.

So far from the Union helping to bring about the Enlightenment, it was the exercise of active Unionism in the course of the nineteenth century, as opposed to the passivity of the eighteenth century, that brought it to an end. The ideals of the democratic intellect in the universities came under attack with pressure on them to conform to the English preference for specialisation. The Chairs in the Scottish universities began to be occupied by men from outside Scotland, bred in a different tradition. Talent, which previously stayed in Scotland or returned to it, was increasingly sucked away to the south. Carlyle's move to London in 1834 was a symbol of the end of an era.

Walter Scott at the High School

(*Blackwood's Magazine*, October 1980)

Arthur Melville Clark says rather sadly in his book *Sir Walter Scott: the Formative Years* that it has to be recognised that Scott and his Edinburgh contemporaries had less devotion to the university than to the High School. They had none of the affection and sense of belonging for the university which they had for the school. This is certainly true, but it is also strange because life at the High School at that period was harsh and demanding. It was not an experience which anyone enjoyed much at the time. 'Did I ever pass unhappy years anywhere?' Scott asked himself in his Journal on 4th April 1826. 'None that I remember, save those at the High School, which I thoroughly detested on account of the confinement', although, he adds, 'I disliked serving in my father's office, too, from the same hatred to restraint.'

His account of the school in the Ashesteil *Memoir* only warms into affection when he speaks of the Rector, Dr Alexander Adam, 'to whom I owed so much' – 'a man so learned, so admirably adapted for his station, so useful, so simple, so easily contented'. Adam's qualities are evident to this day in Raeburn's portrait of him, which is radiant with benevolence. But Scott goes on to speak of a 'savage fellow, called Nicol, one of the undermasters' who insulted Adam and challenged his authority. 'This man was an excellent classical scholar, and an admirable convivial humorist (which latter quality recommended him to the friendship of Burns); but worthless, drunken, and inhumanly cruel to the boys under his charge.' This was, indeed, the Willie who 'brew'd a peck o' maut', but who was plainly abominable as a schoolmaster. Years later, Scott wrote about the school with greater warmth, especially in the first chapter of *Redgauntlet,* published in June 1824. In October of the same year, he spoke at the opening of the Edinburgh Academy. He was at pains to emphasise that the new foundation was not intended to damage the High School, the 'pride and boast of our city'.

Henry Cockburn, who went to the High School eight years after Scott, was one of those who suffered under Nicol. 'Out of the whole four years of my attendance there were probably not ten days in which I was not flogged at least once.' He too admired Adam – 'born to teach Latin, some Greek and all virtue ... inspiring ... enthusiastically delighted with every appearance of talent or goodness ... and constantly under the strongest sense of duty'. But, he adds, 'the hereditary evils of the system and of the place were too great for correction even by Adam; and the general tone of the school was vulgar and harsh ... Two of the masters, in particular, were so savage, that any master doing now what they did every hour, would certainly be transported.' Scott did not think that it was as bad as all that. 'I was indifferently well beaten at school,' he wrote in his Journal on 13th December 1826, 'but I am quite certain that twice as much discipline would have been well bestowed.'

But there was clearly more to the High School than the harshness of some of the masters, which was common enough in schools everywhere for at least another hundred years. When Samuel Johnson came to Scotland in 1773, he was determined to find fault with everything and not least with the state of scholarship, the universities and the schools; but, says Boswell, 'I brought him to confess that the High School of Edinburgh did well.' Boswell, although, exceptionally, he did not go to the school himself, took a close interest in it. On 16th September 1780, for example, 'Mr Fraser, one of the masters of the High School, drank tea with us and examined the young Campbells excellently well, to settle what classes they should attend'. This was Luke Fraser, Scott's first master at the school, whom he calls 'a good Latin Scholar and a very worthy man'. Then, on 19th September, Boswell was 'present at Mr Fraser's opening his class with a decent prayer, after which I heard him examine some of the boys on a passage of Caesar. I was much pleased with his perfect investigation of the elements of the Latin and with his instruction in the sense, particularly the geography'. (Although neither Boswell nor Scott mention meeting the other, Scott was a member of Luke Fraser's class from 1778 to 1782 and was presumably there on that day.) On 22nd September, Boswell was at a dinner-party with Dr Adam: 'Found my association of ideas in my boyish days as to the High School dissolved. Saw it as a good place for education'. The following year, on 21st February 1781, Boswell 'went to *Henry IV, First Part,* and saw all the High School in the theatre. It was a fine scene of boyish amusement and tumult. The profits of the play went to pay for the new school. So all the masters and all the boys were there'. It all gives a very different impression of the school from Cockburn's account.

The school, 'the most important in Scotland, and intimately connected with the literature and progress of the Kingdom', was, Lord Brougham said in a speech in 1825, 'invaluable ... because men of the highest and lowest rank of society sent their children to be educated together.' Probably the pre-eminence of the school was due to its long monopoly in the capital of the country, but, whatever the reason, a list of the men educated there reads like a biographical dictionary of the country's achievement. (It is particularly strong in literature – a tradition which continues with poets from William Drummond of Hawthornden in the sixteenth century to Norman MacCaig and Robert Garioch in the twentieth.) The mixture of classes was both an expression and a reinforcement of the constant Scottish tendency towards egalitarianism. 'I used to sit between a youth of a ducal family and the son of a poor cobbler', wrote William Steven in his *History* of the school, and this was typical of the healthy practice of mixing classes until it was destroyed by the aping of English behaviour in the nineteenth century when wealthier people started to send their sons to English class-conscious and class-exclusive schools. This is one of the ways in which so much that was valuable in Scottish traditions has been damaged by English inter-vention and example.

The traditions of the school, the egalitarianism, even the rigours and the sizes of the classes – there were 100 boys in each – all contributed to a strong feeling of community, the sense of belonging that Melville Clark noticed. At the school itself, there was a lively spirit of academic competitiveness, with boys constantly changing in precedence according to their performance. This was taken so seriously that even Scott was driven to a trick to gain a place. By the time the boys left, they knew one another so well and had been through so much together that there was a bond between them for life. Among the literati of the eighteenth century, as among the Edinburgh Reviewers, and between Scott and his friends, there was an atmosphere of easy familiarity, mutual trust and friendship, a desire to help and co-operate. At least part of the reason is that so many of the people involved were at the High School together.

Scott had a special need for community of this kind because of the isolation of his childhood, when he was cut off from other children by illness. Even the return to life with his own brothers in Edinburgh was a shock. How was this cosseted and lame child to cope with a 'robust and competitive' school? Initially, it seems, by making up in spirit what he lacked in physical agility. He had a determination to overcome his lameness which enabled him for years to compete with anyone on foot or horseback. In the first chapter of *Redgauntlet,* there is a footnote about the escapades of the boys of the High School on the Castle rock, in which Scott recalls that he was once one of those 'juvenile dreadnoughts'. But he had another resource, drawing advantage from the hours which his lameness had forced him to spend in dreaming, reading and talk. 'In the winter play-hours, when hard exercise was impossible, my tales used to assemble an admiring audience round Lucky Brown's fireside, and happy was he that could sit next to the inexhaustible narrator.' He had already started, like a latter-day minstrel to use his imagination and the stores of his memories to entertain.

John Fleming, in his admirable book on Robert Adam, says of the High School of about this time (Robert Adam was there about a generation before Scott), that a boy emerged from it 'with a sound knowledge of Latin grammar and literature, especially Cicero, but of nothing else. For nothing but Latin was taught at the High School'. The only difference by Scott's time was that a little Greek had been added to the Latin. This concentration on Latin was not as crazy as it sounds. In the first place, the sort of analysis of a complex Latin sentence which is necessary to extract its meaning, is about as good an exercise in logical thought as anyone has been able to devise. It encourages the habit of searching for the meaning and thought behind the surface of the words. The next step, the translation of Latin text into one's own language, is a good exercise in the manipulation of words. You cannot translate from one language into another without deciding what it is you are trying to say, and this is an excellent antidote to vague thought and imprecise speech. On the other hand, the sentence structure of Latin is infectious with its tendency to run into an elaborate construction of dependent clauses. It is the style that Scott falls into when he is writing at speed, an echo of the years spent construing Cicero on the benches of the High School. And, of course, Scott continued to read Latin for pleasure and information for the rest of his life, even if he read more medieval chronicles than classical writers, and his favourite Latin poet was the sixteenth century Scot, George Buchanan.

But Latin was more than a linguistic exercise. Boswell talks about 'instruction in the sense, particularly the geography'. Both Scott and Cockburn say that Dr Adam ran into trouble at the time of the French Revolution because he seemed to be supporting revolutionary principles when he talked about ancient Rome. 'He was no politician; insomuch that it may be doubted whether he ever knew one public measure or man from another. But a Latin and Greek schoolmaster naturally speaks about such things as liberty, and the people, and the expulsion of the Tarquins, and republics, and this was quite sufficient for the times; especially as any modern notions that he had were popular, and he was too honest, and too simple, to disguise them.' Adam's book *Roman Antiquities* was reprinted many times and is described by Melville Clark as 'still useful'. In addition to a book on Latin and English grammar and a Latin dictionary, he also wrote about classical biography. Obviously, therefore, his interest in Latin studies was not confined to the language and literature but included history, geography and politics, and his teaching did the same.

If Latin literature was so used to illustrate a whole society, it was also used to encourage certain ideals and standards of behaviour. Cockburn in his famous phrase about Dr Adam, quite naturally mentioned 'all virtue' in the same breath as Latin and some Greek. This association between the morality of Presbyterian Scotland and of Republican Rome may seem paradoxical, but the resemblance between the two moral codes is very close. R. H. Barrow in his book *The Romans* lists the qualities which the Romans admired and liked to think that they possessed: *pietas, gravitas* ('a sense of the importance of the matters in hand'), *constantia, firmitas, disciplina, industria* ('hard work'), *virtus* ('manliness or energy') and *frugalitas* ('simple tastes'). 'It might all be summed up,' Barrow says 'in *severitas,* which means being stern with oneself.' Add to these a respect for learning and you have a catalogue of the Scottish virtues. Boswell was always preaching these qualities to himself in his Journals: 'Remember everything may be endured ... Have constant command of yourself ... Be firm, and persist ... Never indulge your appetite without restraint.' So was Scott, although with more of the restraint in practice to which Boswell only aspired. *'Agere atque pati Romanum est',* as he said in his Journal, and he clearly used the word, Roman, as a term of the highest praise. 'A Roman,' says Scott talking of Davie Deans in *The Heart of Midlothian,* 'would have devoted his daughter to death from different failings and motives, but not upon a more heroic principle of duty.' It is the same sort of comparison which Stevenson causes Glenalmond to make of Hermiston: 'He has all the Roman virtues: Cato and Brutus were such.'

In his *Scott and Scotland,* Edwin Muir says that he will be content if he can show 'that the discipline of Scots law was not an adequate complement to Scott's riotous imagination and violent feelings, that something else was required, and that the Scotland of his time could not supply it'. Like so many of Muir's statements, part of this asserts something which can neither be proved nor disproved, and another part disregards the facts. As we can see from the novels, the effect of Scots law on Scott's imagination was important, as a stimulus as well as a complement. I do not know how it is possible to decide whether or not it was adequate as a complement. But it was far from being the only one which the Scotland of Scott's time supplied. The first in time, and quite possibly in importance, was the Romano-Scottish influence of the High School, which might almost have been designed to curb the excesses of unbridled imagination.

There is something strange in basing a whole system of education on a language and civilisation which flourished almost 2,000 years

ago. Scott himself thought so. In his speech at the opening of the
Edinburgh Academy, he spoke of the advantages of adding such
things as mathematics, literature, history and one's own language.
'He would have the youths taught to venerate the patriots and heroes
of our own country along with those of Greece and Rome; to know
the histories of Wallace and Bruce, as well as those of Themistocles
and of Caesar; and that the recollection of the fields of Flodden and
Bannockburn should not be lost in those of Plataea and Marathon.'
No one, I suppose, would now defend the exclusive preoccupation
with ancient Rome. Even so, the old High School system must have
had some virtue, if we can judge by the qualities of mind and character
in the men it produced.

The Democratic Intellect and the Pressure of Anglocentric Attitudes

(Paper for AdCAS conference, 22 May 1982.
First published in *Scottish Review*, November 1982)

It is, of course, deliberate and significant that in the heading of this item of the agenda we use the phrase 'the democratic intellect' which George Davie used as the title and the theme for his great book on the Scottish academic tradition. It is one of the most important books written in Scotland in this century and essential reading for anyone who is concerned about the questions which we are discussing here today. It is a book about events in the nineteenth century, but it is vitally concerned with the issues that are still at the root of the problem. In recent years, while the tradition of the wide-ranging approach to education continues to be eroded in Scotland, its virtues are increasingly appreciated elsewhere. When C. P. Snow reviewed George Davie's book in the *New Statesman*, he said this:

> I have been thinking and talking about some of the topics which, over 100 years ago, preoccupied these Scottish professional men. They too were worried about divisions in the intellectual life, the relations of intellectual people to society, and so on... There is precious little that I have managed to say on these matters which they did not say before.

C. P. Snow again, in a speech in Edinburgh in 1961, said of the city:

> It is, I think, one of the most beautiful towns in Europe; and it has many other glories. For 150 years ago it had probably the best university in the world, with a deep and serious intellectual tradition, which still exists in this country, although I could wish that Scottish education had remained a little more different from English rather than the reverse because the Scots have always believed in democratic education and in the generalised intellect in a way that my more empirical countrymen have never quite believed.

And another Englishman, Professor V. H. Galbraith, a distinguished occupant of the Chair of British History in this university, said this in a speech when he retired:

> I am perfectly sure that the future of Scotland lies in a sort of tremendous development of its own affairs and having the

power to do that ... No proposal with regard to education
which comes up here from England is worth a damn to you.

Of course, over the last 150 years or so, since Edinburgh, in
C. P. Snow's words, was 'probably the best university in the world',
we have acted in a sense completely contrary to the advice of Snow
and Galbraith. We have progressively succumbed to the proposals
from England. George Davie's book is an account of the steady
pressures from the South which eroded the ideals of the democratic
intellect. In addition, the Scottish educational system as a whole has
largely ignored the serious study of our own history, languages and
literature and accepted English assumptions and an Anglocentric view
of the world. As Robert Sutherland puts it in a book published in 1976:

> The result has been that as a nation we have neglected our own
> history; it has tended to become at times an antiquarian
> browsing in the picturesque, or else the subordination of
> scientific reality to the doctrine of the inevitability and immutable
> providence of the incorporating Union. Not only have we in
> Scotland been for generations permeated with English historical
> interpretations in our schools and universities, but the very
> study of the history of our own country, even as a speciality
> among scholars in our universities, has been – and continues to
> be – hampered and neglected as a consequence of inherited
> attitudes about what really matters, and by the dominance of
> English historians and teaching, in our university departments
> of history and over school curricula.

Our position was well summarised by a sentence in *The Scotsman*
in February 1979: 'In every country, except Scotland, it is taken for
granted that national history and literature should be well taught in
the schools'. I do not need to remind this audience how far we are
from that basic need.

Of course, we should not ignore English history and English literature. The two countries have impinged so constantly on one another
that we need to know something about English history, just as the
English – although they are rarely aware of it – should know
something about ours. English literature is one of the great literatures
of the world, but it is not the only one. What we have to eradicate is
intellectual isolationism, intellectual monopoly. The Anglocentric
monopoly has been provincialising, narrowing and stultifying. We
do not want to narrow, but to broaden, the scope of Scottish
education and to develop an awareness of the whole world. Our own

academic tradition aimed at precisely such an all-embracing view.

To look at ourselves through others' eyes certainly has a useful function. It might be a useful corrective to insularity and complacency. But to look solely through the eyes of one other country, especially of one which is peculiarly insular in its outlook, to ignore the accumulated experience embodied in our own history and literature, even to do our best to suppress our own languages, is quite literally suicidal. It is a recipe for the destruction of a view of the world which has its own unique value and which has made an important contribution to civilisation. We should not be too modest about this. It was an American, Harold Orel, who said recently that no nation of its size had contributed so much to the culture of the world.

The Scottishness of the Scottish universities has been undermined also by their subordination not to any authority in Scotland but to the arbitrary and mysterious workings of an external body, the University Grants Committee, which divorces the universities from the schools. It has another consequence, which has been described by Dr John Hulbert:

> As a result, a veritable torrent of Englishmen were appointed to the professorate of Scottish universities, until the Scots were outnumbered on their home ground. It was as if the required qualifications for a professional chair in Scotland were to be under 40 years of age, to be educated at an English school and then Oxbridge, and finally to have next to no experience of Scotland.

One might add in parenthesis, that a similar idea of qualifications, especially the last, seems to apply to many important jobs in Scotland, even to those which from their nature make the occupant the spokesman for a whole aspect of Scottish life. Dr Hulbert concluded:

> The loss of a complete cultural identity, such as our Scottish university system, is like the loss of a language or the extinction of a species of animal or bird, a loss for anyone. It is a diminution of that variety which is both stimulating and essential for survival.

One might well ask why it was that this anglicisation of the Scottish universities began about 150 years ago, precisely at a time when the reputation of the Scottish universities was at its zenith and that of the two English universities was at a very low level. It was not long after the time when Edward Gibbon spoke of Oxford as 'steeped in port and prejudice' and Adam Smith, who had experience of both, compared the English universities very unfavourably with the Scottish. In these circumstances, one might have expected some recognition that our universities had something that was distinctive and valuable to offer.

To the American sociologist, Michael Hechter, the process of anglicisation was essentially an act of colonialism, as he explained in his book *International Colonialism: The Celtic Fringe in British National Development*. 'A defining characteristic of imperial expansion', he writes, 'is that the centre must disparage the indigenous culture of peripheral groups ... One of the consequences of this denigration of indigenous culture is to undermine the native's will to resist the colonial regime... Conversely, the renaissance of indigenous culture implies a serious threat to continued colonial domination.'

Well, there was certainly a denigration of our indigenous culture and an undermining of our will to resist. I am not sure if Hechter saw this as a consequence of conscious and deliberate policy. He speaks of it as proceeding 'not only by government fiat, but through the voluntary assimilation of peripheral élites'. Again, we are all familiar, to this day, with the voluntary assimilators. In my view, neither the policy nor the assimilation were wholly conscious or deliberately planned. I think that they were the spontaneous consequences of the extraordinary success of the English State in the nineteenth century, when in economic, military and imperial terms it was the predominant power in the world. This bred an arrogance and self-confidence which at its height was overwhelming and which still lingers on even today, despite the material justification having vanished for ever. We have seen recently in some responses to the Falkland Islands crisis that the old jingoism is not yet dead.

This pressure to adopt an English view of the world did not only apply to Scotland. In the days of the Empire, it was found wherever the map was red (the word 'red' in those days had a different connotation from the one it has now). In India, Canada, Australia and in the hundreds of dependent territories, English history and literature were the staples of education. Now, of course, they give priority to their own, and they are right in this because no one can begin to understand the world without first understanding their own past and the experience of their own predecessors. No people can have self-confidence without some knowledge of their own achievements. Scotland is the odd man out. We are still burdened by an anachronism, a relic of the eighteenth century imperialism. In the nineteenth century, we allowed an obsession with Imperial Rome to be replaced by another imperial obsession and we have not yet escaped from the consequences. The result is that the Scottish people at large are hampered by an inadequate understanding and that leads inevitably to a debilitating lack of self-confidence.

There is another consequence of this Anglocentrism. It tends to cut Scotland off from the rest of the world. London is interposed as a barrier, or at least a filter or bottle-neck, between us and the rest of the world. This is the real separatism from which we suffer, and it is the unionists who are the separatists. This has the effect of diluting the stimulation of contact with other countries, which has always been a vital part of the Scottish intellectual tradition, from the days of William Dunbar and George Buchanan, no less than those of David Hume and Adam Smith. Culturally, Scotland has always been part of Europe in a way which insular and self-sufficient England has never been. In John Buchan's *Life of Scott*, there is a passage describing Edinburgh in his time: 'Edinburgh was a true Capital, a clearing-house for the world's culture, a jealous repository of Scottish tradition'. It is a reproach to our educational system that we can no longer make such a claim. We have to recover lost ground. We should set ourselves these dual aims: accessibility to the ideas of the whole world and a firm base in our own traditions.

The Crisis of the Scottish Universities

(*The Scotsman*, 12 October 1981)

The proposals by the University Grants Committee for cuts in the expenditure on the universities have been received in Scotland with a mixture of despair and derision. Of course, any cut of this kind would be unpopular, but in this case the injury has been compounded by discrimination between one university and another, and between one subject and another, in a manner which defies reasonable explanation, and which makes nonsense of the myth of academic independence. It is arbitrary exercise of power of the worst kind, because it is the result of decisions taken in secret, without public discussion and without any attempt to explain the reasons which lie behind them.

The Court of Stirling University said that the proposals were extreme, unfounded and impracticable. The Principal of Strathclyde University said that there was 'no sign of a coherent plan for the 1980s, but rather a seemingly inane shuffling of subjects between universities'. Professor Tom Patten of Heriot Watt said that the UGC had betrayed an 'astonishing and disappointing lack of awareness'. 'They suffered', added the Principal of Glasgow, from an 'Oxbridge mentality.'

There is, of course, nothing new in this sort of situation. For over 150 years the Scottish universities have suffered from misguided interference from the South by men bred in a different academic tradition and generally hostile to the democratic intellectualism of Scotland. When the process started early in the last century, the Scottish universities were in the forefront of world scholarship. They were making an essential contribution to, if not actually creating, modern philosophy, historiography, chemistry, geology, medicine, economics and sociology. At the same time, Oxford and Cambridge were only just emerging from their eighteenth century stupor, 'steeped', as Edward Gibbon said of the Oxford of his day, 'in port and prejudice'. That did not prevent a determined campaign to force the Scottish universities into the English mould, and who can say that this has been to the benefit either of Scotland or of scholarship generally?

Professor V. H. Galbraith, an Englishman who was a distinguished occupant of the Chair of British History at Edinburgh, said in a speech when he retired from it in 1964 (*The Scotsman,* March 2, 1964): 'I am perfectly sure that the future of Scotland lies in a sort of tremendous development of its own affairs, and having the power to do that ... No proposal with regard to education which comes up here from England is worth a damn to you.' Another Englishman, C. P. Snow, well known not only for his novels but for his concern over bridging the gap between the arts and the sciences, said of Edinburgh in 1961 (*The Scotsman,* September 5, 1961): 'It is, I think, one of the most beautiful towns in Europe; and it has many other glories. For 150 years ago it had probably the best university in the world, with a deep and serious intellectual tradition, which still exists in this country, although I could wish that Scottish education had remained a little more different from English rather than the reverse, because the Scots have always believed in democratic education and in the generalised intellect in a way that my more empirical countrymen have never quite believed'. Unfortunately, such an understanding of the Scottish academic tradition has not been widely shared by the countrymen of Galbraith and Snow. The whole sorry story may be read in detail in George Davie's classic work, *The Democratic Intellect,* which should be read and pondered by everyone concerned with the Scottish universities. It is a safe bet that the members of the UGC have never heard of it. Certainly their latest moves are in the tradition of arrogant disregard for Scottish needs, achievements and aspirations.

The principals of the eight universities at a meeting on October 2 pledged themselves to continue the struggle against the cuts, describing them as 'a tragedy for the country'. As a group they have not challenged, so far, the basic conception of the UGC; but it is this institution which has been found inadequate for the immensity of the task imposed on it.

It seems to me that there is a very obvious need for a simple change in the present procedure. The funds available for the Scottish universities, that is the fair proportion according to population of the UK total, should cease to be the concern of the UGC but should be handled by a separate Scottish committee set up for the purpose by the Secretary of State for Scotland. The committee would include representatives of all the Scottish universities.

The case for this is threefold:

1. In the first place the task imposed on the UGC at present is beyond the capacity of any group of ordinary mortals. They are asked to make themselves familiar with the activities of 43 universities and make judgments between them on which their future development, or even survival, depends. Since they cannot possibly be aware of all

the complexities involved in this, they can only follow their own instincts and prejudices and hope for the best. We see the results. On the other hand, the eight Scottish universities are a manageable group, fully capable of co-operation and give and take between themselves. When cuts are inevitable, they could avoid the worst effects on academic standards by some pooling of facilities and merging of departments by agreement between themselves.

2. Secondly, this degree of academic independence would enable the universities to develop in accordance with their own traditions and in response to Scottish needs. I need hardly say that there is nothing narrow or insular about these traditions, which have always been of world-wide interest and scope. Greater independence would enable the universities to make a more valuable contribution to scholarship, which is more likely to flourish in freedom and diversity than under imposed uniformity. Nor would it limit the free movement of staff and students between Scotland and the rest of the world.

3. Finally, it would end the harmful divorce which at present exists between the schools and the universities in Scotland, with the schools administrated as a separate Scottish entity and the universities dependent on an external body, pulling in a different direction. In any rational system, the schools and the universities should form part of a coherent whole, each responding to the needs of the other.

Education generally, and the universities in particular, have traditionally enjoyed high esteem in Scotland. It seems that this has diminished to the point where the universities feel that they can no longer count on the support of an informed and concerned public. Perhaps part of the reason for this is that the educational system has suffered such interference from outside, that it is no longer possible for the Scottish people to take the pride in it which they were once justified in taking in their own distinctive contribution to our common civilisation. The more the Scottish universities are identified with the community which surrounds them, the more each can serve, stimulate and support the other.

When the last Labour Government was drafting the Scotland Bill, there was an academic lobby which resisted the devolution of responsibility for the universities. Their argument, ironically enough, was that their interests would be better served by trusting the UGC. Like so many other 'No' campaigners, they have learned a bitter lesson. Certainly, Scottish responsibility for the Scottish universities must form part of any adequate measure of Home Rule. But we do not have to wait for that. This is something which can be done on its own without delay.

The Royal Society of Edinburgh

(*Books in Scotland*, 21 December 1983)

In his Foreword[1], Lord Cameron says accurately and appropriately: 'of the fruits of the Enlightenment in Scotland not least has been this Society'. The RSE is indeed one of the embodiments of the Scottish Enlightenment, one of the great eighteenth century clubs, surviving and flourishing in our own day. Its activities have impinged in diverse ways on the world at large. It was, for instance, at one of their meetings that James Hutton read his paper on 'The Theory of the Earth', from which modern geology derives. Much that is known about the lives of some of the giants of the Enlightenment, is contained in the obituary notices written by one member of the Society on another, such as Dugald Stewart on Adam Smith, or Adam Fergusson on Joseph Black.

In spite of the prominence of so many of its members, and the importance of the Society as one of the great intellectual ornaments of Edinburgh, the RSE has remained curiously unknown to the public. Its ethos has been very much that of a private club, cherished by its members, but avoiding publicity. It flourished as a forum of free debate, but it does not take a corporate view, officially at least, on any question whatever. Perhaps it would benefit us all if they were less reticent.

This book is therefore much to be welcomed because it gives us a chance to learn a little about what goes on behind those discrete doors in George Street. The authors modestly tell us that this is not an attempt to write the full-scale history of the Society for which Sir Robert Christison called more than a hundred years ago. Even so, it does give a succinct account of its origins, development and future aspirations. It is a pleasantly anecdotal book and is handsomely produced and illustrated.

When it was first established in 1783, the RSE took as its function 'the advancement of learning and useful knowledge'. By this, in the spirit of the Scottish Enlightenment, they meant the whole range of intellectual activity, not only the sciences. From the beginning, the Society had a 'Physical Class', including mathematics, physics, chemistry, medicine and natural history, but also a 'Literary Class' covering 'literature, philosophy, history, antiquities, speculative philosophy and other useful knowledge'. A wide brief indeed. This width of view was reflected by the original membership, men like Blair, Robertson, Fergusson and Smith, as well as Cullen and Munro. Sir Walter Scott was President from 1820 to 1832.

In the course of the nineteenth century, the sciences flourished, but the Literary Class sadly declined. Lord Moncrieff said around 1882 that it had 'perished of inanimation'. It seems that the literary fellows were ill-chosen among men who devoted themselves to pedantry of the narrowest kind. 'The papers', wrote Lord Moncrieff, 'dwindled to somewhat pedantic dissertations on grammar, on modes of verbs, on pronouns, on the Greek letter signs, and were not animated in themselves nor likely to excite enthusiasm on a general audience.'

It is good news that, within the last ten years or so, the RSE has been taking steps to revive the literary side of its activities. Lord Cameron was elected President in 1973, the first non-scientist to hold the office for more than a hundred years. They could hardly have made a more appropriate choice. Lord Cameron, like a latter-day Lord Kames, is a distinguished judge with wide interests, artistic as well as literary, a man very much in the best traditions of the legal literati of Edinburgh. In 1977, the Society set up working parties on Arts and Letters and Technology and Industry to see how these matters could be integrated into its activities.

There has never been a time when Scotland, and society as a whole, has had greater need of the kind of intelligent, informed and dispassionate scrutiny and debate which the RSE is well equipped to encourage. There is no shortage of themes. To give only one example, and one of the most fundamental: we have all an uneasy feeling that education in Scotland has lost its way. There are plenty of committees charged with the examination of isolated elements of the system, but no single body to examine the overall philosophy and purpose as they apply at all levels. Professor Nigel Grant is working, under the auspices of the Advisory Council for the Arts in Scotland, to establish a forum for precisely this purpose. Is this not the sort of thing to which the RSE could apply its prestige and facilities, and co-operate to great effect?

In 1986, attention will be focused on the Scottish Enlightenment, because of the great joint effort of scholarship, IPSE 86, which the Institute for Advanced Studies in the Humanities of Edinburgh University is arranging. It would be very appropriate if the RSE could be associated with this in launching a major new debate on man and society of the kind with which both the Scottish Enlightenment and the RSE began.

'Remaking a Nation'

(*The Scotsman*, 4 April 1986)

The 50th Anniversary of the Saltire Society, which was founded on 23 April 1936, is being celebrated in ways which are as diverse as the activities of the Society itself. Among them is an exhibition in the National Library of Scotland. One of the exhibits is an article which John Oliver wrote for the *Scottish Journal* in 1953. Dr Oliver, the editor of a standard anthology of Scottish poetry and the author of some delightful comic verse, was a founder member of the Society. His article is a useful summary of what these founders set out to achieve half a century ago.

Oliver describes the Saltire Society as 'the one body that, during the last fifteen years, has spoken for Scotland'. He continues: 'Those who, in 1936, founded the Society were not trying to form a hotbed of genius; what they did was to invite all who were sincerely concerned for the welfare of Scotland to unite in forming a body which could stimulate a decent pride among Scottish people, resist the gradual obliteration of the Scottish tradition by centralising tendencies, restore something of what had been lost in that tradition, and encourage its development in new directions. Of course, all these aspirations have not been realised: they can only be realised when the whole nation has been stirred to effort. The remaking of a nation is not a thing that can be done within a few years'.

Another early description of the Society appears in a Saltire Book, *Building Scotland* by Robert Hurd and Alan Riach, published in 1944. It was founded, they say, 'by a group of people who wished to see not a mere revival of the arts of the past, but a renewal of the life which made them, such as the Scots themselves experienced in the eighteenth century'. These two versions are different ways of saying very much the same thing. Both are notably ambitious; the 'remaking of a nation' or a renewal of creative energy on the scale of the Scotland of the Enlightenment.

The founders of the Society set their sights high because they were conscious of a need to respond to an urgent crisis. It was widely felt at the time that Scotland, as anything more than a geographical expression, was threatened with extinction. A whole series of books

had reached this gloomy conclusion. One of them, with the significant title, *Scotland in Eclipse*, was published in 1930 by Professor
Dewar Gibb who became the main driving force behind the formation of the Society. George Malcolm Thomson was not alone in
arguing in his *Caledonia* that all serious intellectual and artistic life
in Scotland had been eroded beyond recovery. Edwin Muir in
Scottish Journey of 1935 concluded that Scotland was a country that
'is becoming lost to history'.

Today, fifty years later, there is still a great deal that is highly
unsatisfactory about the cultural life of Scotland. It is still possible to
go through the entire system of Scottish education, both school and
university, and learn almost nothing about the history, literature and
languages of Scotland. There is still no Chair of Scottish Literature in
any Scottish university, which is a national disgrace, and something
disturbing and mysterious recently happened in Glasgow in this
respect. The reaction of some academics to the desirable recom-
mendations of STEAC (Scottish Tertiary Education Advisory Committee) for the autonomy of the Scottish universities shows that
(unlike most people), they have learned nothing from our experiences
since the Referendum. Broadcasting, and particularly television, is
still dominated by London.

At the same time, there is no doubt that there has been very real
progress since the 1930s in the direction that the Saltire Society set out
to encourage. Literature, publishing, the theatre, music, architecture,
and historical scholarship have all been reinvigorated. Our cultural
life is in a much less depressed condition than our economy. It is now
inconceivable that anyone would describe the Scottish situation in
such terms of despair and hopelessness as G. M. Thomson and others
used in the Twenties and Thirties. There has been a radical change of
atmosphere. In his book on Francis George Scott, Maurice Lindsay
suggested that this 'vastly improved state' of affairs was 'a measure
of the success of the pioneering efforts' of the Society. Of course,
many other people and institutions have been involved, but it is
remarkable how many new developments can be traced back to a
Saltire initiative or proposal. To give just two examples. The reputation of Charles Rennie Mackintosh is now well established, but it
was a Saltire exhibition which first drew attention to his work. Many
publishers are now producing cheap reprints of major works of
Scottish literature, but the Saltire Society started this at a time when
no one else was prepared to do so.

There are several things about the Saltire Society which taken
together, probably make it unique. The first is the range of its
interests, everything that affects the quality of life in Scotland from
civil engineering to poetry, from law to folk-song. Secondly, the

prestige and influence of its many award schemes. It is widely recognised, for example, that the Housing Award has led to a real improvement in standards of design and construction throughout the country. Thirdly, and it may seem surprising for a body of such diverse achievement, it is an entirely voluntary organisation, open to all, run by its members and financed by their subscriptions. Many of the activities would be undertaken in other countries by state institutions. In Scotland, in the face of the indifference or hostility of Westminster, our national interests are very often left to private endeavour. So it is with the Saltire Society.

Since control is in the hands of the members, anyone with the necessary talent and energy can take an active part and help to decide policy. Anyone who has ideas about ways in which life in Scotland can be improved can work for their achievement through the Society. The more people who join, the more influence and effect the Society will have. For this reason, Nigel Tranter said, 'If more people supported its aims, Scotland would be a better place.' The time is ripe for a new generation to give the Saltire Society a new impetus and make it even more productive in the next fifty years than in the last.

Scotland and International PEN

(*The Scotsman*, 13 September 1987)

International PEN (the initials mean poets/playwrights, essayists/ editors and novelists) is a remarkable organisation that grew sponta- neously from a small beginning. After the First World War, an almost unknown English novelist, Catherine Amy Dawson-Scott, had the idea of starting a writers' club in London. She hoped that if similar clubs were formed in other European capitals, writers on their travels would be able to meet their colleagues in other countries. With this very modest ambition, English PEN held its first formal meeting in October 1921 with John Galsworthy as its first president. More than sixty years and another World War later, PEN continues to flourish, with organisations, which are called by that all-purpose word 'cen- tres', in fifty-eight countries. One of the earliest was the Scottish Centre, founded by Hugh MacDiarmid in 1927.

PEN has become a sort of United Nations for the writers of the world. It has a charter which commits it to work for 'good under- standing and mutual respect between nations', the unhampered transmission of thought within and between nations, and to oppose censorship. Since 1971, it has been active particularly in helping writers who have been imprisoned or persecuted because of their opinions. Within each country, the PEN centre has its own programme of social and literary events. Internationally, the work is carried on mainly through congresses and less formal conferences which are held in a different country each year. Congresses have been held in Scotland in 1934 and 1950 and a conference in 1970. One of the most lively accounts of a PEN Congress can be found in Douglas Young's book *Chasing an Ancient Greek* which, among other things, is about the Congress in Venice in 1950 at which he was one of the repre- sentatives of the Scottish Centre.

Earlier this summer, I had an opportunity of attending one of these congresses for the first time, the fiftieth, which was held in Lugano with the formidably hospitable Italian Swiss as the hosts. Sixty-six Centres were represented (some very large countries with more than one language had more than one Centre).

These congresses fall into two parts, an extended debate on some literary theme and an Assembly of Delegates to resolve questions of policy and business. Naturally the first of these is the more interesting and it takes up more time, three and half days with only one for the other. Many distinguished writers from many countries in the world take part. The theme this year was *Writers and Border Literature,* or in French, because as it was remarked during the debate, the implications are not precisely the same, *Ecrivains et littératures de frontière.* It was obviously a theme with marked relevance to Scotland, since the Border strikes such a strong resonance in our literature and our consciousness generally. It also raises the issue of the apparent contradiction between removing the barriers to the free circulation of ideas and preserving diversity against the sterile uniformity which threatens all of us. We have had a long experience of this in Scotland, and indeed the first important statement of the problem is in Sir Walter Scott: *The Letters of Malachi Malagrowther* of 1826.

Many of the speakers in the Lugano debate, no doubt unconsciously, were echoing the thoughts, and sometimes almost the words, which Scott used 160 years ago; Alain Bosquet, for instance, who pleaded for us all to be allowed to keep our differences, or Lassi Nummi who argued that our real wealth lay in diversity. Several speakers discussed whether one should stay true to one's local particularity or seek a wider universality. Most, like Czeslaw Miloscz and Anthony Burgess, concluded that the universal could only be reached through the particular. Many discussed the greatly increased pressures towards uniformity from mass consumerism and its allies in the media. Burgess said that English was the great centralising tongue and George Steiner added that it was now becoming a threat to the survival of all other languages.

For the Assembly of Delegates, the Scottish Centre had tabled a resolution in advance which, as it turned out, was very much in the spirit of these debates. This resolution called for the defence of the languages, literature and culture of the smaller countries and language minorities in the face of the pressures against them and proposed that PEN should set up new machinery for this purpose. This was passed unanimously except for one abstention which, no doubt consistently enough, was by the English delegation. In future, therefore, PEN may be expected to put its international weight behind the struggle of countries, which like Scotland or Pierre Trudeau's Canada find themselves, in his words, 'in bed with an elephant'.

It was clear to me from this experience in Lugano, that International PEN is a very useful organisation, and a force for good in the world. Outside the realm of sport, it is also one of the few international bodies where Scotland has its own full and equal voice. We should make more use of it. In particular, we should see that our best writers are invited to take part in the debates in these international congresses. Above all, it is time for Scotland once again to offer to be host to a congress or conference. Few things can do more to make the writers of the world aware of Scotland, and with all sorts of benefits, from our general standing, to our tourist trade. In Lugano, I met people who still speak of the last conference in Scotland in 1970. (One of them, incidentally, is a Hungarian who is making a new translation of the Waverley novels in Hungarian.) The ability of the Scottish Centre to achieve these things depends on the support it is given by our writers. At present about 140 of them are members, but there are potentially many more. PEN needs the help of all of them.

Universities and Literature: The Scottish Paradox

(Paper for International PEN Conference, Cambridge, April 1988)

Cairns Craig in his Introduction to the Twentieth Century Volume of the *History of Scottish Literature* which has just been published by Aberdeen University Press, has this to say about literature and the universities:

> Literature in every country in the twentieth century has developed a symbiotic relationship with the universities and schools in which it is taught and studied and in which, increasingly, it is created. In Scotland, though, literature has had to operate without those educational supports: 'literature' in Scottish educational establishments, as in English ones, is taught under the title of 'English', and the Scottish literary inheritance has been only a marginal component of the subject when it has not been ignored entirely. It is only since the 1960s that there have been departments in Scottish universities devoted to Scottish studies, and even these are few and small in scale.

Or, to put it in blunter language as *The Scotsman* newspaper did on 8 February 1979: 'In every country, except Scotland, it is taken for granted that national history and literature should be well taught in the schools'. Can it really be true, you might ask, that Scotland can be so far behind other countries in these respects?

At first sight, this seems very curious. Scotland, after all, has long prided itself on its distinctive, and we used to think, superior, educational system. We were the first country in the world to attempt, from the end of the sixteenth century, to set up a school in every parish. Scotland is also a country with a very rich literary tradition in four languages, Latin, Gaelic, Scots and English. So how does it come about that this interesting and rewarding literature should be largely ignored by our schools and universities?

We have, of course, to realise that the academic study of any of the vernacular literatures in Europe is a fairly recent development. Until late in the nineteenth century, the only literatures taken seriously by schools and universities were those of classical Greece and Rome, and this was as true of Scotland as of anywhere else. Of course, the schools and universities have to be considered together. The schools can teach only what the teachers are taught in the universities. The watershed in the academic attitude towards English literature was as recent as 1921 with the Report from the Board of Education, *The Teaching of English in England*. It is usually known as the Newbolt Report, after Sir Henry Newbolt who chaired the committee of enquiry, which included such well-known scholars as Arthur Quiller-Couch, Dover Wilson and W. P. Ker.

This report is remarkable for two things. First of all, it is very strongly marked by English nationalism: 'for *English* children no form of knowledge can take precedence over a knowledge of English, no form of literature can take precedence over *English* literature ... to form the only basis possible for a national education'. Secondly, it has great confidence in English literature as a humane force which would impart ideas of beauty, good and morality, draw out the personality of the child and unite all classes of the nation.

Although this report was specifically directed towards the teaching of English *in England*, the zeal and enthusiasm of the authors for their revolutionary idea was such that it tended to become a doctrine for the whole Empire, an institution which existed at the time. English literature was to be used as a tool which, in the words of Cairns Craig, would 'promote an ideal of English civilisation which the peoples of the Empire would accept as representing the highest values to which they could aspire'.

Such confidence, such arrogance, is breath-taking, but Sir Henry Newbolt did, after all, write 'Drake's Drum':

If the Dons sight Devon, I'll quit the port o'Heaven,
      an' drum them up the Channel as we drummed them long ago.

At all events, the idea of English literature as a sort of imperial cement was widely accepted, at least for a time. In Canada, Australia, India and Africa, a generation or two of schoolchildren were soundly indoctrinated in virtue and Englishness by Palgrave's *Golden Treasury*. Scotland went along with the rest. You might say that our schools moved from an obsession with Imperial Rome to an obsession with Imperial London.

Nearly everywhere this has now changed. It is, after all, obvious enough that if it is true (as I think it is) that for English children 'no form of literature can take precedence over English literature', then the same is true of Canadian literature for Canadian children and so for all the rest of us. Almost everywhere in the schools of the English-speaking world, the literature of the country takes precedence over the literature of England. This has accompanied a movement for the expression of cultural independence in Ireland, Scotland, North America, India and Australasia. There was a feeling in all of these countries that the literature of England was in many ways alien and largely irrelevant for them. Also many people in these countries, and in Africa and the Caribbean, felt that the language in England itself was moribund and that the forms of it spoken and written elsewhere in the English-speaking world had more force and vitality. In these matters, it is always confusing that the same word, English, applies to the people of one small country but also to a world-wide language of infinite variety and sometimes to the literature written in it. It is a pity that we do not have different words for these very different things.

In Scotland, we have been slower than elsewhere to emancipate our schools and universities from the ethos of Newbolt. They still devote themselves to English in all senses of the term, with only a marginal concern for our own languages and literature. Things are improving, but slowly. Perhaps we are too close to the fount of Englishness. We are under stronger influence because of its proximity, and because of the effect of predominantly English television services. Ever since one of our Kings, James VI, succeeded to the English throne, took his Court and royal patronage with him, and authorised a translation of the Bible into English, a certain social prestige has attached to the language and literature of our southern neighbour. Above all, of course, we have only a very imperfect control over our own affairs, even in matters of education.

The consequence of all this is that Scotland offers a test case of what happens when a literature is not sustained by an academic establishment. Has Scottish literature shrivelled and died because of academic neglect? Not in the least. On the contrary, Scottish writing in this century, particularly in the Twenties and Thirties and in the last twenty years or so, has been very vigorous in three languages, Gaelic, Scots and English. The period in which we are living now may well be regarded by our successors as one of the most fruitful in our literary history.

Literature, therefore, does not need the attention of the universities. There is nothing surprising in this because literature survived for centuries without it. But if it is not indispensable, it is nevertheless beneficial. Since our universities and therefore our schools largely ignore our own literature, many of our people grow up in ignorance of it. This is a pity because the literature which is likely to mean most to people, especially when they are young and experiencing it for the first time, is the literature about the people and places which they know best. For most of us, it is better to start with the familiar and work outwards from a firm base. If we deny to children a knowledge of the literature of their own country, we are denying them the books that are most likely to give them pleasure, stimulate their interest and arouse their imaginations. We would be stifling the development of potential readers and writers. If we give the impression that all the best books are written in a different country by and about people who are different from ourselves, we are breeding an inferiority complex and a sense of alienation. We are telling children that literature is not for them because it is external to their lives and circumstances.

By a different route, we have reached one of the main conclusions of Sir Henry Newbolt's committee. They were right to suggest that schools in England should give precedence to English literature, but for the same reasons, Scottish schools should give the same precedence to Scottish literature. To avoid confusion between country, language and literature, we should find some name other than English for the subject.

I have heard it said that Scottish literature is flourishing precisely because it is ignored by the schools; but this was not meant to be taken very seriously. Without help from the schools and universities, we are all left to discover our own literary background and tradition largely by chance. This is precarious, wasteful and uncertain. The schools should help with the process of discovery, and they can only do this if the teachers in their turn have been given appropriate help themselves by the universities. For literature, the universities are neither patrons nor parasites, but a valuable ally in the maintenance of a literary tradition.

The Thinking Nation

(Rectorial Address, Dundee, 24 April 1989)

I am very conscious of the honour and responsibility that the students of Dundee University have conferred on me by choosing me as their Rector. Dundee is a modern university, but by preserving this office in its constitution, it expressed its sense of continuity with the medieval universities of Scotland and the rest of Europe. It is an office of more than symbolic value and a lively democratic tradition. We should make more use of it and not less. I think that it is lamentable that the Government should propose to curb the rights of the Rectors of the four ancient universities, as an afterthought in a Parliamentary Bill already deplorable for the damage which it proposes to inflict on Scottish education.

In a previous incarnation as a diplomat, a sort of licensed international vagrant, I had some experience of universities in a diversity of countries. They are hospitable places and usually allow you to use their libraries. Also, one of the best ways to get to know a country is to take a university course or two in their history and literature. (Something, by the way, from which many people in Scotland itself would benefit.) With this sort of experience, I have no doubt that the vigour and vitality of its universities is one of the best indicators of the intellectual and cultural health of any country and therefore of the confidence with which it can face the future. Similarly, governments can, and should, be judged by the way they treat their universities.

In this respect, Scotland in the past had a proud record. It used to be said that England had two universities and so had Aberdeen. Fraserburgh nearly had one as well. For centuries, Scotland had four flourishing universities and England still had only two and they were very often, as Edward Gibbon said of Oxford in the eighteenth century, 'sunk in port and prejudice'. It was precisely in that century that the Scottish universities became for a time probably the most innovative and influential in the world. Modern economics, sociology, psychology, medicine, chemistry, physics, engineering, accountancy and banking, indeed almost every human activity or line of enquiry, owes an enormous debt to the discoveries and the thought of our universities at the time of the Scottish Enlightenment.

There are several characteristics of this great burst of innovation and understanding from which we can still draw useful conclusions. I should like to comment on three of them.

In the first place, there were no hard and fast divisions between academic disciplines and everyone involved in these matters in this small country knew virtually everyone else. Neil McCallum in a recent book about the Scottish eighteenth century said, 'Today the poet does not rub willing shoulders with the biologist, nor the mechanic with the academic. That is their mutual loss.' It was otherwise in the Scotland of the eighteenth century. 'This momentous generation was in constant converse with itself.' When James Watt began his work on the steam engine, which made the first industrial revolution, he was the instrument maker to Glasgow University. It was said of his workshop that it became 'a kind of academy whither all the notabilities of Glasgow repaired, to discuss the nicest questions in art, science and literature'.

There is a famous remark by Amyat, the King's Chemist, who was described as 'a most sensible and agreeable English gentleman' and who lived in Edinburgh for a year or two about the middle of the eighteenth century. 'Here I stand', he said, 'at what is called the Cross of Edinburgh, and can, in a few minutes, take fifty men of genius and learning by the hand ... In Edinburgh, the access of men of parts is not only easy, but their conversation and the communication of their knowledge are at once imparted to intelligent strangers with the utmost liberality. The philosophers of Scotland have no nostrums. They tell what they know, and deliver their sentiments without disguise or reserve.'

Voltaire was being ironic at the expense of Lord Kames when he wrote: 'It is a wonderful result of the progress of human culture, that at this day there comes to us from Scotland rules of taste in all the arts from epic poetry to gardening'. But Voltaire had noticed one of the qualities of the Scottish literati of the time; they were interested in everything and believed that no subject could be studied adequately in isolation from everything else. Kames, indeed, wrote about both epic poetry and agriculture as well as about history, law and philosophy. In Scotland there was nothing unusual about that. The Scottish universities took the same wide approach with their belief that education required exposure to a diversity of disciplines, not premature specialisation in any one of them.

We still believe in the virtues of this general approach and vestiges of it remain in our schools and universities. We have, however, been under attack in this, as in other matters, since early in the nineteenth century to conform to the English model which was addicted to specialisation. This is the theme of George Davie's great book *The*

Democratic Intellect, which anyone concerned with the Scottish universities, or with our intellectual traditions generally, should read and consider. The attack began at a time when the Scottish universities were at the height of their international reputation, but that did not deter the anglicisers. They believed, as Sir Walter Scott said in the *Letters of Malachi Malagrowther,* that everything English is right and that anything which is not English must therefore be wrong. That was in 1826, but this quaint belief is now being applied to us with more arrogance and insensitivity than ever before.

When I was first a student at Edinburgh University, the Professor of British History was a distinguished English historian, V. H. Galbraith. When he left Edinburgh in 1944 he said in a speech: 'I am perfectly sure that the future of Scotland lies in a tremendous development of its own affairs, and having the power to do that ... No proposal with regard to education which comes up here from England is worth a damn to you'. He was right then and he would be right, with even more force and urgency, today.

I turn now to the second of my three characteristics of the Scottish Enlightenment, the European connection. These achievements were the outcome of centuries of development in the Scottish universities and of constant and direct interchange with the universities of continental Europe. The country immediately to the south was closed to us as enemy territory for more than 300 years, but Scots were at home all over continental Europe, not only as merchants, soldiers and diplomats, but as students and professors. In the sixteenth century, for instance, George Buchanan was regarded all over Europe as the finest poet in Latin since classical times. He studied and taught in Paris, Bordeaux and Coimbra, as well as in St Andrews and Edinburgh. No less a man than Montaigne, as well as Mary Queen of Scots and James VI, were among his students. It is said that students at Edinburgh at graduation are still capped with part of George Buchanan's breeks. I am told that St Andrews claims the same distinction.

Dugald Stewart, the first historian of the Scottish Enlightenment and the most celebrated university teacher of his time, attributed the eighteenth century achievement largely to this European connection. 'It deserves to be remarked', he wrote, 'as a circumstance which throws considerable light on the literary history of Scotland during the later half of the eighteenth century, that, from time immemorial, a continued intercourse had been kept up between Scotland and the Continent ... The constant influx of information and of liberality from abroad, which was thus kept up in Scotland in consequence of the ancient habits and manners of the people, may help to account for the sudden burst of genius, which to a foreigner must seem to have sprung up in this country by a sort of enchantment, soon after the Rebellion of 1745.' It is, of course, for the same reason that Scots law, educational philosophy and much else is closer to the mainstream of European tradition than is the more insular experience of England.

It has been one of the worst consequences of the unfortunate Union of 1707 that this direct contact with the diversity of European cultures was gradually impeded and frustrated. This process has been described by Eric Linklater: 'in earlier days Scottish students had gone for instruction to France and Holland and farther afield. But now they went to England. In a like fashion their cousins and brothers enlisted or took commissions only in the English army, where aforetime they had done their soldiering with France and Sweden, with Germany and with Russia. By reason of its association with England, Scotland became insular. Its political frontier was broken down, and its mind was walled up. Geographical or political enlargement, beyond certain limits is nearly always accompanied by intellectual shrinkage'.

The current impulse towards Scotland becoming once again a full and independent member of the European family of nations is therefore an impulse towards a return to our ancient associations which served us so well in the past. We want Scotland to become independent once again not as an act of separation but as its precise opposite. We want to play a full and direct part in the affairs of Europe and the rest of the world, with the same rights and responsibilities as any other member of the European Community, no more and no less. It is our present dependent and semi-colonial status that is the separation from which we want to escape.

It is in the interest, not only of Scotland, but of England and of the rest of Europe and the world generally that we should recover our independence. In a book which T. S. Eliot wrote in 1948, he said that it was 'to the advantage of England that the Welsh should continue to be Welsh, the Scots Scots and the Irish Irish'. Consciously or otherwise, Eliot was repeating something which Walter Scott had argued in the *Letters of Malachi Malagrowther* more than 100 years earlier. Both were asserting the value of cultural diversity, which is now becoming rarer and more precious under the increasing threat of a sterile uniformity imposed by the mass media.

That cultural need is a powerful reason for independence, but there are also economic, political and administrative reasons. Andrew Fletcher of Saltoun, one of the leaders of the opposition to the Parliamentary Union of 1707, was also the first major figure of the Scottish Enlightenment. At a time when it was generally believed that a country could only become rich by beggaring its neighbours, Fletcher recognised the interdependence of all countries. 'I am of opinion,' he wrote, 'that the true interest and good of any nation is the same with that of any other. I do not say that one society ought not to repel the injuries of another; but that no people ever did any injustice to a neighbouring nation, except by mistaking their own interest.' So it is with England's relations with Scotland. It does not do them any good when they try to ram their views and sense of values down our reluctant throats. We shall have a much happier, more friendly and co-operative relationship, to our mutual advantage, when we are both free to get on with our own affairs as we each think best.

The third characteristic of the Scottish Enlightenment is that it was a consequence of the value placed upon education by the community at large and by their representative institutions: Parliament and the General Assembly of the Kirk. The Scottish Parliament encouraged education as early as 1496 when they passed an act requiring the eldest sons of barons and freeholders to attend grammar schools until they had perfect Latin and thereafter to spend three years at the schools of art and law, in other words the universities. John Knox's First Book of Discipline in 1560 called for a school in every parish and a college in every notable town. From then onwards, the Scottish Parliament, as long as it existed, passed a succession of laws towards the attainment of this objective. Of the last of these, the Act of 1695, the great historian, T. B. Macaulay, wrote: 'Before one generation had passed away, it began to be evident that the common people of Scotland were superior in intelligence to the common people of any country in Europe ... Scotland made such progress ... in all that constitutes civilisation, as the Old World had never seen equalled, and as even the New World has scarcely seen surpassed.

This wonderful change is to be attributed, not indeed solely, but principally, to the national system of education'.

Girls as well as boys went to these Scottish schools but formal higher education was for centuries, as in other countries, confined to men. I am happy to say, however, that there is evidence that many women in Scotland even at that time somehow managed to educate themselves. Captain Edward Topham, an English officer who was in Edinburgh in 1774 and '75, was clearly very impressed by the women that he met there. He said of them in one of his letters that few nations excelled the Scottish ladies, 'in beauty, as in advantages derived from disposition and education ... nor are they rivalled by the French in the talent of agreeable conversation; for which they seem to be better calculated, as well from their superior knowledge of the world, as from their more extensive acquaintance with books and literature'.

In case you think that the gallant captain was beguiled by the bright eyes of these Edinburgh ladies, let me give you another example. Elisabeth Grant of Rothiemurchus in her entertaining *Memoirs of a Highland Lady* tells us about another officer who in 1818 sought the hand of one of her sisters. 'He was a fine looking young man,' she wrote, 'truly amiable, played the flute to Jane's pianoforte, a performance suitable in every respect and unimprovable, for in spite of daily very lengthened practicings neither artist made much progress. He had a handsome private fortune ... But his knowledge of history was so defective! It was not possible for a moment to think seriously of a companion for life with whom there could be no rational conversation. So the handsome Cavalry officer walked away – no, rode.'

Now, you might suppose that Jane Grant was something of an intellectual snob. Perhaps she was, but I suggest that the episode shows that she had a proper sense of priorities and knew that an intelligent and enlightened mind was more important than a fine military figure or a healthy bank balance. She realised in fact that one of the functions of education is so to stimulate and furnish the mind that we are less likely to bore ourselves or other people, and so become more agreeable and useful members of society in consequence. There is nothing so unnecessary as boredom and nothing more socially dangerous and destructive. Many of the social evils which we suffer are products of boredom. The cure is the stimulation of curiosity, which is also the source of all progress. Without it we should still be living in the Stone Age. 'Disinterested intellectual curiosity', G. M. Trevelyan wrote, 'is the life-blood of real civilisation.' It is, or should be, the function of a university to arouse such a curiosity and to pursue it in all the directions that it might take. The effect, to quote Lord Macaulay again, is 'to open, to invigorate, and to enrich the mind'.

Most important discoveries begin with disinterested curiosity. Take James Clerk Maxwell, for example. He was one of the greatest men of science of all time and he ranks in importance with Newton and Einstein. His philosophical and sceptical approach and the breadth of his intellectual interests derived from his Scottish education and especially from the philosophy of Sir William Hamilton. During the whole of his life he was devoted to pure science, not to its practical application, but his work on electromagnetism was the foundation of the electronic revolution, which is as fundamental to our century as Watt's work on the steam engine was to the nineteenth.

This disinterested curiosity is, of course, the basis of our generalised approach to education, the belief that you cannot hope to understand or cope with the complexities of life if you approach it with a mind trained to think in only one channel. The present British Government wants to put the clock back in this, as in other matters. They would like to confine our schools and universities, except perhaps for a privileged minority who can afford to pay for something better, to the subjects which seem to have a direct commercial utility. They call this 'the enterprise culture'. There is another, more traditional and more appropriate name; it is barbarism.

Even for strictly practical purposes this narrow, commercial approach is mistaken. Let me quote to you the whole passage from which that remark of Macaulay comes. In 1854 (for the Government wants to put the clock back for more than a century), he wrote a famous report about the reform of the Indian Civil Service and in it he said:

> We believe that men who have been engaged, up to twenty-one or twenty-two, in studies which have no immediate connexion with the business of any profession, and of which the effect is merely to open, to invigorate, and to enrich the mind, will generally be found in the business of every profession, superior to men who have, at eighteen or nineteen, devoted themselves to the special studies of their calling.

That is an admirable statement of the Scottish approach. It is also the principle which the British Civil Service has followed for recruitment into its own higher branches since the time of Macaulay.

It is not surprising that the present British Government does not believe in disinterested intellectual curiosity, or in the stimulation of the sceptical intelligence. You would expect nothing else when you consider the alarming totalitarian tendencies which it displays in so many ways. It is centralist and authoritarian, obsessed with secrecy, intolerant of criticism and indifferent to public opinion, especially when it is Scottish. Among the countries of the West, the United Kingdom is uniquely vulnerable to elected dictatorship because it has an unfair electoral system, no written constitution to restrain the Government and no laws to guarantee the rights of the individual, no Bill of Rights, no Freedom of Information Act, no legal guarantees of the freedom of speech and the press. This ramshackle system has so far preserved a large measure of freedom because Prime Ministers and the Governments, which are their creatures, have traditionally observed conventions of moderation, restraint and fair shares for the opposition, as well as respect for the rights and institutions of Scotland which were left intact and indeed guaranteed by the Treaty of Union. The present Government openly despises these conventions in its zeal to transform society in accordance with its own dogma and because of its insensitivity, if not contempt, towards Scottish opinion. The result is the impending constitutional crisis. All of this was analysed in *A Claim of Right for Scotland* which was issued last year and in which I had the honour to be involved. Out of it

grew the Constitutional Convention which had its historic first
meeting at the end of March. It reasserted in resounding terms the
Constitutional principle which has been upheld in Scotland for more
than 600 years that sovereignty rests, not with the monarch or with
Parliament, but with the people, or in the famous phrase of the
Declaration of Arbroath of 1320, the whole community of the Realm
of Scotland.

It is now impossible to talk about education in this country
without talking in political terms. Like almost everything else,
education is under political attack from the Government and can be
defended only by political means. For the first time in history, our
universities can no longer count on the support and encouragement
of an approving Government. On the contrary, the universities are
under pressure to cut staff, curtail their activities and abolish whole
departments. We have seen with a sense of pain and outrage, the
intellectual vandalism inflicted on the University of Aberdeen. Here
in Dundee, we have largely lost Modern Languages and Geology and
the Dental School is still under threat. The staffs of our universities,
instead of being left to the vital work of teaching and research, are
constantly harassed and distracted by the need to resist attacks of this
kind, as well as those on their standards of living. Similarly, life is
made more difficult for students by cuts in the real value of their
grants and by the new threat of a loan scheme which will discourage
all but the wealthy. We are told that the universities are to be
subjected still further to the ethos of the market place, as though they
were in the business of selling soap powder or running a grocery shop
in Grantham.

It is not only the universities which are under such an onslaught.
Research institutes of all kinds are being reduced or abolished.
Newbattle, the only adult residential college of its kind in Scotland,
has a proud record of achievement. In spite of that, and in spite of
widespread protest, the Secretary of State for Scotland has decided to
cut off its funding. The National Library for Scotland is being slowly
starved of funds to buy books from abroad. Our intellectual institutions, on which our civilisation depends, have never before had to
live in such a hostile climate. Previous governments, even in the days
of arbitrary royal power, have always recognised a responsibility to
cherish and encourage the universities, and the other institutions of
higher learning. We are now faced with the most anti-intellectual, the
most philistine, government in our history.

This is happening at a time when our need for universities is greater
than ever before. Technology is developing at unprecedented speed,
and so are the dangers and complexities that surround us. We need
more, and not fewer, trained minds to keep pace with change, seek

solutions and expose the attempts of mass commercialism, advertising and propaganda to turn us into a generation of mindless puppets. Physical pollution is bad enough, but intellectual pollution is still worse. The Government White Paper on Broadcasting in the Nineties opens up hideous possibilities of this kind.

Government meanness over funding does not apply only to universities and the other institutions of our intellectual and artistic life. It applies to virtually everything except nuclear submarines (which we would be better without), the police, and government propaganda, which is a new growth industry – perhaps the only one we have. Services of all kinds are deteriorating, our streets are dirtier, our railways more dangerous. Private affluence, or the excessive wealth of a minority, is no compensation for public squalor. If we allow our people to grow up in sordid, decayed and dilapidated surroundings, it is to be expected that their minds and characters will reflect the same qualities. If we set up greed, competition and acquisitiveness as our ideals, is it surprising that we encourage crime and the breakdown of the spirit of community and cooperation?

Recently the English novelist, A. N. Wilson, wrote an article about this in *The Spectator*. Both he and that magazine are generally regarded as adherents of the political Right, but Wilson told us that he had changed his mind. 'Trains, museums, operas, hospitals, universities', he writes, 'cannot exist without public funding and those of us who pay high rates of tax have a right to expect something better than the present government offers.' He continues, 'It is impossible to resist a feeling of distaste and shame at the sheer unimaginative meanness of this administration where the poor are concerned ... We face a future with dud trains, dud libraries, dud museums, dud hospitals, and the poor getting poorer.' He might have added dud universities, because that will certainly be the consequence if the Government pursues its present policies.

The incredible fact is that this environment of decay and squalor is not the result of necessity but of deliberate choice. It is not because the Government cannot afford to pay for flourishing universities that it imposes decline and misery on us, it chooses to reduce public expenditure in all directions as a matter of dogma, to which it clings with obsession. The Treasury coffers are bulging with money, largely because of revenue from the oil in Scottish waters and the proceeds of selling off national assets of enormous value, like BP or the telephone system. At the time of the last Budget about a month ago, the Chancellor was faced with a surplus of 14 billion pounds and could not think what to do with it, except to keep it in reserve to bribe the electorate with tax cuts before the next General Election.

We have all been so concerned to oppose particular iniquities, like the Poll Tax or the Education Bill, that we have not sufficiently exposed the dogma, the set beliefs politely called an ideology, which lie behind all the acts of this Government. I think that on examination they will be found to be intellectually misguided and simplistic, socially harmful and divisive, and morally repugnant.

The dogma resolves itself into a handful of propositions: free market good; government intervention bad. Private ownership good; public ownership bad. Private profit good; government expenditure bad. Businessmen good; civil servants bad. It is accepted that the Government will have to pay for some services because the people who need them cannot afford to pay to enable anyone to make a profit out of them. This includes social security, health and education. Here the tendency is to encourage private insurance, private health care and private education for those who can afford to pay, leaving a residual and inferior service for those who cannot. This entire attitude runs counter to our egalitarian traditions and it is to the credit of the people of Scotland that they have constantly refused to fall for any of it, despite all the blandishments and the expensive electioneering, financed to the tune of about 9 million pounds by the businessmen who expect to benefit from the policies, an unholy alliance. We reject the crude appeal to selfishness and greed, jingoism and snobbery because they are qualities which we find alien and unattractive.

The advocates of this dogma attribute it to Adam Smith. I can only suppose that they have never read *The Wealth of Nations*, to say nothing of *The Theory of Moral Sentiments*. It is true that Smith advocated free trade, but the restraints that he argued against were those of the mercantilist system and the remnants of the practices of the medieval trade guilds. He was writing at the beginning the industrial revolution when the power of the multinationals and the massive destruction of the environment by industry were unimaginable. There was no manipulation of demand by sophisticated advertising. The conception of social services was rudimentary and industrialisation had not yet created the problems that arose with the congregation of large populations in the towns. Since then life has become more complex and dangerous and Governments have had to accept responsibilities for the health and well-being of their people. They cannot simply be handed over to the tender mercies of private enterprise and the profit motive. For a Government in the modern world to abdicate these responsibilities by appealing to Adam Smith, is as absurd as it would be for an industry to base its technology on the description of a process in the first edition of the *Encyclopaedia Britannica*, which was published in Edinburgh only five years before *The Wealth of Nations*.

In any case, the attitudes of Adam Smith, who was a kindly, humane, intelligent Scot, were utterly opposed to those of the people who now claim to follow him. Smith regarded labour as the source of all wealth and his sympathies clearly lay with the workers. 'No society', he wrote, 'can surely be flourishing and happy, of which the far greater part of the members are poor and miserable. It is but equity, besides, that they who feed, clothe, and lodge the whole body of the people, should have such a share of the produce of their own labour as to be themselves tolerably well fed, clothed, and lodged.' On the other hand, he had a low opinion of landowners, who, he said, 'love to reap where they never sowed'. He distrusted those whom he called 'merchants and master-manufacturers' or, as we should now say, businessmen. 'Any proposal for a new law or regulation which comes from them', he wrote, 'ought always to be listened to with great precaution, and ought never to be adopted till after having been long and carefully examined, not only with the most scrupulous, but with the most suspicious attention. It comes from an order of men whose interest is never exactly the same with that of the public, who have generally an interest to deceive and even to oppress the public.' In another passage he says that 'people of the same trade seldom meet together, even for merriment and diversion, but the conversation ends in a conspiracy against the public, or, in some contrivance to raise prices'.

This is all very different from the attitude of a Government which does its best to pack all public bodies, even those concerned with the arts, education or training, precisely with these 'master manufacturers' because they are the paymasters and therefore the natural allies of the Conservative Party. Adam Smith detested monopolies above all other institutions. What would he have thought of a Government which by privatisation, an ugly word for an ugly process, has created a whole series of private monopolies? Smith spoke of the 'wretched spirit of monopoly' and said that 'the price of monopoly is upon every occasion the highest which can be got'. Customers of British Telecom know how right he was.

An even more astonishing and barefaced example is the Poll Tax, first proposed by a body which has the temerity to call itself the Adam Smith Institute. This violates the first of Smith's principles of taxation which is that all taxation should be levied in proportion to the ability to pay. It would be difficult to find another piece of legislation, at any time in any country, so cynical, so flagrantly aimed at narrow party advantage and so contrary to natural justice.

Are we then to despair because we are the prisoners of a Government which the people of Scotland has repeatedly rejected at the polls, and which is so alien to our instincts and aspirations? I think not because there are many encouraging signs which exist, not because of the Government, but in defiance of it. The feeling of national identity was consolidated in Scotland, as probably the first nation in Europe where such a feeling emerged, in response to the seven military invasions of Edward I. The repeated attempts of the Thatcher Government to impose on us policies and ideas which we find repugnant have had a similar result in making us more aware than ever of the things which we value and have to defend.

The disillusionment of the Referendum of 1979 seemed for a time to destroy self-confidence and hope. There was, I think, a widespread feeling of shame that we had allowed ourselves to be cheated so easily, cheated by the scaremongers who played deliberately on the fear of change, cheated by those, including a past and a future Conservative Prime Minister, who told us that the best way to get a Scottish Parliament with real power was to vote against the particular Act then on offer, cheated finally by those who told us that a majority of over 77,000 was not a majority at all, although for every other decision in our political history, a majority of one has always been regarded as sufficient. Because of the shame of all this, the Press and the population at large seemed for a time to lose all interest in the constitutional question and all hope for the future of Scotland.

The demand for constitutional change, however, was always there beneath the surface. In the last ten years it has become more articulate, more coherent, better informed and thought-through in all its implications. It has not been discouraged, but on the contrary stimulated, by the Government's attempts first of all to try to pretend that the demand did not exist, and then, when that failed, to announce that they would refuse to listen to any such proposal. These ostrich tactics are no longer tenable. The more the demand is denied, the more irresistible it will become.

It is not only in this matter that Scotland has advanced in the last ten years. There is a close link between the instinct for political freedom and the instinct for self-expression. It is another aspect of the same upsurge that Scottish literature, music, the visual arts, historical research, journalism and publishing are all now more vigorous and assertive than at any time since the collapse of intellectual nerve at about the end of the 1830s. The recovery in both political and cultural terms began about 100 years ago and has been gathering pace ever since.

This recovery of self-confidence and achievement has now advanced so far that it was possible for Professor Peter Jones to make a challenging proposal in the pages of the *Glasgow Herald* just over a month ago. 'Scotland', he wrote, 'must proclaim itself as unashamedly intellectual – the thinking nation,… recognising no position as final, all claims as provisional, defiantly open to new avenues, steadfastly sceptical of current understanding, resolutely resistant to the narrowing categories of established boundaries of investigation.' In other words, Professor Jones, having no patience with the commercialism and other distortions that are now being inflicted on our universities, is calling for a new Scottish Enlightenment. He is suggesting that we should once again not hesitate to give a lead to the rest of the world in the exercise of critical intelligence and innovative thought. Professor Jones knows what he is doing because he knows as much as anybody about the Scottish Enlightenment. He is Professor of Philosophy at Edinburgh, a leading authority on David Hume, and, as Director of the Institute for Advanced Studies in the Humanities, was one of those who conducted the great international enquiry into the Scottish Enlightenment in 1986.

Compton Mackenzie had a similar ambition for Scotland. In 1931 he was elected Rector of Glasgow University as one of the first successes of the then recently formed National Party of Scotland. In October of that year, he gave one of the most celebrated of Rectorial Addresses. In it he spoke of Scotland assuming a role of spiritual and intellectual leadership and said this:

> It is not because I believe that Scotland is dying, but because I believe that Scotland is about to live with a fullness of life undreamed of yet, that I count it the proudest moment of my career to be standing here today.

That expresses my own feelings precisely. For a country as small as ours leadership in any field is perhaps over-ambitious, but I have no doubt that an independent Scotland, free to follow its own instincts, would make a valuable and distinctive contribution. I believe that we now have within our grasp a free Scotland, playing a full and important part in Europe and the world, a Scotland of greater prosperity, self-confidence and social justice, a Scotland which encourages and sustains its schools, colleges and universities as the most important of its institutions, the thinking nation, the source of a new Enlightenment. All of that is within our grasp, but we must first resume control of our own affairs through our own independent Parliament. The way forward is through the ballot box. We need only follow the example of the electors of Govan.

I believe that Scotland has a bright future in which the students and young generation of today will have an important and satisfying role. Those of you who are students of Dundee are particularly fortunate because this is a university which has already achieved a distinctive character, an enviable reputation and a very agreeable atmosphere. The new Scotland will have more need of your knowledge and your skills than the old dependent Scotland in which so many of its brightest and most active citizens had to seek their fortunes abroad. I hope that you will find great satisfaction in contributing to the revival. I hope too that our friends from other countries who study here will have warm memories of Dundee and of Scotland and with us will help to establish that universal friendship to which Robert Burns looked forward 200 years ago. 'Its comin yet for a that.'

V

The Language Question

'This Illustrious and Malleable Tongue'

(The Scots Magazine, September 1982)

In 1764, James Boswell wrote in his *Journal*: 'The Scottish language is being lost every day, and in a short time will become quite unintelligible ... To me, who have the true patriotic soul of an old Scotsman, that would seem a pity. It is for that reason that I have undertaken to make a dictionary of our tongue.' Nearly 100 years later in 1853, Lord Cockburn wrote much the same: 'Scotland can only live in the character of the people, in its native literature, and in the picturesque and delightful language. The gradual disappearance of the Scotch accent and dialect is a national calamity.' By 1887, when he wrote the introduction to *Underwood*, R. L. Stevenson thought that the total extinction of the language was not far off: 'The day draws near when this illustrious and malleable tongue shall be quite forgotten; and Burn's Ayrshire and Dr MacDonald's Aberdeen-awa', and Scott's brave, metropolitan utterance will be all equally the ghosts of speech'.

How justified were Boswell, Cockburn and Stevenson in their pessimism, regret and nostalgia? In many ways, Scots has shown itself to be more teuch and endurable than they supposed, Boswell wrote before Burns published his first book at Kilmarnock and before the birth of Walter Scott or Galt. Cockburn and Stevenson evidently did not imagine that in the century after them, Scots would not only still survive, but increase its range and strength as it has in the works of MacDiarmid, Smith, Garioch, Gibbon and McLellan and many others. The dictionary to which Bosworth aspired has now been achieved on a scale and depth of scholarship beyond his wildest imaginings in the ten volumes of the *Scottish National Dictionary*. Work continues, though under financial threat, on the *Dictionary of the Older Scottish Tongue*. The substance of both will soon be made available to a wider public in a concise edition. Of course, the written language is a dead thing unless it is also spoken, but good Scots words and the distinctive rhythms and flavour of Scots speech can still be heard every day on our streets.

The pressures against Scots also continue and intensify. Their roots lie deep in the past with the adoption of the Authorised Version of the Bible by the Reformed Kirk, and the transfer of the centre of gravity of patronage, political power and fashion to London in 1603 and 1707. In consequence, our schools, especially in the heyday of the British Empire, saw their essential mission in the indoctrination of English standards of speech. Anglocentric attitudes became a massive exercise in brainwashing. Already by Lord Cockburn's time, there was additional pressure from the larger population in the south through new means of transport. 'Railways and steamers, carrying the southern into every recess', he wrote in 1844, 'will leave no asylum for new native classical tongue.' Since then, mobility has increased immeasurably, and films, radio and television have deluged our ears with almost any language but Scots. If Boswell was pessimistic about the survival of Scots in 1764, more than 200 years later, and against such infinitely more pervasive pressure, we need more than a dictionary if the language is to survive at all.

The first question, of course, is does it matter if Scots does disappear? In most countries it is taken as axiomatic that a national language is a precious possession to be preserved, or if necessary restored, at all costs. But we should consider what in fact is at stake. In Scotland we have two such languages, Gaelic and Scots, and similar considerations apply to both in their appropriate areas of the country. My present concern is with Scots or Lallans, the language of Lowland Scotland.

The first point arises from the sheer endurability of the language. Scots would not have survived, against all the massive pressures against it, unless it served some purpose or was seen to have some value. A language is a means of communication or it is nothing. The language which a child uses naturally, within his family and among his peers, is the one in which he can communicate most readily. For generations of Scottish schoolchildren, and to this date in wide areas of the country, that means a speech heavily tinged with Scots. When they are told that this is 'wrong' and they are compelled to speak in a way which is unnatural to them, they are forced into a feeling of verbal insecurity. With this loss of self-confidence in speech, comes an impoverishment of the ability to communicate. The 'inarticulate Scot', of which much has been written, is the result. This linguistic mutilation is an act of cultural vandalism.

Secondly, it is not only the ability to communicate in general that is lost with this gag on natural speech, but possibly also the ability to say certain things that cannot be said so clearly, or said at all, in any other language. In his book on Walter Scott, D. D. Devlin says:

> It is often remarked that Scott's strength lies in the handling of the vernacular. What perhaps needs saying is that his strength lies here not simply because he had an ear for lowland speech,

but because he endorsed those qualities of mind and character which the vernacular so accurately conveyed.

Similarly, Edwin Muir said of the Border Ballads that 'they enshrine the very essence of the Scottish spirit, and they could have been written only in the Scottish tongue'. Every language develops vocabulary to express peculiarities of the native climate, scene and habits. In Scots, words like *snell, cranreuch* and *haar* evoke the feel of the Scottish winter in a way which no other language can. This is true not only of physical description but of processes of thought. Scots is particularly rich in vocabulary to prick pretension and emphasise that we are all Jock Tamson's bairns. To take an historical example, *Toom Tabard* has a quite different connotation from its nearest English equivalent, *stuffed-shirt*. Our preference for precision in speech emerges, for instance, when we speak of infusing, not making, tea, and in the whole range of Latin words naturalised in Scots. Qualities of mind and character, in Devlin's phrase, are so intimately bound up with language that, if we lose the language, the qualities which it expresses are well on the way to being lost as well.

The third point is the pleasure and expressiveness of Scots words in themselves. The language is full of words that convey their meaning forcefully by their very sound and are delightful to say and hear. Words like *gloaming, stravaig* and *glaur*. Often they have no precise equivalent in English. They give colour and smeddum to speech. They are what Cockburn had in mind when he said that he felt sorry for 'the poor one-tongued Englishman'. They are a national asset which we should not be blate to use.

Fourthly, if we lose the language, we lose access to a rich literature, uniquely valuable to us because it expresses our own historical experience, but valuable also to the world at large for its own sake. We have literatures in Latin, Gaelic and English as well as Scots, but the contribution in Scots is solid and irreplaceable. If it were to become accessible only to a few scholars studying it as a dead language, and both Boswell and Cockburn foresaw that possibility, our distinctive contribution to civilisation in general would be eroded almost to invisibility. Dunbar, Henryson, Fergusson, Burns and the best parts of Scott and Galt, to say nothing of the moderns, would become almost a closed book.

This brings me to my fifth and final point. Cockburn said that the loss of Scots would be a national calamity. It would be more than that. Civilisation needs the stimulation and enrichment of diversity, of different ways of thought and expression. The loss of a species of animal or plant is an impoverishment of the planet. Much more so would be the loss of a language and literature and all the centuries of thought and experience which they embody.

What then do we do about it? That is another and complex question. For the moment, may I just say that we can all play a part by studying, reading and using Scots at every opportunity, and by demanding more of it in the theatre and on radio and television.

MacDiarmid

(*The Story of Scotland*, no. 48, December 1988)

When A. C. Davis and I edited a book of essays about Hugh MacDiarmid in 1980, we had no hesitation in calling it *The Age of MacDiarmid*. We had no doubt that in many respects he set the tone, or at least the agenda for discussion, which has prevailed in Scotland with fluctuating intensity for the last fifty years or so. If you want to set a date for the start of this period, you might choose 1922, the year that the young poet, Christopher Murray Grieve, first took the pseudonym, Hugh MacDiarmid, by which he is now generally known. It was also, as it happens, the year when Joyce published *Ulysses* and T. S. Eliot *The Waste Land*, those two other landmarks of the modern age. Alternatively, you might take 1926, the year of the first publication of his long poem, or sequence of poems, *A Drunk Man Looks at the Thistle*.

The continuing force of MacDiarmid's influence has been widely recognised. Just after his death on 9 September 1978, *The Scotsman* said in its first leader: 'There is very little written, acted, composed, surmised and demanded in Scotland which does not in some strand descend from the new beginning he made.' Shortly afterwards, David Murison, the editor of the *Scottish National Dictionary*, wrote about him: 'There is one other Scot, at first blush an unlikely candidate for comparison, who is his spiritual ancestor – John Knox; in him we have the same uncompromising aggression, the same argumentativeness ... After MacDiarmid, as after Knox, Scotland will never be the same place again.'

And yet, in many ways, this is surprising. In spite of Shelley ('Poets are the unacknowledged legislators of the world'), poets do not often have such a direct and immediate effect on the climate of opinion of their time. By his own repeated admission, MacDiarmid was no populariser, but an intellectual and an élitist. He gloried in extremes and contradictions. 'I'll hae nae hauf-way house, but aye be whaur / Extremes meet.' He accepted that he often spoke nonsense. As he said in a famous letter to another poet and BBC producer, George Bruce: 'My job, as I see it, has never been to lay a tit's egg, but to erupt like a volcano, emitting not only flame, but a lot of rubbish.' At various times MacDiarmid was active in four political parties, the National Party of Scotland, the ILP, the SNP and the Communist Party, and he was expelled from two of them. He stood for Parliament three times, but was never elected. None of this sounds like an obvious leader of opinion.

The fact, however, is that beneath all the extremity, the élitism and the contradictions, MacDiarmid consistently advocated a very clear set of ideas about Scotland. He expressed them, for instance, in a letter in 1967 towards the end of his life: 'I have devoted many years to seek to overcome the inability of the academic authorities and literary circles in many countries to recognise that Scotland has an independent literary tradition at odds in many vital respects with the English tradition.' He saw a need 'for Scotland to build on its own separate traditions without regard to England, and in particular to revive our native languages, Scots and Gaelic'.

Alan Bold in his excellent biography, *MacDiarmid*, tells us that these ideas go back to the time when Grieve as a young man was a soldier in the First World War. 'By the time he left Salonika early in May 1918 Grieve's nationalist views were pronounced. He was hostile to English people as representatives of imperialism ... Grieve was weary of the assumption that the British troops were fighting exclusively for the honour of England. Scotland, he was sure, had a future too.'

For his entire adult life, and he lived until he was 86, MacDiarmid campaigned tirelessly for these ideas. Of course, they were not original. Many people before him had advocated Scottish self-government and the need to assert the cultural identity of Scotland, including the Scots and Gaelic languages. MacDiarmid was able to bring two qualities to the campaign: his formidable intellectual energy and the prestige of a poet of genius who had himself revived and enlarged the tradition that he was defending. It is probably due more to MacDiarmid than to anyone else that the large majority of the Scottish people are now in favour of a measure of self-government and that hardly anyone would now deny that Scotland has a distinct cultural tradition which should be upheld.

Christopher Murray Grieve was born in Langholm, only a few miles from the border with England, on 11 August 1892. He was the son of a postman who lived in the building which housed a public library founded by Thomas Telford, the great civil engineer. His early voracious appetite for these books laid the foundation for the wide reading and erudition that was reflected in much of his later poetry. After school, he was for a time a student-teacher at Broughton School in Edinburgh, where two other poets in Scots, J. K. Annand and Albert Mackie, were his near contemporaries. During the First World

War he became a sergeant in the Royal Army Medical Corps, serving in Salonika and France. His head was already full of literary projects.

At the end of the War, he married and worked as a journalist in Montrose. There he began to edit and publish anthologies of contemporary Scottish poetry and a series of magazines devoted to Scottish literature, art and politics. His own early writing was in English, but at about the time when he adopted the pseudonym, Hugh MacDiarmid, he turned to writing in Scots. His aim was to rescue poetry in the language from what he saw as a decline into rusticity and sentimentality that had affected it since Burns. He wanted to do two things that might seem contradictory. Firstly, he wanted to enlarge the vocabulary of Scots by recovering words from the poets of the fifteenth century, when Scots was a full and copious language used for all purposes by all classes of society. Secondly, he wanted to extend the intellectual range of poetry in Scots and bring it back into the mainstream of contemporary European literature.

MacDiarmid then began to write short lyrical poems in Scots embracing both of these aims and powerfully expressing emotion and metaphysical thought which ranged from the local and particular, to the cosmic and universal. He published these poems, beginning with 'The Watergaw' in 1922, in his periodicals and anthologies. Collections of them as books followed with *Sangshaw* in 1925 and *Penny Wheep* in 1926. It soon became apparent that Scottish literature was being revitalised by a new force. The great Gaelic poet, Sorley Maclean, for instance, has written about his 'instinctive and overpowering' response to these poems and of his conviction that MacDiarmid was a 'much greater poet than Eliot, Yeats or Pound'. Already in 1923, the *Glasgow Herald* published a leader about MacDiarmid and the group around him, headed 'A Scottish Literary Renaissance'. The following year, Denis Saurat gave wider currency to the same term when he used it in an article in a French review about MacDiarmid and his contemporaries.

A Drunk Man Looks at the Thistle followed in 1926. In the words of the distinguished critic, David Daiches: 'It is not only MacDiarmid's finest sustained performance but also the greatest long poem (or poem-sequence) in Scottish literature and one of the greatest in any literature.' It is an extended reflection on the state of Scotland and on the human condition, in language which ranges from the colloquial to an intense lyricism, and in thought from the commonplace to the mystical. Much of it is a satirical and passionate denunciation of the sorry decline of contemporary Scotland.

In 1929, MacDiarmid went to London to edit a magazine about radio, founded by Compton Mackenzie, which did not long survive. He had a serious accident when he fell from the top of an open double-decker bus. His wife left him and he began a period of prolonged poverty and hardship. In 1933, he moved to virtual exile with his second wife, Valda Trevelyn, on the Shetland island of Whalsay. He was conscripted during the Second World War to work in a factory in Glasgow. In 1950, he was granted a Civil List pension of £150 a year by the Attlee government. For the rest of his life he lived with his wife in a small, and at first fairly primitive, cottage near Biggar.

During the whole of this time, MacDiarmid produced a steady stream of poetry and prose and engaged with vigour in political and cultural controversy. He was invariably courteous and considerate in personal relationships, but he gave no quarter in public dispute. The most notorious case was the controversy provoked by the poet, Edwin Muir, with a book, *Scott and Scotland*, published in 1936. Muir ignored all that MacDiarmid had achieved in Scots and indeed argued that serious poetry was impossible in it because it had become a medium only for feeling and not for thought.

In his own practice, MacDiarmid began increasingly to write poetry in English, which he sought to expand by including terms from science and lines and phrases from a diversity of other languages. He sought 'the union of poetry and science', to give expression to his philosophical communism and to give increasing weight to the importance of Gaelic in the Scottish tradition. Several of his poems in English, such as 'On a Raised Beach' and passages from the longer ones are impressive; but the general view is that his best work is the poetry in Scots of the Twenties and Thirties.

When MacDiarmid started to write, Scottish culture and national consciousness were at a low ebb and it was reasonable to suppose that they were about to disappear in a complacent acceptance of provincial mediocrity. In his book *Scottish Eccentrics*, of 1936, MacDiarmid listed the requirements for national revival: a struggle to defend the Scottish literary tradition and the Gaelic and Scots languages, the serious study of Scottish history and an effective nationalist movement. None of these have yet achieved all of MacDiarmid's aspirations, but they are all very much stronger than they were 60 years ago. He was not alone in calling for these things but his was the strongest and most persistent voice. MacDiarmid certainly played a major part in laying the foundations for the present recovery of Scottish national self-confidence.

The Lorimer New Testament

(*The Scotsman*, 22 October 1983)

For some 300 years the Authorised Version of the Bible was easily the most widely read book in Lowland Scotland, and not only read but heard in every service in every kirk. It was, of course, in English, and English at its most dignified, sonorous and memorable. We may speculate about the spiritual or psychological effects of this deluge of splendid words, but of its consequences for the development of Lowland Scots, there is no doubt. Who, in that religious age, could argue with the word of God and that word was invariably in English. Scots had already lost prestige by the flitting of King and Court to London. The same King's Authorised Version stifled the development of Scots prose for any serious purpose. It was otherwise with speech and poetry, of course; but they too suffered from this double blow to the status of the language. Probably no other language has been so much affected by the influence of a single book.

Now, 300 years too late, we have this magnificent translation of the *New Testament* by William Lorimer.*

There is a passage in the *Acts of the Apostles* (Chapter 2) which in this translation reads:

> They saw like tungs o fire, at sindert in twa an sattelt on ilkane o them, an they war aa filled wi the Halie Spírit an begoud speakin in fremmit leids, accordin as the spírit gae them the power tae mouband their thochts.
>
> There wis wonnin in Jerusalem at this time gudelie Jews at hed come there frae ilka kintra aneth the lift. Whan this sound gaed throu the place, they aa gethert in a croud an war fair bumbazed, ilkane o them, tae hear the Apostles speakin in his ain leid.

The Scots, when most of them have all but lost the leid, now have the opportunity to be bumbazed in the same way.

This is a translation with many substantial qualities. In the first place, it is of sound scholarship. William Lorimer spent most of his life teaching Latin and Greek at University College, Dundee and the University of St Andrews, but also from his childhood he studied Scots and as much from spoken as from written sources. His translation is, of course, directly from the Greek and he prepared himself for it by studying a great many translations in as many as 23 different languages. He then devoted the last ten years of his life to the task. There have been previous translations of the *New Testament* in Scots, but none with anything approaching this detailed and scholarly planning and preparation. Lorimer's translation even reflects the differences in style between the writers of the different books.

Of course, scholarship is not enough. It might easily be worthy, painstaking and dead. If it does not give new life to the familiar text and speak movingly and memorably to us, it would remain a curiosity for the linguistic scholar. William Lorimer had a more ambitious purpose. His son R. L. C. Lorimer, who has skilfully edited the translation for the Press, says this of his father's intentions: '... further study had convinced him that if Scots was ever to be resuscitated and rehabilitated, two great works must first be produced: a good modern Scots dictionary, and a good modern Scots translation of the New Testament.' [In making the translation]...'he was well aware that in doing so he would also be setting out to resuscitate and recreate Scots prose.'

His purpose then was even more ambitious than MacDiarmid's, who widened the dimensions of poetry in Scots. Lorimer was attempting not only to re-establish the lost traditions of Scots prose, but to restore to the language as a whole something of the range, status and acceptability which it began to lose in the seventeenth century. We now, of course, have the dictionary, the ten volumes of the thorough and comprehensive *Scottish National Dictionary*. Work continues on the *Dictionary of the Older Scottish Tongue*, establishing the historical roots of the language. We are about to have for popular use the *Concise Scots Dictionary* which will combine the scholarly resources of the other two.

If one of Lorimer's requirements is thus fully met, how well does his translation meet the other? It is certainly too late in the day for a *New Testament* alone to make the major impact on speech habits which it once would have done. Even so, a successful work on this scale and level could still radically transform attitudes to the language, and its chances of survival, usage and development.

Lorimer's translation is not merely scholarly but is a great literary achievement in its own right. It gives a fresh impact and vigour to the familiar story which not only restores life to Scots but to the *New Testament* itself. Passages which had become an empty litany of words in the customary versions, regain the excitement and significance which they must have had for those who first read the original Greek.

The dialogues in particular become conversations between living people, not abstractions. They have the zest of real debate:

'... tell us your mind anent the imperial poll-tax: have we líshence tae pey it, or hae we no?

Jesus saw weill their sleeness, and said tae them, 'What for seek ye tae girn me, hýpocrites at ye ar? Shaw me ane o the coins ye pey the tax wi.' They raxed him a merk, an he speired at them, 'Wha's heid is that? Wha's name read ye there?'

'The Emperor's,' said they.

'A-weill, than,' qo he, 'pey the Emperor what perteins tae the Emperor, and pey God what perteins tae God.' That left them dumfounert; an, onsaid mair til him, they gaed their waas. (Matthew, 22)

Scots used as Lorimer uses it positively benefits from the fact that it has become a language of poetry and speech, not of prose. It is a language quite free from the tired associations of bureaucracy and ad-speak. It demands to be read aloud. It is colloquial, vivid and direct, with varied pace and rhythm, and it surges to heights of nobility and power.

Inevitably, Lorimer uses some words which are no longer familiar. If Scots is to be restored, the reader as well as the writer will have to enlarge his vocabulary by recourse to the dictionary. He will find that Lorimer invariably uses words with precision. 'Ye will finnd a new-born bairn swealed in a barrie an liggin intil a heck' (Luke, 2). What is a barrie? You will find in the *SND* that it is a 'garment in which a baby is wrapped'. Two small points may cause some difficulty at first, the use of the enclitic 'na' at the end of a verb to express the negative (as in 'I dinna') and the conjunction 'at' (equivalent to 'that').

Once you get used to these, which are more unusual in written than in spoken Scots, the language will give little difficulty to anyone with some feel for Scots, especially if it is read aloud.

The publication of this book is an important date in our literary and linguistic history. Buy a first edition while you have the opportunity. Many people have already heard how magnificently the Lorimer version sounds in the readings by Tom Fleming. I hope that our ministers will not be slow to follow his example.

The New Testament in Scots (1983). Translated by W. L. Lorimer, edited by R. L. C. Lorimer.

The Concise Scots Dictionary

(*The Scotsman,* 10 August 1985)

For reasons with which we are all familiar, Scots, once the language of the whole nation outside the Highland Line, as well as the medium of a great literature, has been in retreat for about 300 years. At various times even its enthusiastic supporters have had moments of despair that it would soon be lost beyond recovery. Lord Cockburn, for instance, wrote in his journal in 1853 that the gradual disappearance of this 'picturesque and delightful language' was a 'national calamity'. R. L. Stevenson, some 30 years later, agreed with him: 'The day draws near when this illustrious and malleable tongue shall be quite forgotten: and Burns's Ayrshire, and Dr MacDonald's Aberdeen-awa, and Scott's brave, metropolitan utterance will be all equally the ghosts of speech'.

For all that, Scots has displayed a remarkable resilience. The retreat has not been without many notable rearguard actions. We have had the eighteenth century revival of Ramsay, Fergusson and Burns, and in the nineteenth, of the richness of the Scots dialogue in the novels of Scott, Galt and Stevenson. In our own century, writing in Scots has been more diverse than at any time for the last 300 years in the novels of Gibbon, the poetry of MacDiarmid, Smith and Garioch, and the plays of Kemp and McLellan, to mention only a few. Within the last two or three years, the enormous success of the Lorimer *New Testament in Scots* and of the Scottish Theatre Company's productions of McLellan's *Jamie the Saxt* and of Lindsay's *Thrie Estaites* has proved again the continuing power of Scots to convey a particularly Scottish response to life.

That, I think, is the real point. If we were to lose Scots, we would lose access to an important literature, but more is at stake than that alone. D. D. Devlin in his book on Scott said his strength lay in his handling of the vernacular and that was not only because he had an ear for it, 'but because he endorsed those qualities of mind and character which the vernacular so accurately conveyed'. Cockburn made a similar point. If we lose Scots, he wrote, 'above all we lose ourselves. Instead of being what we are, we become a poor part of England.' I think that they were both right. There are 'qualities of mind and character' which can only be conveyed adequately in Scots. If you doubt that, try translating a poem of Burns, or a dialogue in Scott or Galt, for instance, into English. You are left with a pale shadow.

Fortunately, the lexicographers and the scholars, particularly David Murison and A. J. Aitken, have been active in the study and recording of the great riches of Scottish vocabulary. In 1931, work began on two full-scale dictionaries, the *Scottish National Dictionary* to cover the language from 1700, and the *Dictionary of the Older Scottish Tongue* from the earliest times until that date. The first of these was completed in ten volumes in 1976. Work still continues on the second, and five volumes have been published so far. These are thorough, comprehensive dictionaries, with the history of every known word illustrated by quotations. From their nature, they are large and expensive volumes, a resource for the library, not for daily use in the home. This need has now been met by the *Concise Scots Dictionary** which is based on the material accumulated by the two parent dictionaries. It collects into one convenient volume the most important words of the language from the time of Henryson and Dunbar to the present.

Of course, in the compression something had to go. It has inevitably meant the exclusion of the quotations, which, as the introduction says, are 'such a rich source of information and pleasure in the parent dictionaries'. Apart from this, the editors have contrived to include an enormous amount of information in their 800 pages without sacrifice of legibility. If you are looking only for a definition, you will find that very readily. But you can also find alternative spellings, distribution of the word by area and time and its etymology. Much of this is conveyed by an ingenious use of typography, punctuation and abbreviation in a system which is described very lucidly in the introduction. The dictionary is a model of clarity for a work of this kind.

The introduction contains also a brief, but notably clear and balanced, history of the language. This stops short of mentioning two forces which have moved powerfully against Scots: the schools and broadcasting. For about 100 years, the schools have taken as their principle task the eradication of Scots and its substitution by Standard English. As I. K. Williamson has shown, this was enforced by the Inspectorate, many of whom were Oxbridge men with no knowledge or appreciation of Scottish language or literature. The recent report, *Scottish Resources in the Schools*, is a welcome sign of a radical change of attitude. The BBC has made some effort to recognize and encourage Gaelic. It has still to do anything comparable for Scots.

We have been systematically brainwashed to suppress Scots and therefore to impair a vital part of our personality and character. It is for this reason that the publication of this admirable dictionary is a major event of more than only linguistic, literary or historical significance. As the editors say in their introduction:

> The present dictionary is intended not only as a record of the copiousness and variety of the resources of the Scots language, but also as a contribution to the self-assurance of the Scottish people about that language, which enshrines their past and lives in their daily speech.

*Mairi Robinson (ed) (1985) *The Concise Scots Dictionary*

VI

Cultural Policy

Cultural Diplomacy

(Paper for International Conference on European Cultural
Co-operation, Edinburgh University, 1–2 June 1984)

Cultural diplomacy, by definition, must mean part of the relationship
between countries in diplomatic relationship with one another and
therefore between sovereign States. Quite a number of the remarks at
this conference suggest that that definition is neither very satisfactory
nor complete. The Scottish experience also suggests that a relationship which concentrates on, or is confined to, the existing sovereign
States is inadequate. Scotland, of course, is in somewhat anomalous
position because it is a country with a very long history of independence.
For instance, it is the accepted and conventional view that the idea of
the nation State started with the French Revolution. Well, in Scotland
we think we invented it in the fourteenth century, in a document
called the Declaration of Arbroath, which we regard as the first great
classic statement of the principle.

Of course, we lost some of the outward attributes of this sovereignty in the eighteenth century when by Treaty between England and
Scotland the two Parliaments were merged. In a sense, this was meant
to be an equal sort of arrangement with the same effects on both
countries, but since the population of England is ten times the
population of Scotland, the effects were in fact different, and England
became the dominant partner. On the other hand, although we lost
the Parliament, we maintained many of the attributes of a State on
which a culture depends, in particular a distinctive Church, legal, and
educational system. Partly in consequence of these things, we have
also maintained our separate tradition in all the arts – music,
architecture, literature and philosophy and in everything else. In these
matters, we have always been conspicuously European in the sense
that we have always been very open to influences from virtually the
whole of Europe, to a much greater extent than England.

For instance, we derived a language from the early influence of
Ireland. The architecture of Edinburgh, until recent times, maintained
a conscious devotion to the influence of classical Greece and Rome;
a symbol of that devotion is the fact that the first translation of
Virgil's *Aeneid* into any other language was one into Middle Scots.
We have been greatly indebted to the influence of Italy and of France,

with whom we were allied for three hundred years – so closely allied that we exchanged citizenship. And we are indebted to Holland from which we derive such typically Scottish manifestations as the game of golf and the Edinburgh Medical School. Our system of law is based on the Roman tradition, and is therefore close to the mainstreams of European traditions.

This has not been a one-way relationship because, as other speakers have mentioned, many Scottish writers and thinkers have had a marked influence on the rest of Europe. Monsieur Missir mentioned *Ossian*, which was Napoleon's favourite reading. The influence of Hume and Adam Smith is enormous, just as Walter Scott's influence on the rest of Europe's literature was pervasive for well over one hundred years. Even the influence on European music is remarkable. Roger Fiske recently wrote a book which demonstrated that all the major European composers for about one hundred years, were much influenced by an idea of Scotland (which may have been mistaken or mythical) which was reflected in their music and which brings in Scottish melodies, and also goes back to the influence of Ossian and Walter Scott. So, we think we too have played an important part in the evolution of European culture.

In the past, Governments played a very minor role in these matters, We sometimes tend to forget that until the twentieth century, Governments did nothing much except make war and raise taxes. All other activities that affect people were either self-generating or were run by some agency such as the Church, as happened in Scotland and other places. But in this century, Governments increasingly began to play a role in every aspect of life, including the business of cultural diplomacy or cultural relations.

Of course, when the British Government started to take an active role in these matters, Scotland increasingly found herself in an unsatisfactory position. Scotland needs direct contact with other countries. When the State intervenes, Scotland tends to be cut off by the intervention of London. Bodies like the British Council certainly make an effort, for which we are grateful, to take account of the Scottish contribution; but they look at it from the outside. Our experience is that even very well-informed and well-disposed Englishmen are remarkable ignorant about everything Scottish. They know little about Scottish culture, do not understand its background or the circumstances from which the various Scottish art forms develop, and even if they do know a bit about them, they look at them from different assumptions and standards. The result is that any representation of Scotland in the cultural field, if channelled through London, is inevitably distorted, misleading, stifling and frustrating.

I am sure this applies to other small nations as well as Scotland.

Therefore, any vision of cultural co-operation in Europe, any programme of cultural exchange in Europe, must take account not only of the sovereign States as they at present exist, but of these other contributions which have their own importance. There is a sense in which we should truly speak not about European cultures but European culture – the things we have in common are much more important than the things which distinguish us. Nevertheless, part of the richness and value of European civilisation lies in its diversity. We shall lose an important part of the cultural richness of Europe if we think in terms which tend to submerge or ignore the smaller countries and nations like Scotland.

Six Immediate Objectives

(Paper for a Conference in Edinburgh City Chambers,
12 September 1987, subsequently published in *Radical Scotland*)

One problem which we are discussing today is not only a Scottish but a universal one. As Henrik Borovik, one of the Soviet speakers in the first week of the recent Edinburgh Festival, said, we are all faced with the choice between the defence of national cultures or acceptance of a multinational cultural desert. At the last international conference of PEN in Lugano in May, many of the most distinguished writers from all over the world spoke in very similar terms. Czeslaw Miloscz and Anthony Burgess argued that the universal can only be reached through the local and particular. Lassi Nummi, Alain Bosquet and many others spoke about the the need to defend diversity against imposed uniformity. A Scottish resolution about the need to defend the smaller cultures and less-used languages, was received with enthusiasm. It was passed unanimously with only one abstention, which was by the English delegation.

When I wrote a pamphlet on this subject as it applied to Scotland, *In Bed with an Elephant*, I took the title from a remark by Pierre Trudeau when he was Prime Minister of Canada. He said that this was the uncomfortable experience of Canada in having to share a continent with the United States. Well, there are quite a few elephants of that kind in the world and many countries and minorities that feel that they are being suffocated by that sort of pressure.

Scotland, with a particularly expansive neighbour with a population ten times larger, has felt this pressure for hundreds of years. It is therefore not surprising that the first important statement of the case for diversity against uniformity, was Sir Walter Scott's *Letters of Malachi Malagrowther* in 1826. This is a book which no one interested in this question, and the Scottish example in particular, should ignore.

Even if there were time, I do not think that I need to demonstrate before this audience that the Scottish contribution to the arts and sciences is rich, diverse and valuable. It was an American, Harold Orel, who concluded that no other country of a comparable size had contributed so much to civilisation. Scottish thought is also very distinctive, involving as it does both the qualities which George Davie described as the 'democratic intellect' and those which Gregory Smith called the 'Caledonian antisyzygy'. Many of these qualities are among those which have a very useful role to play in the modern world. I mean such things as egalitarianism, irreverence, a polymathic distrust of watertight barriers between subjects, a taste for first principles and for following the argument wherever it might lead.

Now, you might suppose that a culture so rich and distinctive as the Scots would be under no great threat and that the educational system and public bodies of the country would be doing everything possible to support and sustain it. You would be wrong and, in fact, the opposite is closer to the truth. An English historian in the nineteenth century, J. A. Froude, wrote: 'No nation in Europe can look with more just pride on their past than the Scots, and no young Scot ought to grow up in ignorance of what that past has been'. The majority of Scots do, indeed, grow up in precisely that state of ignorance. This is because our educational system is, incredibly, still caught up in the old imperialist habit which caused schools all over the Empire to devote themselves to English language, history and literature and to disregard their own. Canada, India, Australia and the rest have escaped from this frustration, but Scotland not yet.

The effect of this is compounded by the domination of our television screens (after all the chief cultural, intellectual and political influence for most people), by programmes which overwhelmingly come from the outside. Only a fraction of the money raised in Scotland to finance television by licence fee or advertising, is spent on programme-making in Scotland. Most of it goes to London.

Of course, there are many other aspects of the insidious erosion of Scottish control in many aspects of our affairs. Many, if not most, of the key posts in institutions which are supposed to express or defend a Scottish interest or point of view, are paradoxically held by people who are not Scottish.

The consequence of all of this is not only the erosion of the national culture but the creation in its place of alienation and an inferiority complex, with disastrous social consequences. You bring people up in ignorance of the realities of the past and encourage them to think that everything of value and importance happened somewhere else. Is it any wonder if they either try to escape or collapse into apathy and despair?

This situation is largely a consequence of the Treaty of Union which the Scottish Parliament was bribed and bullied into accepting in 1707. Like most things in Scotland, we shall be hampered and restricted in any attempt to deal with the problem until we resume responsibility for our own affairs. There are, however, a number of objectives which we can set ourselves even before we achieve self-government or independence. Most of them have been studied in detail by AdCAS. Let me end with a list of them:

1. We should begin in the schools, by encouraging them to emancipate themselves from an obsession with England and to give far more attention to Scottish conditions, literature, languages and history. The best way to achieve this is by a gradual modification of the questions in the Scottish Certificate of Education examinations.

2. The Scottish universities should have their own funding arrangements through the Scottish Office as proposed by STEAC (Scottish Tertiary Education Advisory Committee) but which the present Secretary of State has so far failed to implement.

3. Broadcasting, both public and commercial, should have an autonomous organisation in Scotland. Money raised here through licences or advertising should be used for programme-making in Scotland.

4. The Scottish Arts Council should be liberated from its dependence on the Arts Council of Great Britain and become responsible to the Scottish Office. It should give priority to the encouragement of the Scottish arts.

5. The Scottish share of the funding of the British Council should be devoted to an organisation for the promotion of direct cultural exchange between Scotland and other countries.

6. The achievements of drama in Scotland should be consolidated and promoted by the early establishment of a Scottish National Theatre.

A Cultural Policy for the Nineties

(Paper for AdCAS Conference, 2 June 1989;
adapted from the last chapter of *Cultural Independence*)

In the Seventies the mere prospect of even a limited measure of
autonomy brought about a marked change in the intellectual climate
in Scotland. There was a surge of confidence and optimism and much
activity in thinking and planning about the new opportunities which
would be open to us when we had control of our own affairs. As part
of this, the Saltire Society in September 1977 held a conference at St
Andrews to discuss the consequences for the cultural life of Scotland.
A resolution was passed, inviting the Society to get in touch with all
the cultural organisations of Scotland to see if there was a general
demand for a joint body to pool ideas and evolve proposals for
cultural policies which they would like a Scottish Government to
adopt. With Professor John MacQueen as Convener and A. C. Davis
as Secretary, the Society then undertook extensive consultations with
about 200 organisations, governmental, professional and voluntary,
involved in diverse aspects of the artistic and intellectual life of the
country. A conference, at which many of these organisations were
represented, was held in February 1979 with Sir Kenneth Alexander
in the chair. It approved a Manifesto for the Arts which suggested
priorities in the cultural field for the Scottish Government. This
included a recommendation for the election of an Advisory Council
for the Arts in Scotland (AdCAS) which would continue to act as a
joint think-tank and a means of exchanging ideas between the
organisations and the new administration.

Shortly afterwards, there was a radical change with the Referendum, the election of a Conservative Government and the repeal of the
Scottish Act. The new ministerial team in the Scottish Office declined
an invitation to appoint representatives to take part in the work of the
proposed Advisory Council, but said that the Government would
'recognize the value of its advice'. On this basis, AdCAS was
established at a further conference in June 1981. Since then, it has
continued to keep policies towards the arts under review and has
made frequent submissions to the Government, Committees of
Enquiry and others. It has successfully pressed, for example, for a
greater Scottish content in the Edinburgh Festival and for paperback

reprints of important Scottish books. It has held public conferences on such matters as a Scottish National Theatre.

The following proposals for a cultural policy for Scotland incorporate ideas which have been discussed and approved by AdCAS in the past.

1. *Ministry for Cultural Affairs*

Scotland already has a formidable range of cultural institutions and organisations although some others are still needed. Those which are funded by the State, such as the National Library of Scotland and the Scottish Arts Council, suffer at present from two disadvantages. They are being progressively starved of funds because of the Tory obsessions with privatisation and sponsorship, and the reduction of Government expenditure. Also, since some are funded through the Scottish Office and others through Departments in Whitehall, it is difficult for them to follow coherent policies. There is an urgent need for a Ministry to bring together responsibility for the funding of all of these organisations, such as the National Library, Museums and Galleries, the Scottish Arts Council, the Scottish Film Council and so on. A Scottish Government would certainly wish to fund all of them more generously than in the past, and to encourage optimism and development, not, as at present, resignation and despair.

Several important Scottish institutions, such as the National Portrait Gallery and the National Library, were established by private generosity with the Government afterwards accepting responsibility for running costs. Successive British Governments have tended to avoid responsibility for cultural institutions in Scotland. It is, for example, scandalous that such things as the *Dictionary of the Older Scottish Tongue*, the School for Scottish Studies and a long overdue proposal to establish a Chair of Scottish Literature in Edinburgh University, and indeed now the entire university system, should have to appeal to public generosity for their very survival. It would be one of the functions of the Cultural Ministry to ensure adequate funding in all such cases.

The Ministry would also be responsible for encouraging the establishment of institutions which are still needed. The most important of these are:

i) A Scottish Broadcasting Corporation and a Broadcasting Authority to regulate the conditions under which independent broadcasting operates. They would ensure the continuation of public service broadcasting and that independent franchises are awarded on merit, not (as proposed in the recent White Paper) merely to the highest bidder.

ii) An organisation, which might be called Scotland International, which would promote cultural exchange with other countries. In particular, it would encourage co-operation within the European Community.

iii) A Scottish National Theatre. It is anomalous that we should have national companies for opera and ballet, but not for drama which is precisely the form of the performing arts in which we have made the most valuable, distinctive contribution. Experience in virtually all other European countries has shown that a national theatre is an effective stimulus to the general cultural life of the country. The AdCAS Conference in May 1987 was the largest and most representative meeting of those involved in, and concerned about, the theatre in Scotland, and was an impressive demonstration of an urgent and widespread desire for a National Theatre. It adopted a resolution virtually unanimously that there was a 'pressing need' for a National Theatre and elected a Working Party to pursue the matter. They issued a Report on 30 November 1987, but there was a serious set-back when the Scottish Arts Council almost simultaneously allowed the Scottish Theatre Company to collapse. Active attempts are being made to find an alternative approach.

All of these new institutions, like those which already exist, would be autonomous with their own councils or boards. They would operate openly and encourage public discussion of their policies. AdCAS, reinforced by government participation and assistance, could act as a channel for ideas about policy.

Funding of the arts, crafts and films, through their appropriate councils, would be particularly directed at new creative work in Scotland and to the revival and performance of important work from the Scottish past, including the great wealth of Scotland in traditional music, song, poetry and dance.

In a more direct governmental role, the Ministry, in association with other appropriate departments, would explore means of encouraging the arts by suitable taxation policies or by purchase and distribution. They would look for useful examples in policies of this kind already followed in other countries, and encourage measures for cultural co-operation and exchange within the European community.

2. Education
There is such a close relationship between education and the arts and sciences that it is arguable that all should come under the same Ministry. Probably, however, this would be too much for one department and it would probably be preferable to have a separate Ministry of Education and Science, working in close collaboration with the Ministry of Culture. Education at all levels should be

integrated into one coherent system. It should be accorded a high priority for government expenditure with a tendency towards expansion and development instead of the cuts and closures of the last ten years. Education will be freely available as a lifelong process for people of all ages. Newbattle will be re-opened as an adult residential college and other colleges of a similar nature will be opened in other parts of Scotland.

The Anglicization of Scottish universities has proceeded relentlessly since the early nineteenth century, as George Davie has described in his great book, *The Democratic Intellect*. This has now reached the point where very little remains of the broad philosophical approach which was the essential characteristic of the Scottish universities, and an excessive proportion of staff and students are English. Under the Thatcher Government, savage cuts have been imposed which have meant large reductions in staff and even the abolition of whole departments. Angus Calder scarcely exaggerates when he said in the Summer 1985 issue of *Cencrastus*: 'The drive from London seems to be towards a situation where elderly English academics in decimated departments teach an Anglocentric view of culture and history to English public schoolboys amid the ruins of the broad Scottish curriculum'.

There are also serious causes for concern for the school system as a result of the recent government policies. In May 1989, the Scottish Centre for Economic and Social Research published *Scottish Education: A Declaration of Principles*, a report by a group of distinguished educationalists invited by AdCAS to consider the position. They concluded that the system was 'being savaged and destabilised on ideological grounds irrelevant to Scotland'.

A Scottish Government will therefore be faced with the urgent and vital task of repairing the damage inflicted on our education at all levels. In Scotland, we have traditionally placed great value on education and at one time gave a lead to the world. The restoration of the democratic intellect with all that it implies, must be a major objective of an independent Scotland.

Scottish history, literature and languages will be given their proper place in the curriculum at all levels and in broadcasting. There should be no attempt to enforce linguistic change by legislation, but an independent and self-confident Scotland is likely to make greater use of its native forms of speech, and reverse the decline which external influences have imposed on them.

3. *Science*
The Scots are an inventive people with a particular aptitude for science and technology. We should build on this strength by encour-

aging research in areas likely to be useful to Scottish industry, agriculture and fishing, as well as in pure science. One of the objects should be to increase the number of intellectually demanding jobs in Scotland and counteract the process under which well-qualified Scots are forced to seek employment elsewhere. For this purpose, a Research Council should be established responsible to a Department within the Ministry of Education.

4. *Important Posts*

Applicants for important posts in the cultural institutions of Scotland should be required to show a good knowledge of the Scottish background in their own field. One might think it self-evident that anyone seeking the post of, let us say, the Director of the National Gallery of Scotland would be expected to have a good knowledge of Scottish painting and an enthusiasm for it. In fact, the extraordinary thing is that this has simply not been so in recent times. This is one of the reasons why our cultural identity is at risk of disappearing from sight behind a solid phalanx of people from elsewhere (and nearly all of them English), with little previous experience of Scottish achievement and Scottish attitudes. We obviously want to avoid intolerance or unfair discrimination and we welcome the greater freedom of movement within the European community, but it is the sheer scale of the influx from a single source which threatens suffocation. England has more than ten times the population and so we are highly vulnerable. We have, therefore, to face up to this very real and embarrassing problem. The simple answer seems to be an insistence on appropriate knowledge or experience, in all job specifications for posts which are important for our cultural identity.

5. *Conclusion*

The entire cultural life of Scotland will be enlivened by the attainment of responsibility for our own affairs. This has been the experience of other countries which have obtained or regained independence. By itself, it is of sufficient importance to justify all our efforts to secure constitutional change.

Cultural policy is uniquely involved with national identity. However thoroughly the European Community may integrate and pool sovereignty in other matters, in the general interest it will always be essential that cultural policy remains a national responsibility. For the same reason, this is the area in which it is most urgent that we liberate ourselves from London control. This does not mean that we should not encourage wide cultural exchange and co-operation. On the contrary, one of the advantages of taking control of our own affairs is that we can then establish direct contact with other countries. It is the bottle-neck of dependence on London which is the real separation.

We should not set our sights too low. Scotland has many natural advantages but chief among them are the qualities of its people and the abilities which they have shown in everything, from gardening to philosophy. We should make a conscious effort through our educational system and all the institutions of our cultural life, to encourage the full development of this potential and to give satisfying careers to our people in their own country.

When Francis Jeffrey gave evidence to the Royal Commission and the Scottish universities in 1826, he praised our traditional system which encouraged students to argue about the basic questions of 'history, literature, physics, metaphysics and everything'. This is a tradition which we should repair and restore. As Professor Peter Jones suggested in the *Glasgow Herald* of 8th March 1989, Scotland should not hesitate to become again 'unashamedly intellectual, the thinking nation', open to new ideas, sceptical of current understanding, recognising all ideas as provisional, and resistant to 'narrowing categories of established boundaries of investigation'. But we should not only be intellectual, but enjoy the refreshment and enlargement of the spirit to be found through the arts. Here too we should be open to the world, but with a firm base in our own traditions. We should avoid slavish imitation, because as Ramsay of Ochtertyre said in one of his letters, 'professed copying ever implies inferiority'.

All of this lies within our grasp if we make the effort. It will enable us to escape from the miserable position of being 'neither quite alive or quite dead', neither quite Scottish or quite anything else. It will free us from agonising doubts about our identity and make us self-confident citizens of the world. By being more Scottish and more universal, we shall make Scotland an infinitely more agreeable and stimulating place for our people and make a more useful contribution to the common civilisation of humanity. By becoming a full and active member of the European community, we shall recover the role which in the past brought so much benefit to Scotland and the rest of Europe.

VII

The Need for Independence

Fletcher and the Union

(*The Scotsman*, 15 April 1978)

Andrew Fletcher of Saltoun (1655–1716), a key figure in the opposition to the Treaty of 1707, has a unique reputation among Scottish politicians. He was admired and respected by his contemporaries of all shades of opinion to an extent which is quite remarkable. 'To sum up all,' wrote Lockhart of Carnwath (who was a Jacobite), 'he was a learned, gallant, honest, and every other way well accomplished gentleman; and if ever a man proposes to serve or merit well of his country, let him place his courage, zeal and constancy as a pattern before him, or think himself sufficiently applauded and rewarded, if he obtain the character of being like Andrew Fletcher of Saltoun.'

From the opposite end of the political scale, John Mackay, who was a Whig and a Hanoverian, was even more lyrical: 'He is a gentleman steady in his principles, of nice honour, with abundance of learning: brave as the sword he wears, and bold as a lion: a sure friend, and an irreconcilable enemy: would lose his life readily to serve his country: and would not do a base thing to save it.'

Later in the eighteenth century David Hume described him as 'a man of signal probity and fine genius', and Sir John Dalrymple as one 'whose mind was inflamed with the love of public good, or all of whose ideas to procure it had a sublimity in them'. Since his own lifetime, Fletcher has been known quite simply as 'the Patriot'.

This universal approval of Fletcher was the more remarkable because he made no attempt to seek popularity. He did not suffer fools, or even contradiction, very easily. He had a quick temper. More than once during the debates in the Scottish Parliament from 1703 to the Union in 1707, he was nearly involved in a duel. When he landed at Lyme as one of Monmouth's chief advisers in the Rising of 1685, he shot dead one of their local supporters in an argument about a horse.

Jonathan Swift never said a good word about any Scotsman, but there was an element of truth, as well as malice, in the comment which he scribbled in the margin of his copy of Macky's 'Characters': 'a most arrogant Conceited Pedant in Politics: cannot indure the least contradiction in any of his Opinions or Paradoxes'.

Fletcher's reputation rested on solid grounds. In a Scottish Parliament which finally succumbed to pressure or bribery, he was one man who could be neither intimidated nor bribed. He had a vision of Scotland that was lucid and passionate. In Macky's words, he was 'a stout pillar for the constitution of the parliament of Scotland', or in Lockhart's 'he shewed a sincere and honest inclination towards the honour and interest of his country. The thoughts of England's domineering over Scotland were what his generous soul could not get away with. The indignities and oppression Scotland lay under gaul'd him to the heart.'

These thoughts he expressed in his pamphlets and speeches in a prose remarkable for its vigour and elegance. He anticipated the Enlightenment in the originality of his thought, the range of his curiosity, his command of language, and even in his zeal for agricultural improvement; but he cannot be accused, as J. G. Lockhart accused the men of the Enlightenment, of allowing his desire for universality to suppress national traditions or ordinary human feelings.

Fletcher, wrote John Clerk of Penicuik, was 'a man of Republican principles'. He meant that Fletcher went further than his contemporaries in advocating the limitation of the Royal prerogative and the assertion of the powers of Parliament, another respect in which he was ahead of his time. It was for him a general principle that investing one man with unlimited powers was a 'mad kind of government'.

In the particular case of Scotland since the Union of the Crowns, it was still worse, because the monarch was an absentee, making or controlling all state appointments in Scotland, but on English advice and in the English interest. Fletcher was not alone in attributing the decline of Scottish trade and prosperity since 1603 to this fact; but it was his speeches which exposed the dilemma with a brilliant clarity. There were two possible solutions. Either Scotland must choose a separate king to succeed Queen Anne or the Royal prerogative must be so limited that effective power passed to the Scottish Parliament. The essentials of this policy were embodied in the Act of Security of 1703, on which Parliament insisted for three tense years, against English pressure and retaliation.

The English Government wanted Scotland to accept the same succession to the throne without conditions, the system which had given them indirect control since 1603. It was only when all attempts to achieve this failed that they decided, in the summer of 1705, to go for an incorporating Union instead. They had their way quite rapidly by a mixture of military intimidation, economic pressure, propaganda, or straightforward bribery, for that period a surprisingly sophisticated exercise of power politics. Fletcher was defeated in the end in Parliament; but he became a legend in the process.

Recently, this legend has been under attack from two sides, or rather deliberate attack from one side and, I think, misunderstanding from another. Trevor-Roper, who is inclined to sneer at most things in Scotland, sneers at Fletcher on the grounds that he advocated slavery, and Tam Dalyell follows him. They echo a passage in Macaulay: 'It is a curious circumstance that this man, the most honest, fearless and uncompromising republican of his time, should have been the author of a plan for reducing a large part of the working classes of Scotland to slavery'.

This is a reference to one of Fletcher's pamphlets, 'The Second Discourse Concerning the Affairs of Scotland; Written in the Year 1698'. In this he draws attention to the miserable state to which Scotland has been reduced by a succession of bad harvests and the disruption of trade by the English wars on the Continent. It is a plea for compassion. Thousands were dying for want of bread. 'Must not every unnecessary branch of our expense, or the least finery in our houses, clothes or equipage, reproach us with our barbarity, so long as people born with natural endowments, perhaps not inferior to our own, and fellow citizens, perish for want of things absolutely necessary to life?'

He goes on to propose a drastic remedy. Slaves in ancient society were happier than people simply allowed to starve to death. This example should be followed, but under conditions which prevented the maltreatment of workers, and provided for them and their families, food, lodging and clothes, education and care in old age. In some ways, it is a sketch of the Welfare State. The future Prime Minister, then an idealistic young socialist, Ramsay MacDonald, responded to this. He wrote in an article on Fletcher in the *Scottish Review* of July 1893: 'No-one who knows the scheme in its entirety, or who is aware of the conditions of labour in Scotland at the time, will regard the proposal as anything but humane – we might almost say enlightened.'

Fletcher was saying nothing new in suggesting that 'vagabonds and sturdy beggars' should be compelled to work. The idea was so commonplace at the time that this part of the pamphlet seems to have provoked no reply from his political opponents and indeed no reaction of any kind. A whole series of Acts of the Scottish Parliament from 1579 to the end of the seventeenth century had made provision for compulsory labour, even if they remained ineffective, except in coal-mining and salt-panning. An article in the *Edinburgh Review* in January 1899, which went into the whole question in some detail, described it as 'the favourite solution during the whole of the seventeenth century of our still pressing problem of the unemployed'. This was not a survival of medieval serfdom, which disappeared in

Scotland earlier than in most countries, but a logical extension of the Calvinist work ethic. John Knox's *First Book of Discipline* said that 'stout and sturdy beggars must be compelled to work'. The work of Francis Hutcheson (1694–1747) was one of the foundations of the Scottish school of philosophy and of the Scottish Enlightenment. He is described in the *Edinburgh Review* article as 'a most ardent and enlightened advocate of freedom', but in his *System of Moral Philosophy* he also proposed the 'perpetual slavery' of 'idle vagabonds'.

To a point, therefore, Fletcher was following the accepted attitude of his time in proposing a desperate remedy for a desperate problem, long before unemployment insurance and the Welfare State were within the remote realms of possibility or imagination. What was new about his approach was his compassion and his concern for the well-being, education, health and provision for the old age of the poor. In any case, the proposal for compulsory labour was not one of Fletcher's favourite themes. It occurs only in this one pamphlet, and some passages may have been written in a spirit of Swiftian irony.

The second attack on Fletcher is more fundamental because it touches on the constitutional questions which are central to his political thought. In an essay published in 1969, T. C. Smout referred to a letter, now in the Scottish Record Office, which Fletcher wrote to a Scottish merchant in Holland in 1689: 'We can never come to any firm setlement but by uniting with England in Parliaments and Traid; as for our worship and particular laws we certainly can never be united to them in this.' Both Smout and William Fergusson have suggested that this means that Fletcher must subsequently have changed his mind when he resisted the Treaty of 1707. Fergusson adds the rider that this was because Fletcher in 1689 still hoped that the revolution of 1688 would lead to a radical constitutional change. There is a much simpler explanation – so simple that it is curious that no-one seems to have remarked on it before.

Fletcher, and other Scottish writers of the time, habitually used the word 'union' in quite another sense from the specialised meaning which it required in 1707. They continued to advocate both 'nearer union' and to oppose the 1707 arrangements which involved the loss of the Scottish Parliament and independence. In this they saw no inconsistency because the word 'union' (as the examples in the OED demonstrate) was generally used in a wide sense to mean the absence of conflict, or any form of association for any common purpose. The word thus carried a stronger suggestion of co-operation between two states than of the incorporation of one in the other.

The distinction is made quite specifically in Fletcher's pamphlets. In the 'State of the Controversy betwixt United and Separate Parliaments', which he wrote in 1706, for instance, he says 'a nearer union will be the only effectual measure to bring these two nations to a peaceable state at home, and to make them formidable abroad'; but he goes on to say, 'the Scots deserve no pity, if they voluntarily surrender their united and separate interests to the mercy of an united parliament where the English shall have so vast a majority'.

This explicit distinction is common in the documents of the time. In the protest against the treaty proposals which the Convention of the Royal Burghs addressed to Parliament in October 1706, for example, they said that they were not against 'an honourable and safe union with England, consisting with the being of this Kingdom and Parliaments thereof'. They were against a British Parliament, 'wherein the mean representation allowed for Scotland can never signify in securing to us the Interest reserved by us, or granted to us, by the English'.

What Fletcher, and others, meant by a 'nearer union' was a relationship established by treaty, which would provide for equitable conditions of trade and for co-operation in matters of defence and foreign policy. The Scottish Parliament would be retained and Scotland would have greater, and not less, independence than they had enjoyed since 1603. 'There are several Interests, and of the greatest consequence too, which are and must be reserved separate to each Nation', Fletcher wrote, '... it seems beyond human Comprehension, how these separate distinct Interests, and Establishments, can be regulated and supported by one Parliament.'

This has been described as a federal arrangement, but in fact the idea was for a much looser structure than is normal in federal states. The Scottish negotiators for the treaty, although appointed by London and not by the Scottish Parliament, made a token attempt to achieve something like this: but they quickly abandoned it in the face of the English refusal even to discuss it. 'They think all the notions about foederal unions and forms a mere jest and chimera', as Mar reported from Whitehall.

Fletcher developed his constitutional ideas in the most celebrated of his works, 'An Account of a Conversation Concerning A Right Regulation of Governments', published in 1704. They were not limited to Scotland and England but included the whole of Europe. He argued in favour of large units for some purposes and small for others. European stability and peace would be more secure if groups of countries were combined together in leagues for their common safety; but within these groups, there should be not one but several centres of government. That would avoid 'the miserable and languishing condition of all places that depend upon a remote seat of Government'.

He saw the essential interdependence of nations. 'The true interest and good of any nation is the same with that of any other. I do not say that one society ought not to repel the injuries of another: but that no people ever did any injustice to a neighbouring nation, except by mistaking their own interest.' Early in the eighteenth century, these ideas were visionary; but it was a vision which now has a very contemporary ring.

The Malachi Episode

(*Blackwood's Magazine*, September 1976)

In February and March 1826, Sir Walter Scott, breaking, as he said, 'a good and wise resolution' not to write on political controversy, sent a series of three long letters to the editor of the *Edinburgh Weekly Journal* 'on the proposed change of the Currency, and other late Alterations, as they affect, or are intended to affect, the Kingdom of Scotland'. They were at once reprinted as pamphlets and ran into several editions. They not only provoked a sensation, debates in both Houses of Parliament and a Government-inspired reply; but, and this must be a rare achievement, actually caused the Government to change its policy. These were the letters which Scott, with his weakness for absurd pseudonyms, attributed to *Malachi Malagrowther*, a character in one of his own novels, *The Fortunes of Nigel*. If the name was facetious, there was no doubt that Scott's purpose was entirely serious. He was concerned not only with the currency question, which was the opportunity and the pretext; but much more with the whole problem of the relationship between Scotland and England, on which he had thought long and felt deeply. It is a subject which is still very much with us in the devolution debate. The *Malachi Letters* deserve to be rescued from Volume 21 of Scott's *Miscellaneous Prose Works*, where they have been hidden for the last hundred years or so in the disguise of ephemeral journalism.

For the Scott bicentenary in 1971, the University of Edinburgh held an important conference at which scholars from many countries read papers on virtually every aspect of Scott's works. As far as I can discover, there was only one reference to Malachi. It was in a paper by Donald Low on 'Periodicals in the Age of Scott'. Dr Low said: '*The Letters of Malachi Malagrowther*, for example ... reveal that he did not always find it easy to combine his support of the Government with his pride in Scotland. The tone of the letters is that of affronted nationalism and political frustration. Yet these powerful feelings are indulged over a subject of limited significance – disagreement as to whether Scottish banks should be allowed to issue their own banknotes. Aggressive emotion is diverted from political actuality to an almost irrelevant area of play.' The first two of these sentences make fair points; but the others are radically wrong on two, if not three, counts. At the time, Scottish banknotes were not of mere symbolic importance, as they may be now, but an essential form of currency and the only means of credit in Scotland. The question was so politically actual that it provoked an unprecedented response from the whole country. Even so, Scott was concerned more with the wide general implications than with the immediate practical issue alone. All of this is obvious from the *Letters* themselves and from Scott's own comments in his *Journal* and private correspondence. That the only reference in the Edinburgh conference should miss the point so completely, shows how far the *Malachi Letters* have been either forgotten or misunderstood.

Scott sat down to write the first *Malachi Letter* on 18th February 1826, and with his usual dispatch (it is forty-two printed pages long) finished it next morning. This was a month, almost to the day, from 'the awful 17th January', when there was no longer any doubt about the collapse of his own financial affairs. The irony was not lost on Scott: 'Whimsical enough that when I was trying to animate Scotland against the currency bill, John Gibson brought me the deed of trust, assigning my whole estate to be subscribed by me; so that I am turning patriot, and taking charge of the affairs of the country, on the very day I was proclaiming myself incapable of managing my own.' The two events, the public and the personal, were connected.

Scott's misfortunes were one incident among thousands in a general crash of the London money market after a period of wild speculation. The Government's proposal which provoked the *Malachi Letters* was a response to this situation. They hoped to impose restraint by forbidding the banks to issue notes of less than £5. This might have been sensible enough in England, where provincial banks had a poor record for stability and issued notes of only local validity. It would have been a disaster in Scotland, where the standing and practice of the banks were quite different, and where their notes financed all economic activity. Scottish banknotes were so widely accepted and trusted in Scotland that they had displaced gold, which was hardly to be found north of the Tweed. With this system of bank credit, the Scottish economy had been flourishing. Why did the Government want to disregard the difference in circumstances and upset something which was working well? To Scott it was the last straw, the latest in a series of measures 'to change everything in Scotland to an English model', uniformity for the sake of uniformity, whether it was to the benefit of Scotland or not. He regarded this policy as both insulting and dangerous. It had been disturbing him for years. 'I am certainly serious in Malachi if seriousness will do good,' he wrote to James Ballantyne. 'I will sleep quieter in my grave for having so fair an opportunity of speaking my mind.'

In the first *Letter*, Scott goes straight to what was for him the heart of the matter: 'I own my intention regarded the present question much less than to try if it were possible to raise Scotland a little to the scale of consideration from which she has so greatly sunk.' His impression was that Scotland had been falling into 'absolute contempt' because English Ministers no longer felt it necessary to take Scottish opinion into account. They were very cautious, and rightly so, about making any change in their own laws. Towards Scotland, they had indulged in 'experiment and innovation at our expense, which they resist obstinately when it is to be carried through at their own risk'. They had acted in accordance with the theory that 'all English enactments are right; but the system of municipal law in Scotland is not English, therefore it is wrong'. There was a 'general spirit of slight and dislike manifested to our national establishments, by those of the sister country who are so very zealous in defending their own'.

It had not always been so. In the first half of the eighteenth century, Scotland had been too dangerous to touch, and 'some thought claymores had edges'. Subsequently, Scotland had been protected from interference by her poverty. In spite of this neglect, or perhaps because of it, Scottish prosperity had increased in a ratio five times greater than the English. Now Scotland had become an 'experimental farm', where English politicians sought to extend the 'benefits of their system, in all its strength and weakness, to a country which has been hitherto flourishing and contented under its own'.

The reference to claymores sounds like a threat. When the *Letter* first appeared, Scott prefaced it, as he was fond of doing, with a verse from an old song. This sounded even more threatening:

Out claymore, and down wi' gun,
And to the rogues again.

He dropped this from later editions when he found that it was being taken too literally in Press and Parliament. In fact, he emphatically rejects any thought of force: 'God forbid Scotland should retrograde towards such a state.' No more talk of old military exploits. Rather than this, it would be better to stay in the Union, 'even at the risk of becoming a subordinate species of Northumberland. But there is no harm in wishing Scotland to have just so much ill-nature ... as may keep her good nature from being abused; so much national spirit as may determine her to stand by her own rights, conducting her assertion of them with every feeling of respect and amity towards England'.

It is only at this point that Scott turns to the banknote question. He explains the difference in both the banking system and the commercial needs of the two countries and attacks the absurdity of applying the same measure to both, merely for the sake of uniformity. 'They might as well make a law that the Scotsman, for uniformity's sake, should not eat oatmeal, because it is found to give Englishmen the heartburn ... The nation which cannot raise wheat, must be allowed to eat oat-bread; the nation which is too poor to retain a circulating medium of the precious metals, must be permitted to supply its place with paper credit; otherwise, they must go without food, and without currency.'

Scott then invokes the Treaty of Union in a passage of Swiftlike irony. (He had edited an edition of Swift, and in writing *Malachi* he probably had *Drapier's Letters on the State of Ireland* in mind.) Unless an old man had been dreaming, there was such a treaty and it contained a clause preventing any alteration of Scots Law, 'except for the evident utility of the subjects within Scotland'. If this treaty really existed, it settled the matter.

These are subjects worth struggling for, Scott continues, and the whole of Scotland should rise in protest. In the case of Captain Porteous, the British Government yielded to the voice of the Scottish mob. Surely, they would not show less deference to a reasonable and temperate remonstrance. He returns again and again to 'evident utility' and suitability to Scotland as the standards by which measures should be judged. 'It would be no reason for planting mulberry-trees in Scotland, that they luxuriate in the south of England. The universal opinion of a whole kingdom ... ought not to be lightly considered as founded in ignorance and prejudice.'

The first *Letter* was published on 21st February and had an immediate effect. On the 24th, Scott wrote in his *Journal*: 'Malachi prospers and excites much attention ... The country is taking the alarm; and I think the Ministers will not dare to press the measure. I should rejoice to see the old red lion ramp a little, and the thistle again claim its nemo me impune.' By the 27th, Rosebery was able to tell the House of Lords: 'Men of all parties who had never agreed on any one subject before, were united in this.' To press home the attack, Scott wrote a second *Letter*, published on 1st March. 'I trust to see Scotland kick and fling to some purpose.' The pamphlet edition had to go out uncorrected, and without last-minute additions, to be on the streets of Edinburgh before a public meeting on the afternoon of 3rd March. This was a triumphant success with only one dissenting voice.

In his *Journal*, Scott described the second *Letter* as 'more serious than the first, and in some places perhaps too peppery'. At the start, his language is cool enough, but the temperature rises as he goes on. He begins with tactics. Now that Scotland has been awakened from her 'passive slumber' and 'the heather is on fire', what is the next step? He addresses the Scottish, Irish and English Members of Parliament in turn. The Scottish members should lay aside distinctions of party and unite against the 'foreign enemy'. They should not take part in any public business until the Government abandons the currency bill, and until then attend the House only when they can conscientiously vote against the Government. He asks the Irish to remember that the disregard of her rights which Scotland was suffering today, Ireland might suffer tomorrow. He proposes a league between Scotland and Ireland for joint defence against any such attempt. Scott then turns to the English. 'We ought not to be surprised that English statesmen, and Englishmen in general, are not altogether aware of the extent of the Scottish privileges, or that they do not remember with the same accuracy as ourselves, that we have a system of laws peculiar to us, secured by treaties.' They will surely withdraw when they realise that they are infringing national right.

So far, Scott has been moderate and even generous; but he does not conceal his feelings when he deals with the wider question of the treatment of Scotland by England. He makes a distinction between the treatment of individuals, which is kind and amicable, and of Scotland, which is jealous, overbearing and illiberal. The English attitude is 'all that is yours is ours, and all ours is our own ...'

'There has been in England a gradual and progressive system of assuming the management of affairs entirely and exclusively proper to Scotland, as if we were totally unworthy of having the management of our own concerns ... What are we esteemed by the English? Wretched drivellers, incapable of understanding our own affairs; or greedy peculators unfit to be trusted? On what grounds are we considered either as one or the other?' It was not as though there were any advantage in 'centring the immediate and direct control of everything in London ... That great metropolis is already a head too bulky'. There is strength in diversity. 'Let us remain as Nature made us, Englishmen, Irishmen, and Scotchmen, with something like the impress of our several countries upon each!'

The third *Letter*, published in the next issue of the *Weekly Journal* on 7th March, need not detain us. It is mainly concerned with the practical difficulty of replacing the paper currency by gold. Scott himself did not much like it, and was ready to suppress it, if Ballantyne agreed. Scott felt that he should have put these detailed arguments at the beginning; to state them now was to 'yield up the question, and to fire from interior defences before the outworks were carried'. Evidently, Ballantyne did not agree and one can see why. Even if this *Letter* is something of an anticlimax after the other two, it is still an unusually lively treatment of financial and economic questions.

It is evident even from this short summary, that the *Malachi Letters* amount to a coherent statement of the philosophy of Scottish nationalism, a set of ideas which has been gaining ground in Scotland during the last hundred years or so. This is the doctrine that diversity is preferable to uniformity and centralisation; that Scottish national characteristics are valuable for their own sake and should not be abandoned without good reason; that government should be responsive to local needs and wishes; that the parliamentary and administrative machine in London is overburdened in any case and should refrain from interfering in Scottish affairs. All of these ideas are expressed repeatedly and emphatically in the *Malachi Letters*, and it would be no exaggeration to describe them as the first manifesto of modern Scottish Nationalism.

It is extraordinary, but no one seems to have noticed this, with the possible exception of John Buchan in his admirable life of Scott, published in 1932. At that time, it was too early for anyone to see the contemporary implications of Scott's position; but Buchan saw the value of *Malachi* and realised where Scott stood politically. *Malachi* would repay study, he wrote, both for its 'acute economic thinking' and its 'sane and honourable nationalism'. He described Scott's political faith: 'Its first element was nationalism. He believed firmly in the virtue of local patriotism and the idiomatic life of the smaller social unit. Whenever Scotland was concerned he was prepared to break with his party, with his leaders, and with the whole nobility, gentry, and intellectuality of Britain. "The Tories and Whigs may go be damned together, as names that have disturbed old Scotland, and torn asunder the most kindly feelings since the days they were invented."' Buchan remarked that Scott's opinions on economics were 'singularly up to date'. This is now even more strikingly true of his political views.

Even since Buchan's time, historians have overlooked *Malachi*. In the last thirty years, there have been three general histories of Scotland on a large scale. The most recent and most substantial of these, the *Edinburgh History of Scotland*, does not mention the *Malachi Letters* at all. G. S. Pryde, in *A New History of Scotland*, gives them one sentence. Agnes Mure Mackenzie, notorious among historians for her robust nationalism, has only two. The two historians[1] of the nationalist movement as such do no better. Sir Reginald Coupland has a short passage, but does not comment on the substance of the *Letters*. H. J. Hanham has only a footnote. In all of these brief references, there is no suggestion that *Malachi* was anything more than a fuss about banknotes. The accepted view is that British chauvinism aroused by the Napoleonic Wars nearly destroyed the whole idea of Scotland in the early years of the nineteenth century. Modern Scottish Nationalism is usually said to have begun about the middle of the century, at about the time when the Association for the Vindication of Scottish Rights was formed in 1853. In fact, virtually all the ideas promoted by the Association had already appeared in *Malachi*, nearly thirty years earlier. It is true that Scott stopped short of calling in so many words for the repeal of the Union; but so did the Association. The Home Rule campaign began later as a response to the increasingly active and centralising role of governments. But there is only a very short logical step between the arguments of *Malachi* against London 'management of affairs entirely and exclusively proper to Scotland' and the demand for Home Rule.

Before we go further into Scott's views on the Union, there are one or two theories about his motives in writing *Malachi* which should be considered. There is, first of all, the persistent idea that the *Letters* were fugitive pieces written to please the Scottish bankers. Grierson in his life of Scott blames this theory on John Wilson Croker (of whom more later), who wrote to the Duke of Wellington on 20th March 1826:

> Walter Scott, who, poor fellow was ruined by dealings with his booksellers, and who had received courtesy and indulgence from the Scotch bankers, thought himself bound in gratitude to take the field for them, which he did in a series of clever but violent and mischievous letters.

But this letter only became known when Croker's correspondence was published in 1884. Before then, Cockburn had made virtually the same point in his *Memorials*: 'Scott, tempted by the bankers, came forward … in the new character of a political pamphleteer. Poets may be excused for being bad political economists.' The whole passage is, for Cockburn, strangely ungenerous. He contrives to celebrate the popular response ('It was really refreshing to see the spirit with which the whole land rose as one man') without giving Scott any of the credit. Presumably the Whig reformer did not like to see the Tory Scott assuming the leadership of a popular agitation.

Grierson could have found his source still further back, in Lockhart and in Scott's own *Journal*. In his biography, Lockhart suggested that three motives were involved in *Malachi*, but not all of equal value:

> Scott, ever sensitively jealous as to the interference of English statesmen with the internal affairs of his native kingdom, took the matter up with as much zeal as he could have displayed against the Union had he lived in the days of Queen Anne. His national feelings may have been somewhat stimulated, perhaps, by his deep sense of gratitude for the generous forbearance which several Edinburgh banking-houses had just been

exhibiting toward himself; and I think it need not be doubted, moreover, that the *splendida bilis* which, as the Diary shows, his own misfortunes had engendered, demanded some escape-valve.

On 22nd February, Scott referred in his *Journal* to the republication of the first *Letter* as a pamphlet: 'The Banks are anxious to have it published. They were lately exercising lenity towards me, and it will be an instance of the "King's errand lying in the cadger's gate".' In other words, he did not write to please the banks, but if the *Letters* were incidentally agreeable to them, so much the better. There is plenty of evidence in the *Journal* that so far from expecting to advance his personal interests by the *Letters*, Scott knew from the start that he was putting them at risk. He expected to offend his friends in high places in England, which apart from anything else might damage the prospects of his son, Charles. When Lockhart wrote from London to say that indeed 'the ministers are sore beyond imagination', Scott's reaction was to write the second and stronger *Malachi*. He did not expect gratitude even from the bankers: 'But I foresaw it from the beginning. The bankers will be persuaded that it is a squib which may burn their own fingers, and will curse the poor pyrotechnist that compounded it.'

Later biographers have followed Lockhart in speaking of the therapeutic, escape-valve, effect of the *Letters* in allowing Scott to demonstrate that he had not been defeated by his misfortunes. Again there is supporting evidence in the *Journal* and correspondence: 'On the whole, I am glad of this brulzie, as far as I am concerned; people will not dare talk of me as an object of pity – no more "poor-manning".' But this too was a secondary consequence, not the motive, for writing the *Letters*. 'The impulse', as Herbert Grierson said, 'came from a deeper source.' On this point, the evidence leaves no room for doubt. The deeper source emerges clearly in his letters to his closest friends. To Lockhart: 'What reason on earth can I have to affront all my friends in power but the deep consciousness that there is a duty to be discharged?' To James Ballantyne (in words already quoted, and they are words which Scott meant quite literally): 'I will sleep quieter in my grave for having so fair an opportunity of speaking my mind.' To Lockhart again: 'My heart will not brook ... to leave the cause of my country ... in a state so precarious without doing whatever one poor voice can to sound the alarm.' This duty, this compulsion to speak, arose from, in Lockhart's words, Scott's 'national feelings'.

These feelings were both strong and complex. One element was a deep regret for the Scottish characteristics which had already been lost because of the influence of England, and a fear that this process would continue implacably. This was the impulse behind most of Scott's best work. It could make him, as little else could, drop the outward composure of the Edinburgh lawyer and Man of the Enlightenment. Take one example from Lockhart. In 1806, when Scott was thirty-five, he had been opposing certain proposals for change in the procedure of the Scottish courts at a meeting in the Faculty of Advocates. Lockhart continues:

> ... when the meeting broke up, he walked across the Mound, on his way to Castle Street, between Mr Jeffrey and another of his reforming friends, who complimented him on the rhetorical powers he had been displaying, and would willing have treated the subject-matter of the discussion playfully. But his feelings had been moved to an extent far beyond their apprehension: he exclaimed, 'No, no – 'tis no laughing matter; little by little, whatever your wishes may be, you will destroy and undermine, until nothing of what makes Scotland Scotland shall remain.' And so saying, he turned round to conceal his agitation – but not until Mr Jeffrey saw tears gushing down his cheek – resting his head until he recovered himself on the wall of the Mound. Seldom, if ever, in his more advanced age, did any feelings obtain such mastery.

There is also the other well-known passage in the introduction to the *Minstrelsy of the Scottish Border*, which shows that Scott approached ballads and banknotes in something of the same spirit:

> By such efforts, feeble as they are, I may contribute something to the history of my native country; the peculiar features of whose manners and character are daily melting and dissolving into those of her sister and ally. And, trivial as may appear such an offering to the Manes of a kingdom, once proud and independent, I hang it upon her altar with a mixture of feelings which I shall not attempt to describe.

In addition to this feeling about Scotland, although perhaps to some extent as a rationalisation of it, Scott argued that all change should be approached with caution. 'Hasty and experimental innovations', he says in the first of the *Malachi Letters*, were liable to have 'unforeseen and unprovided for consequences'. At the same time, he was ready to admit that change could often be beneficial. He was receptive, in the spirit of the Scottish Enlightenment, to technological improvement. As Virginia Woolf noticed, Abbotsford was one of the first houses to be lit by gas. Perhaps simply because he was a lawyer himself, or perhaps because he thought that changes in the law were liable to have more complex and unpredictable effects, he was more anxious about legislation than technology. Above all, he was worried about the effect on social stability of the loss of traditional values and ideas. He developed this thought mainly in letters to Lockhart and Croker, where he suggested that the erosion of the Scottish identity would disturb people and provoke a destructive, revolutionary spirit, which would make Scotland a dangerous neighbour. This was the sense of the celebrated remark in a letter to Croker: 'If you unscotch us, you will find us damned mischievous Englishmen.'

Of course, Scott's attitude to change has affinities with political conservatism and defence of class interest. In the last year of his life, when he was worn out by overwork and illness, his panic reaction to the Reform Bill looked very much like a simple response of that kind. Normally he was pulled in opposing directions. His emotional Jacobitism and regret for Scotland's turbulent and feudal past were balanced by respect for Hanoverian peace and progress, his Toryism by affection for the common man, even his nationalism by impulses of post-Napoleonic British chauvinism. As someone has said, the Last Minstrel was also the first Chairman of the Edinburgh Oil-Gas Board. The appropriate reaction to change, the resolution of conflict, were the constant preoccupations of both the Enlightenment and of the major Waverley novels. These conflicts, between the emotional and the rational, the romantic and the Augustan, the past and the future, were involved in almost everything that Scott thought and wrote. No simple, unqualified statement about any of his attitudes is therefore likely to be found adequate. Scott himself was perfectly conscious of the tension: 'It is difficult to steer betwixt the natural impulse of one's national feelings setting in one direction, and the prudent regard to the interests of the empire and its internal peace and quiet, recommending less vehement expression. I will endeavour to keep sight of both. But were my own interests alone concerned, d—n me but I would give it them hot!'

Scott's attitude to the Union is no exception, and no less subject to internal conflict. Strangely enough, a tradition has grown up, repeated uncritically from writer to writer, and bolstered by selective quotation, that this is one case where Scott's views were simple, definite, and all of one piece. This accepted wisdom is paradoxical: that Scott was at the same time an intense Scottish patriot and a strong supporter of the Union. Both Coupland and Hanham say as much, although with very little in the way of supporting evidence. Often Bailie Nicol Jarvie is called as a witness, as if Scott's opinions could be deduced from the words of one of his characters: '"Now, since St Mungo catched herrings i' the Clyde, what was ever like to gar us flourish like the sugar and tobacco trade? Will onybody tell me that, and grumble at the treaty that opened us a road west-awa' yonder?"' Andrew Fairservice's reply is less frequently mentioned: '"It was an unco change to hae Scotland's laws made in England; and that for his share, he wadna for a' the herring-barrels in Glasgow, and a' the tobacco-casks to boot, hae gien up the riding o' the Scot's Parliament … What wad Sir William Wallace, or auld Davie Lindsay, hae said to the Union, or them that made it?"' Or, for good measure, Mrs Howden in the *Heart of Midlothian*: '"When we had a king, and a chancellor, and Parliament o' our ain, we could aye peeble them wi' stanes when they werena gude bairns – But naebody's nails can reach the length o' Lunnon."'

David Daiches suggested recently that 'where Scott thought he stood on this question in the last part of his life' can be seen in the first chapter of his *Tales of a Grandfather*, where he speaks of 'this happy union'. Scott's views are set out much more explicitly in the three chapters (60–62) which deal with the negotiation of the Union and its consequences. Once again, Scott's feelings break through the even tenor of his prose. The English were 'more desirous to subdue Scotland than to reconcile her', and insisted on an incorporating union. 'The Parliament of Scotland was bribed with public money belonging to their own country.' Phrase piles on phrase: 'The total surrender of their independence, by their false and corrupt statesmen; degradation of their country; loss and disgrace to be sustained by the ancient kingdom which had so long defended her liberty and independence against England.' It all sounds as though Scott was much more in sympathy with Andrew Fairservice than with the Bailie. In fact, his account of the Union in these three chapters suggests very clearly that, like the Scottish negotiators, he would have preferred a 'federative union' with Scotland retaining 'her rights as a separate Kingdom, making as heretofore her own laws, and adopting her own public measures, uncontrolled by the domination of England'. As it was, he thought that 'the interests of Scotland were considerably neglected in the Treaty of Union', although 'all leagues or treaties between nations, which are designed to be permanent, should be grounded not only on equitable, but on liberal principles'. Scott conceded that the Union had 'beneficial effects' in the 'happy change from discord to friendship', and in opening the English colonies to Scottish trade; but these advantages might have been obtained by federation instead of union. He began the *Tales* about a year after *Malachi*, and the two are consistent. He accepted the Union, with regret, in the political conditions of his own time, but hoped that interference in Scottish affairs could be restricted. This was not unrealistic at a time when the activity of governments was very limited. One of the most revealing sentences in *Malachi* is in the passage where Scott abjures the use of force: 'We do not want to hear her prate of her number of millions of men, and her old military exploits. We had better remain in union with England, even at the risk of becoming

a subordinate species of Northumberland, as far as national consequence is concerned, than remedy ourselves by even hinting the
possibility of a rupture.'[2] In other words, Scott disliked the Union, but
he disliked violence even more. Certainly, his romantic imagination
was stirred by the panoply of war. He was never happier than when
he was charging on Portobello sands in the guise of a dragoon, and
his vocabulary ran easily to military metaphors, as in *Malachi* itself.
But if this was one of his conflicts, it was one that was firmly resolved.
He was too much of a realist, and too knowledgeable an historian, to
imagine that any good could come of force. Again and again in the
Tales, he stresses the virtue of the Union in ending conflict between
the two countries. To him, this was its greatest merit. Again, this
arose from the circumstances of his time. He had talked to men who
had taken part in the 'Forty-five, and he had lived through the period
of the French Revolution. The possibility of violence between Scotland and England, or that political agitation could turn to extremity
and bloodshed, were very real to him. They affected his reaction both
to talk of Reform and to the Union. In the pre-Reform House of
Commons, there was no possibility at all that the Union could be
modified or repealed by constitutional means. Agitation against it
was therefore bound to turn to frustration and perhaps to violence.
In these circumstances, the only prudent course was to accept the
Union as an accomplished fact. This is Scott's predominant attitude,
even if he also wanted Scotland to show enough national spirit to
assert her own rights.

Political argument, and political compromise apart, Scott contributed to Scottish national feeling even more powerfully by the
effect of his imaginative writing. No one has ever doubted or disputed
this. He created an image of the Scottish past which welded the
Highlands and Lowlands together in a heightened national consciousness, and made the rest of the world aware of it for the first
time. This is something quite different from the pamphleteering of
Malachi Malagrowther; but there was a common impulse behind
both.

By a curious coincidence, the idea of writing the *Tales of a
Grandfather* was suggested to Scott by the example of a similar book
about English history by the very man who was chosen by the
Government to reply to *Malachi*. This was John Wilson Croker, a
sort of latterday Pepys, who was Secretary of the Admiralty for
twenty-two years and a protégé of Wellington. He attracted notice in
1809, aged twenty-nine and a new Irish member of the Commons,
with a poem on the Battle of Talavera in the metre used by Scott in
Marmion. Scott congratulated him by letter and in a review in the
Quarterly. From then onwards, Scott and Croker kept up a close and

friendly correspondence. It was to Croker that Scott turned when he wanted the permission of the Prince Regent to search for the Scottish Regalia. When Croker was working on an edition of Boswell, Scott supplied him with anecdotes which have now become part of the Johnson legend. Croker was therefore presented with a difficult conflict of loyalties when the Government asked him, as the ablest controversialist at its disposal, to reply to *Malachi*. He acquitted himself with dexterity. His pseudonym, Edward Bradwardine Waverley, was ingenious in itself by implying the reconciliation in his own person of the sympathetic Englishman and the true Scot. It enabled him to make a distinction between *Malachi* and Scott, 'their common parent', and play one off against the other. But his reply to Scott was a *dialogue des sourds*. He started with such opposed assumptions that he hardly came into contact with Scott's arguments at all. He accused Scott of a 'radical error' right from the title-page, which referred to the Kingdom of Scotland. Croker wrote: 'If Scotland were indeed a Kingdom – a separate and independent sovereignty – the question of uniformity and assimilation might be open to some, though certainly not to all, the observations you make.' At the same time, Croker wrote to Scott to assure him that his personal friendship was undiminished, and Scott replied in the same spirit. He had been tempted to hit back, but would not 'endanger the loss of an old friend for a bad jest'.

Scott objected more to a letter written 'at' him by his still older friend, Lord Melville, who, as the Minister responsible for Scottish affairs, felt himself to be the chief target of *Malachi*. Scott's objection was not so much to the content as to the procedure. Melville wrote to his kinsman and Scott's colleague in the Court of Session, Sir Robert Dundas, and asked him to show the letter to Scott – without giving him a copy – and to other Party friends in Scotland. To Scott this seemed, in Johnson's phrase, 'a sign to hate'. The letter itself accused *Malachi* of an 'inflammatory tendency ... gross misrepresentation', and 'insulting taunts and unfounded attacks on the present government'; but it did admit that the arguments on the Scottish banks and paper currency were 'very much to the purpose, and deserving of great consideration'. In his reply, Scott admitted that some passages in *Malachi* ought perhaps to have been modified, 'but I desired to make a strong impression, and speak out, not on the currency question alone, but on the treatment of Scotland generally ... So much for my Scottish feelings – prejudices, if you will; but which were born, and will die with me'.

In the passage in his *Memorials* about the *Malachi* affair, Cockburn says that Scott 'was mentioned in Parliament by his own friends with less respect than one would ever wish to be shown him'. *Hansard* and the Press reports of the time, although admittedly neither is verbatim, suggest that the references were in fact very decorous. Several members criticised Scott on a vulnerable point, his imprudent reference to claymores (although, strangely enough, no one seems to have reacted to his still more provocative phrase, 'foreign enemy'). 'The cry of alarm – the call to resistance – could not have been greater ... there had been some mention ... of the claymore,' said a Mr Tierney. But talk of this kind was put in a more sober light by Robinson, the Chancellor, in his Budget speech: 'I shall look without terror on the flashing of the Highland Claymore, though it be evoked from its scabbard by the incantations of the first magician of the age.' This mingling of criticism and praise is typical of both Parliamentary and Press response.

Scott's prestige was so great that he could not be ignored, and anything that he wrote had to be treated with respect. There would have been agitation against the currency proposals in any case. The first of the petitions against them reached Parliament even before the publication of the first *Letter*; but they became a flood afterwards – from every town and county in Scotland. Faced with such an outcry, and such an opponent, the Government responded quickly. On 16th March, it set up a committee to consider the question, and two months later it was decided to accept its verdict and 'not meddle with the currency of Scotland'. 'The principles, if not the reasoning, of *Malachi Malagrowther* have triumphed ... and are "crowned with complete success,"' said the *Edinburgh Weekly Journal*. Despite Cockburn, no one at the time seems to have had any doubt that the credit was due to Scott. *The Scotsman* in its report of the protest meeting in Edinburgh on 3rd March quoted a speaker: 'The gratitude of the country was due to him if ever gratitude was due to any man,' and added: 'Great applause – all looking towards Sir Walter Scott.' Even the editor of Croker's papers, L. J. Jennings, concludes: 'In the end, the Ministry withdrew its scheme, so far as it applied to Scotland, and the victory rested with the author of *Waverley*'.

And what of the reaction of Scott himself to this famous victory? Lockhart in the Conclusion of his biography says: 'Whenever Scotland could be considered as standing separate on any question from the rest of the empire, he was not only apt, but eager to embrace the opportunity of again rehoisting, as it were, the old signal of national independence; and I sincerely believe that no circumstance in his literary career gave him so much personal satisfaction as the success of *Malachi Malagrowther's Epistles*'. He might have quoted chapter and verse from Scott's own *Journal*: 'The consequence will in time be, that the Scottish Supreme Court will be in effect situated in London. Then down fall – as national objects of respect and veneration – the

Scottish Bench, the Scottish Bar, the Scottish Law herself, and – "there is an end of an auld sang". Were I as I have been, I would fight knee-deep in blood ere it came to that. But it is a catastrophe which the great course of events brings daily nearer ... I shall always be proud of *Malachi* as having headed back the Southron, or helped to do so, in one instance at least'.

John Buchan: 'A Decent Man in the Wrong Party'

(*New Edinburgh Review*, Summer 1982)

In the opening sentences of his introduction to *John Buchan, A Memoir*[1], William Buchan tells us that he is not attempting to write a 'proper biography' of his father. As he rightly says, that is unnecessary because it has already been done superbly by Janet Adam Smith. He describes his book as 'a memoir, a personal recollection'. It is that certainly, because there is some fine evocative writing about how it felt to be John Buchan's son, in his manor house at Elsfield, on family holiday at Broughton in Peeblesshire, or in Vice-Regal splendour in Ottawa. If there were nothing else, this would still be a fascinating book, but it would be incomplete. John was already forty-one before William was born and had much of the most interesting part of his life behind him. William gets over this difficulty by writing not so much a narrative as an extended commentary. He writes, in effect, a series of essays on the diverse phases of Buchan's life and on some, but not all, of the questions that they provoked. He has interesting points to make about such questions as the place of religion in Scottish life at the end of the last century, the nature of the English establishment, idealistic imperialism and, repeatedly, the clash between Scottish and English attitudes.

William Buchan admits quite frankly that he has been provoked into writing the book by the general tone of recent comment on Buchan. Much of it, he says, has been 'both obtuse and dismissive, where not actually malicious'. This forces him, he concedes, into a defensive tone. He is disturbed because the respect with which John Buchan was regarded in his own lifetime has turned sour. 'His ambitions have been judged excessive, his achievements trumpery, his ideals stuffy, his literary work almost an irrelevance.' For this is not one of these books written by a son to purge his resentment, hostility, or contempt for his father. It is the opposite, which is much rarer and no doubt much more difficult to write. William Buchan's love and admiration for his father is apparent on almost every page. He describes him as a 'lovable, fascinating, mysterious man', with a powerful intellect and a formidable capacity for work. It is a rare achievement to write such a book convincingly without ever seeming either boastful or mawkish.

The picture of Buchan which emerges (although the book never makes the point), shows an astonishing resemblance to Walter Scott. Both were born outside the Borders, but both spent part of their childhood there and acquired a strong sense of belonging to it. The imaginations of both were nurtured on Scottish history in general, but on the ballads and traditions of the Borders in particular. They were both proud of their family connections which gave them deep roots in the Scottish past. Both had great stamina and energy, although often in uncertain health, and both were devoted to strenuous country pursuits. They trained in the law, and although enormously prolific writers, neither made literature a full-time occupation. Neither took his own novels very seriously, but both made fortunes from them; and both achieved a remarkable position in the life of their times, largely because of their writing. Buchan himself said that he had the same sort of 'reverence and affection for the plain people' as Walter Scott himself; but both also had a weakness for titles and grand society. Politically, both were their own brand of Tory. In the preface to his *Life of Scott*, Buchan said that it was a book which he was bound to write because he 'had the fortune to be born and bred under the shadow of that great tradition'. He seems almost to have followed in Scott's footsteps.

Of course, there were also great differences. No one would suggest that Buchan as a writer comes into the same league as Scott in originality, achievement or influence. Nor did he reach anything like Scott's towering position in the life of Scotland, despite his peerage and his appointment to the decorative roles of Lord High Commissioner to the General Assembly and Governor General of Canada. But it is not merely a difference of degree. For some reason, it is difficult not to feel that there is some essential difference between the two men, despite the extraordinary coincidence of the similarities. Certainly, the attitude towards them in Scotland is very different. There has never been anything approaching the wholehearted approval for Buchan which Scotland for so long accorded to Scott.

William Buchan suggests that some Scots disapproved of his father simply because he left Scotland to live in England. He makes two points in reply. Firstly, he says very justly that Buchan continued to take an interest in Scotland and wrote about a dozen books on Scottish themes even after he had established himself in his manor house at Elsfield. Secondly, he argues that 'Buchan found the very nourishment he most needed and could best absorb within walking distance of the university town which had first shown him the accessible marvels of the world'.

On the first of these points, William Buchan could have made a stronger case than the one he makes by merely listing the books on Scottish subjects. Two of these, *Montrose* and *Sir Walter Scott,* are among the most valuable and enduring of Buchan's works. In the latter in particular, he broke new ground in understanding not only of Scott's writing but of his views on politics and on the state of Scotland. Buchan's anthology of Scottish poetry, *The Northern Muse,* is one of the most eclectic and sensitive of all such anthologies, and it ranges from Dunbar to MacDiarmid. This is remarkable enough when one remembers that it was published as early as 1924. Buchan was, in fact, responsible for persuading Blackwood's to publish *Sangschaw,* MacDiarmid's first collection of lyrics in Scots, and *A Drunk Man Looks at the Thistle.* He wrote a preface to *Sangschaw* in which he said: 'a new spirit is today abroad in the North, which, as I have said, is both conservative and radical – a determination to keep Scotland in the main march of the world's interests, and at the same time to forego no part of her ancient heritage'. It would be no exaggeration to say that Buchan was one of the earliest protagonists of MacDiarmid's Scottish Renaissance. The broad base of Buchan's approach to Scottish affairs is illustrated too by another point, mentioned by Janet Adam Smith but not by William Buchan, the friendship between John Buchan and the 'Red Clydesiders' in the House of Commons. They regarded him, says Miss Adam Smith as 'a decent man who had got into the wrong party'.

The other side of the coin appears in the second of William Buchan's explanations, Buchan's need to be near Oxford as the original source of his intellectual stimulation. This is curiously at variance with John Buchan's own description of his feelings when he went from Glasgow University to Brasenose: 'The lectures which I attended seemed jejune and platitudinous, and the régime slack after the strenuous life of Glasgow ... I felt that I had been pitchforked into a kindergarten.' On the other hand, it is on a par with John Buchan's dismissal of his education at Hutcheson's Grammar School in Glasgow. He did not mention the school in his entry in *Who's Who* and went so far in his autobiography, *Memory Hold-the-Door,* as to say: 'I never went to school in the conventional sense, for a boarding school was beyond the narrow means of my family'.

It is clear from John Buchan's own account that the active and formative part of his education, and the foundation of his scholarship, was at his school and university in Glasgow. Oxford gave him something quite different, a taste for the lifestyle of the English upper classes and the entrée into the English establishment. Both of these he embraced enthusiastically and to them he owed all the appointments that launched his astonishing career, even his job with the late, lamented Scottish publisher, Thomas Nelson. I suspect that through-

out his life, and perhaps increasingly as he grew older, he also felt the
contrary pull of the Scottish and Calvinist traditions in which he grew
up. There are hints of this throughout William Buchan's book,
particularly in the references to John Buchan's mother. Buchan was
very close to her throughout his life, for she survived until about two
years before his death. She did not approve of his slipping into English
ways and his departure from the Romano-Scottish ideal of *severitas*,
high endeavour and plain living. Buchan's children, with their
English habits and English voices, were uncomfortable with her. She
is the one member of the family about whom William Buchan is less
than enthusiastic. 'She was adept', he says, 'at creating moral
discomfort over almost any matter, however small.' I suspect that in
voicing her moral disapproval, Mrs Buchan was expressing the sort
of reservation that many people in Scotland have always felt about
Buchan. It was not, as William Buchan supposes, because he went to
live in England; that has been the fate of many good Scots. It was
because of an uneasy feeling that he was wasting his talents and
betraying both his potential and his origins.

There are many signs that Buchan himself shared these misgivings.
His last book was the novel, *Sick Heart River*, which he wrote in the
last few months of his life. 'Thought by many people to be his best',
writes William Buchan, 'it is certainly the most self-revealing.' One
of the characters in the novel is a French Canadian who became
discontented with the poverty-stricken life of his native Quebec. 'In
the city he had occasional glimpses of comfort and luxury, and of a
wide coloured world and these put him wholly out of temper with his
home.' So he went to the United States to make his fortune. Towards
the end of his life he was troubled by disquiet. 'But presently he
realised that the trouble was not nostalgia for his dead boyhood, but
regret for a world which was still living and which he had forgotten.
Not exactly regret, either; rather remorse, a sense that he had behaved
badly, had been guilty in some sense of a betrayal.' Were these
Buchan's own feelings towards the end of his life about himself and
Scotland?

When John Buchan died in Ottawa in 1940, many of his books and
papers were bequeathed to the Douglas Library of Queen's University at Kingston in Ontario. Among them is the typescript of a speech
or article which Buchan seems to have written in the 1930s or shortly
after the formation of the SNP. As far as I know, it has never been
published, but it is an important key to understanding Buchan's
feelings about Scotland. They could perhaps be deduced from his
approval of Walter Scott's *Malachi* letters, but here Buchan is spe-
cific:

Every true Scotsman and Scotswoman should be a Scottish
Nationalist ... We do not want Scotsmen merely to be distin-

guished and prosperous up and down the face of the earth; we want Scotland itself, the home of our race, to be healthy and prosperous, and to retain its historic national character ... We do not want to see Scotland become merely a northern province of England ... We want to save our nationality while yet there is time. If that is the aim of Scottish Nationalists, then there is no stronger Nationalist than I.[2]

William Buchan from his frequent references to Anglo-Scottish tensions evidently realises that his father was deeply affected by them. But he still seems to be as puzzled as he was as a child by the mysterious disapproval of his Scottish grandmother. Perhaps Eton and Oxford distort his vision on Scottish matters. For all that, he has written a delightful and rewarding book, which gives a fresh and indelible picture of John Buchan as a man.

John Mackintosh

(*The Scotsman*, 31 July 1982)

John Mackintosh was 48 when he died in July 1978. It was only 7 months before the Referendum of March 1979 which might have been the culmination of his strenuous campaign of more than 30 years for the devolution of political power. The might-have-beens of history are usually a futile indulgence, but this was one of the most tragic. His early death removed the only leader in the Labour Party in Scotland with the intellectual conviction, dialectical skill and lucidity of argument to explode the emotional confusion deliberately created by the 'No' campaign. He had intended to stand for the Scottish Assembly. It was widely assumed that he would be its first Prime Minister. He was confident that the Scottish people would have no patience with the semantic attempts to downgrade the significance of the Assembly. 'It will call itself a Parliament. The leader will call himself Prime Minister.'

As these two books* abundantly demonstrate, John Mackintosh achieved a standing and influence in our political life which was unique for a back-bench MP. He combined the practice of politics both with academic study and popular exposition. His book *The British Cabinet* is the definitive modern study of British constitutional practice. His broadcasts and newspaper articles carried his ideas outside Parliament and the universities. The selection from his lectures and journalism in the two volumes now before us, make it easy to understand why they were so influential.

Mackintosh's writing is free both of the verbiage and evasion which is the usual stock in trade of the politician and of the ponderous language and sweeping generalisation customary in the comments of the pundits. He is invariably lucid, concrete and precise. He writes with elegance and wit. Almost always, his writing carries the conviction of opinions strongly, even passionately held; but based on rigorous examination of the facts and the strenuous exercise of logical thought. I am constantly reminded in reading Mackintosh of Andrew Fletcher of Saltoun, both in his style and intellectual approach. There can be no higher compliment than that.

In his Introduction, Henry Drucker says that Mackintosh's style

and approach were in many ways 'a product of the Scottish educational system and the Scottish intellectual tradition'. In his autobiographical essay *Forty Years On* (in the Marquand volume) Mackintosh himself says, 'I am grateful for the echoes of Carlyle and the
Scottish worthies of the past with their constant emphasis that
nothing worth doing is ever easy, and that the value of any endeavour
lies as much in the effort made as in the end result.' Mackintosh was,
as he says in the last paper in the Drucker volume, 'an old believer in
the value of rational thought about problems'. He was firmly
addicted to the Edinburgh habit of argument, or *pruritus disputandi*,
as Walter Scott called it.

His Scottish intellectual approach was even more fundamental
than any of these things. He rejected English pragmatism or 'mud-
dling through'. He was convinced that you could get nothing right in
politics or elsewhere unless you had first arrived at a clear philosophy
which established what you were trying to do. 'I believe that the first
requirement of any theory is that it must be logically coherent and
that it must explain current situations and provide a guide for action
which will meet not only our practical problems but those instinctive
feelings we have about the values underlying human life.' So wrote
Mackintosh, consciously or unconsciously reflecting the outlook of
the Scottish Enlightenment, and he continued: 'All through the 1960s
we in Britain tried to reform our institutions without such a philosophy
and the results were confused, inadequate or just trivial'.

As that last quotation suggests, Mackintosh became increasingly
disillusioned both with his own party and with the British political
system. As he wrote in 1977, 'The Labour Party, like the nation of
which it is a part, seems to have lost its way'. His analysis of the system
in *The British Cabinet* had shown that, contrary to the accepted
myth, power had been increasingly concentrated in the hands of the
Prime Minister (what would he have said of the Thatcher Government!) and Parliament had been reduced to a machine for carrying
out the will of the Executive. Part of the answer, he saw in restoring
democratic control through devolution. Originally, as in his book
The Devolution of Power (1968), he saw this as a British-wide
arrangement. This was a blueprint of the sort of proposal which is
now being promoted by the SDP. In 1964 he had thought that most
Scotsmen would accept 'that the general pattern of financial, social
and economic policy must be settled for the whole country in
London'. Gradually, the logic of the arguments and of events moved
him closer to the position of the SNP.

The obituary in *The Times* said of Mackintosh: 'As a keenly
patriotic Scotsman he believed that the country required greater
control over its own affairs. From time to time there was speculation

that his heart was really with the Scottish Nationalists, speculation that was indeed on occasion fanned by his own words'. Drucker, of course, comments on this aspect of the matter and, in particular, draws attention to a statement by Mackintosh in 1977: 'The message from the House of Commons was that if the Scots wanted devolution the only hope of getting it was to vote SNP'. This is a point which Mackintosh made repeatedly. (There are three examples in the book.) The implication is obvious to anyone who, like Mackintosh, thought logically, or, like Mackintosh again, passionately wanted devolution, or, as he preferred to call it, Home Rule or Self-Government.

Drucker also prints an exchange of views between Mackintosh and Stephen Maxwell, in which Mackintosh said that he was inhibited from going all the way with the SNP because he had a sense of dual nationality, British and Scottish. Now there are, of course, two answers to this. In the first place, 'British' implies reciprocity and this has been denied by the English who have never understood the distinction between British and English. Secondly, autonomy or independence does not preclude a secondary or wider loyalty. The Norwegians have not less, but more feeling for Scandinavia since they became independent. The Canadians, Australians and New Zealanders became independent without losing all feeling for the Commonwealth, residual as that institution has become. In any case, as Mackintosh frequently argued, the Scots have stronger reasons and a longer tradition than the English for involvement in Europe, which is an additional reason for the need to regain a distinctive Scottish voice.

Unaccountably, and it is a serious omission from the book, Drucker does not include Mackintosh's fullest statement of his attitude to Scotland, 'The New Appeal of Nationalism', published in *The New Statesman* in September 1974. In this Mackintosh described the 'precise moment and issue' when his own conversion to the nationalist idea occurred:

> For all these reasons a point comes at different times with different individuals when they suddenly wonder if this nationalist idea which they have first ignored and then belittled does not make some sense after all. The precise moment and issue when this reaction occurs varies with the person concerned. For me, it came at an international conference when I had just heard a middle-ranking minister explain the present Government's position. He said that Britain must unilaterally rearrange the Treaty of Accession to the Common Market which had recently been ratified by Parliament. Britain was going to be much poorer than had been anticipated and could not afford her budgetary contributions. Other concessions were also

needed. Till these were granted, Britain would continue to
boycott the European Parliament and, if the concessions were
not adequate, then the Treaty might have to be breached. My
feeling of shame deepened with every word and when the
chairman turned and asked me to speak, almost involuntarily,
I found myself saying: 'I am from Scotland and I must dissociate
myself from all that you have just heard.' As I left, the Parisian
taxi driver said: 'From your accent, I gather you are not French
– where do you come from?' Again, I found myself saying
'Scotland'. 'Ah', he replied, 'I hear it is a beautiful country with
brave people; what a pity you have to cross England to get
there.' I could not but agree.

So nationalism is making converts in many places for many
reasons. It is the answer to so many of the present discontents.
One must hand it to the SNP that their challenge is the central
issue of this election in Scotland. They have forced the other
parties to fight on ground chosen by the SNP: namely, what can
these parties do for Scotland? And anything that they suggest
will always be inadequate, be it more regional economic
advantages or assemblies or a percentage of oil revenues: it will
all be inadequate so long as there is no proper pride in being
British. Only one thing will halt or reverse the onward march
of the SNP and that is a period of government in London which
is really successful so that it ends with a satisfied electorate
eager to vote positively for a party that has once again restored
the feeling that Britain is a successful, worthwhile country to
belong to for those who do have other places where they can go
and other traditions and titles to which they can turn.

John Mackintosh
* Henry Drucker (ed) (1982) *John P Mackintosh on Scotland*; David Marquand (ed)
(1982) *John P Mackintosh on Parliament and Social Democracy*

A Confused Disaster: The Referendum of 1979

(*The Scotsman,* 12 December 1981)

'The Union of 1707 had been an awkward way of doing things,' Trevor Royle wrote in 1977, 'and many Scots still smarted with shame at the nature of the joining together of the two very different peoples.' The shame has been so strong that it has been difficult for us to face the facts and examine dispassionately the nature and causes of the Union. As Hume Brown said, 'by a kind of unconscious instinct, Scotsmen deliberately averted their gaze'.

The Referendum of 1979 is in danger of falling into a similar limbo. We have an embarrassed feeling that we were outsmarted and that we made fools of ourselves on a grandiose scale. In the seventies, Scotland had reappeared as a country to be taken seriously both by Westminster and the world at large. The prospect of the return of even a limited measure of self-government quickened the national life. Optimism was in the air and institutions of all kinds, Scottish and others, were making plans to extend their activities in Scotland. Edinburgh was about to become a real capital again. These hopes were deferred by the Referendum, not because we did not say 'Yes' but because we did not say it loudly enough. Plans were thrown in the waste-paper baskets all over Europe. Westminster decided with a sigh of relief that it no longer had to take Scotland seriously. As someone said at the time, we had snatched defeat from the jaws of victory.

It is not surprising that such a confused disaster should have been followed by an embarrassed silence, and that we turned away once again by unconscious instinct. The hopes and issues of the seventies now seem like another age; they have vanished like snow off a dyke.

This new book*is a valuable contribution to the study of what happened in 1979 and an antidote to the conspiracy of silence; but it is only part of the answer. The editors and contributors are all academic political scientists, and the book has all the strengths and weaknesses of their particular discipline. Its main strength is that it makes a strenuous effort to seek objectivity, and search for the sort of facts which can be measured and preferably displayed in a comparative table. It suffers from the corresponding weakness that the rigorous distrust of polemics and rhetoric, means a concentration on form at the expense of content, or on procedures at the expense of politics. There is a risk that this involves deliberately ignoring the most interesting and important questions, especially as the main focus of the book is on the referendum as a constitutional device.

This technique might have led to an abstract, academic thesis. In fact, the deliberate stripping away of the rhetoric exposes more clearly than ever before the devices of the small group of people in the Labour and Conservative parties who set out actively to frustrate the Scotland Act. Not unnaturally, they have been very quiet since the Referendum, but this book leaves them no hiding place.

First, there was no need for a referendum at all. Since all political parties had fought the previous General Election with a commitment to devolution, and since all public opinion polls since they began had consistently shown a strong majority in favour of it, the Government could not have had a clearer mandate. In any case, the referendum is not part of established British constitutional practice. One had been held in Northern Ireland in 1973 and the only other precedent was the one held by the Labour Government in 1975 over the EEC question, which James Callaghan frankly described as a 'rubber life-raft' to save his party from their internal difficulties. The 1979 Referendum had the same purpose, to reconcile dissident Labour MPs to the policy of their own party. In the particular case of the Scotland Bill, opposition came from a small, but noisy, minority of Scottish members of the party, who opposed the measure on the grounds that it was bad for Scotland, and from a larger group of members from the North-east of England who took the opposite point of view.

Having achieved the concession of a referendum on the issue, the dissidents systematically set about obtaining every possible contrivance to make it difficult for it to win a positive result. The most notorious of these was, of course, the requirement of 40 per cent, not of those voting but of those theoretically entitled to vote.

But the 40 per cent was not all. The government were also forced to concede that there should be an interval of four months between the dissolution of Parliament and the Referendum so as to avoid synchronisation with a General Election which would have made high participation more likely. Contrary to the precedent of 1975, there was no provision for the publication of campaign accounts, no financial aid to the campaigns, no distribution of their leaflets by the Government and no publication of an explanatory leaflet.

This deliberate bending of the rules to favour the 'No' side continued during the campaign itself. Brian Wilson and Tom Dalyell brought a petition to the Court of Session to prevent the IBA going ahead with their programme of party political broadcasts. Andrew

Heron managed to prevent the Church of Scotland issuing a call to vote 'Yes', though the Church had advocated Home Rule for more than 30 years.

All of these contrivances are painstakingly described by the contributors to the book, but they give rather more attention to the activities of a minority in the Labour Party than they do to those of the majority of the Conservative party. This is surprising because, as they point out, the Referendum happened to be held at a time when support for both Labour and the SNP was at a low ebb but for the Conservatives was unusually high. One feature of the book which is valuable for the historical record, is a collection of reproductions of the posters and leaflets issued during the Referendum campaign. The official Conservative Party leaflet emphasises that a 'No' vote would not be a vote against devolution and that in the event of a 'No' majority, they would 'propose the immediate calling of a constitutional conference'.

Two consequences seem to me to follow from these Conservative tactics. In the first place, they made it impossible to know how many of the 'No' votes were a repudiation of the idea of an elected Assembly, and they so confused the issue that they largely deprived the Referendum, and certainly the 'No' votes, of any intelligible significance. Secondly, they probably explain the apparent diminution during the campaign of the long-established strong majority for an Assembly. For the Conservative Party, the Referendum was an opportunity to embarrass the Labour Government by frustrating a major piece of their legislation and perhaps even forcing their downfall.

The authors expose the inadequacies of the Referendum, yet they admit that it will cause surprise that they think that it was a success; but they explain that they mean this only in the mechanical sense that it was found possible to hold it with a substantial degree of public interest and participation. James Kellas in another chapter concludes more realistically that it was ambiguous in its effect and gave no more than 'a particular preference expressed by voters on a particular day'. Few people would dissent from the general conclusion of the book that, if there are to be any more referenda, there must be firm rules in advance of the kind which the opponents of the Scotland Act contrived to prevent on this occasion. It is ironic that the use of a constitutional device which is supposed to give more power to the people should have resulted in the frustration of their clear desire for more Scottish control over Scottish affairs.

This is a book which should be read by everyone concerned with Scottish politics or interested in the referendum as a constitutional device. It deals more in fact than in speculation, but it implies a vast range of salutary lessons. Both as a contribution to the historical record and as a stimulant of clearer interpretation, it is a valuable introduction to the next phase of our still unresolved constitutional problem.

*John Bochel, David Denver, Allan Macartney (eds) (1981) *The Referendum Experience: Scotland 1979.*

Adam Smith and the Thatcherites

(*Glasgow Herald*, 17 September 1987)

When the Thatcher Government first took office, it is said that Sir Keith Joseph sent a reading list of essential books to all the members of the Cabinet and that among them Adam Smith's *The Wealth of Nations* had a prominent place. From many statements of leading Tories, you might think that Smith was their great teacher and prophet and the foundation of their philosophy. Mrs Thatcher even claimed him as the founder of Thatcherism during her recent visit to Scotland. One of the right-wing think-tanks, the Adam Smith Institute, wraps itself in the prestige of his name. All of this is very curious; I wonder how much of Adam Smith any of them have actually read. You cannot read very much without discovering that in very many ways, he is fundamentally opposed to Thatcherite attitudes and practice.

Paradoxically, the Marxists also acknowledge an intellectual debt to Smith and with rather more reason. In the first place, *The Wealth of Nations* was one of the first books to develop at length a theory about the fundamental importance of economic factors in determining human behaviour and the structure of society. Then, his whole analysis was based on what has since been called the labour theory of value which is basic to communist ideology. This is the idea, in Smith's words, that 'labour is the real measure of the exchangeable value of all commodities.' (I/27*). In fact, the very first sentence of *The Wealth of Nations* is: 'The annual labour of every nation is the fund which originally supplies it with all the necessaries and conveniences of life which it annually consumes.'

Smith makes it very clear that his sympathies were much more with the workers than with the owners of land or capital. Some examples. 'A great number of people do not labour at all, many of whom consume the produce of ten times, frequently of a hundred times, more labour than the greater part of those who work.'(I/2) 'No society can surely be flourishing and happy, of which the far greater part of the members are poor and miserable. It is but equity, besides, that they who feed, cloth and lodge the whole body of the people, should have such a share of the produce of their own labour as to be themselves tolerably well fed, clothed and lodged.'(I/70) 'The property which every man has in his own labour, as it is the original foundation of all other property, so it is the most sacred and inviolable.'(I/110)

Of landowners, 'mere country gentlemen' as he calls them (I/362), Smith usually speaks with contempt. Feudal land ownership he describes as a 'barbarous institution' (I/343) and 'landlords, like other men, love to reap where they never sowed'. (I/44) They are the only order of society whose income 'costs them neither labour nor care ... That indolence, which is the natural effect of the ease and security of their situation, renders them too often, not only ignorant, but incapable of that application of mind which is necessary in order to foresee and understand the consequences of any public regulation.'(I/ 230)

His attitude towards the capitalists, or 'merchants and master-manufacturers', as he often calls them, is one of extreme distrust. He does not think that they are ignorant and stupid, like the landowners; but their superiority 'is not so much in their knowledge of the public interest, as in their having a better knowledge of their own'. (I/231) Any proposal for a new law or regulation which comes from them should always be treated with 'great precaution' and 'the most suspicious attention ... It comes from an order of men whose interest is never exactly the same with that of the public, who have generally an interest to deceive and even to oppress the public.' (I/232) For example, they 'complain much of the bad effects of high profits. They are silent with regard to the pernicious effects of their own gain. They complain only of those of other people.' (I/88) For all these reasons, Smith was at the opposite extreme from those who believe that governments should have particular deference for the views and wishes of businessmen. Indeed he thought that: 'The government of an exclusive company of merchants is, perhaps, the worst of all governments for any country whatever'. (II/68)

Since Adam Smith distrusted capitalists so much, it is not surprising that he was highly critical of capitalist society as a whole. 'All for ourselves and nothing for other people, seems, in every age of the world, to have been the vile maxim of the masters of mankind.' (I/ 366) 'The violence and injustice of the rulers of mankind is an ancient evil, for which, I am afraid the nature of human affairs can scarce admit of a remedy. But the mean rapacity, the monopolising spirit of merchants and manufacturers, who neither are, nor ought to be, the rulers of mankind, though it cannot perhaps be corrected may very easily be prevented from disturbing the tranquillity of any one but themselves.' (I/436)

In a letter which Smith sent from his home in Kirkcaldy to a friend

in Denmark he said that his book had made a 'very violent attack ...
upon the whole commercial system of great Britain'. In fact, his
criticism is much more far-reaching than that. He questions the whole
nature and purpose of established authority, law and order: 'The rich,
in particular, are necessarily interested to support that order of things
which can alone secure them in the possession of their own advantages ... Civil government, so far as it is instituted for the security of
property, is in reality instituted for the defence of the rich against the
poor, or of those who have some property against those who have
none at all'. (II/203)

Smith's analysis of capitalism is so devastating that you might
expect that the Tories would be more inclined to suppress *The Wealth
of Nations* than to praise it. It is more damaging to them than
Spycatcher and they are not very tolerant of criticism. Why then do
they wave Smith's name like a banner, when he is so destructive of so
much that they stand for? The answer, of course, lies in the vague
general belief that Smith was an advocate of unbridled abandonment
to market forces. They are appealing, in fact, to Smith's famous
analogy of the 'invisible hand'. This is a passage where Smith argues
that in many cases a man following only his own self-interest is 'led
by an invisible hand to promote an end which was no part of his
intention ... By pursuing his own interest he frequently promotes that
of the society more effectually than when he really intends to promote
it.' (I/400) This sounds like a very comfortable doctrine for the greedy
and unscrupulous; but Smith says only that it applies 'frequently', not
invariably.

This idea of the 'invisible hand' may not sound very convincing,
but it was a sort of shorthand for one of the central themes of *The
Wealth of Nations*. It was a sustained argument in favour of leaving
the economy to work by its own intrinsic laws, or what he called: 'the
obvious and simple system of natural liberty' in which 'every man, as
long as he does not violate the laws of justice, is left perfectly free to
pursue his own interest his own way'. (I/180) The condition on which
this depends is important. Smith was a moral philosopher before he
was an economist, and if we want to discover what he meant by 'the
laws of justice', we have to go to his earlier book, *The Theory of Moral
Sentiments*. Here he makes it clear that he regarded selfishness as a
vice and benevolence as the key to virtue. Anyone who seeks to
interpret *The Wealth of Nations* as a licence for unbridled greed, or
for surrender to market forces without regard to the consequences,
is distorting Smith's intentions. As he said himself of mercantilism,
'they who first taught it were by no means such fools as they who
believed it'. (I/436)

We must also remember, of course, that *The Wealth of Nations* was published in 1776. He was writing at a time when most people were employed in labour intensive agriculture and the new industrial age was only beginning to transform society. Urban conglomerations, mass unemployment, industrial pollution, powerful multinationals and many other such problems were still unknown. Governments had not yet assumed responsibility for the health and welfare of their citizens. Smith notes, for instance, as a simple fact of life that a large part of the children of the workers would inevitably die in childhood because their parents could not afford to feed them. (I/71) In this simpler but harsher world, Smith was bound to take a more restricted view of the role of government than would make any sense in the twentieth century.

The forms of intervention in the economy to which Smith particularly objected have long since disappeared, at least in the form in which they existed in his day. In the first place, they were the vestiges of the medieval guild system intended to reduce competition in certain trades. (Smith observed that Scotland was less oppressive in this respect than any other country in Europe. (I/110) Secondly, he was opposed to mercantilism, under which governments tried to regulate trade to keep the greatest possible stock of gold and silver within their own borders, a belief, said Smith, that national interest 'consisted in beggaring all their neighbours'. (I/436) On the other hand, privately owned monopolies are very much still with us as a result of the privatisation of Telecom and the rest. Smith objected above all to the 'wretched spirit of monopoly' (I/406) which sacrificed the people at large to the selfish interest of the few.

Smith also had strong views on poll taxes which he regarded as 'arbitrary and unequal'. (II/329) They violate the first of his four maxims about taxation which was that all taxes should be related to the ability to pay. (II/307) We might apply two other of his conclusions to the Scottish question. He warns us that 'no nation ever voluntarily gave up the dominion of any province' (II/113); but he observed that the 'liberty to manage their own affairs in the way that they judged was most suitable to their own interest' (II/64) was the reason for the rapid progress of some colonies in the past.

I think that it is clear from these extracts, as it is from everything that Smith wrote, that he was egalitarian, compassionate towards the poor and oppressed, and concerned always with moral principles. These are not the most conspicuous of values among the Thatcherite Tories, but they are all very much part of the Scottish tradition. They are values which Scottish literature has asserted and defended for more than 500 years and which have become instinctive to us. Perhaps this is the main reason for the Scottish rejection of Thatcherism.

*References are to volume and page in the two-volume Everyman's Library Edition.

The Awful Phase

(*The Scots Magazine*, November 1987)

The poet Edwin Muir, in a letter* to James Whyte of 10 September 1931, discussed the contemporary state and future prospects of Scotland. He thought it quite likely that Scotland would ultimately be absorbed 'into a larger spiritual group' (a phrase which he did not explain), and that Scottish literature as such would disappear as well. He then said: 'But the really awful phase is the present one: we are neither quite alive nor quite dead; we are neither quite Scottish (we can't be, for there's no Scotland in the same sense that there is an England and a France), nor are we quite delivered from our Scottishness, and free to integrate ourselves in a culture of our choice.'

Of course, Muir was an Orkney man who never quite felt that he was Scottish and who tended in any case to take a pessimistic view of things. Also, although Scotland in 1931 was already stirring in both politics and literature, it was still an an early stage in the modern revival of both. I do not suppose that anyone writing today would dismiss either the Scottish identity or Scottish literature with quite the uninhibited ease that came naturally to Muir at that time. Even so, I think that there is something in what he said about being 'neither quite alive nor quite dead', neither quite Scottish nor quite anything else. Most people who live in Scotland are conscious, I think, of some degree of tension and confusion over this sort of question.

We are pulled in two opposite directions. Most of the obvious, official and financially powerful forces want to make us British. In the last analysis, it is difficult to distinguish that from English, especially as the English themselves hardly ever make a distinction. The schools do their best to make their pupils speak standard English; such history and literature as they teach is mainly English. The whole apparatus of State propaganda, with the Royal Family as its chief resource, is firmly British or English. So is most of the output of the BBC and of the commercial television channels. The English popular press, and there is nothing more chauvinistically English than that, is fighting hard to increase its penetration of the Scottish market. Most of our political parties and trade unions are British. We have largely lost control of industry and commerce; English multiple stores dominate our shopping streets. There is a powerful internal column in the large number of important jobs in Scotland which have passed into English hands. This applies even to very many jobs, in local government and arts administration for example, which from their nature are supposed to represent or defend a Scottish interest or point of view.

Since the Union of 1707, three institutions which survived more or less intact have sustained the Scottish identity, the Church, the Law and the Universities. They are not as strong as they once were. The Church of Scotland ceased to be the main cohesive force in Scottish society when it split in two at the Disruption of 1843. It has never recovered its old position, partly because of the increase in the strength of the Catholic Church, and partly because life generally has become more secular. Scots Law is increasingly overlaid by modern legislation common to the whole of the United Kingdom. Under the influence of the University Grants Committee, the Universities have been anglicised, demoralised and impoverished.

On the other hand, there are innumerable Scottish institutions, mostly created during the last 100 years or so, which affect almost every aspect of life in Scotland. The most important is the Scottish Office, through which much of the activity of the Government in Scotland is channelled. It may function, as at present, as more of a device to impose the will of Westminster on Scotland than to assert a Scottish point of view. Even so, its existence is a recognition by the Government that Scotland has a separate identity with rights as well as obligations derived from the much violated Treaty of Union. Many other organisations with 'Scottish' in their title are little more than branches or sub-committees of British institutions, but many are completely distinct and autonomous. Among them are some created by their members to assert and expand the Scottish identity. They include the Scottish National Party and such bodies as the Saltire Society and the St Andrew Society. Many of these were founded in the 1930s, within a few years of Edwin Muir's letter to James Whyte and as part of the reaction to the situation of which his letter is a reflection.

The struggle between Britishness and Scottishness is therefore one of great complexity, with the individual buffeted in both directions by all sorts of factors. Sport, especially the two forms of football, is one of the most strident. Oral tradition is less blatant but perhaps more pervasive. It is not surprising that many people find themselves in the 'awful phase' of not being quite sure of their own identity. Some veer between Britishness and Scottishness or try to combine the two; but this does not work very well because they are in many ways incompatible and contradictory.

Does the outcome of this struggle matter either to us or to anyone else? Edwin Muir was ready to await the outcome with detachment. 'I cannot even quite exclude the thought', he said in the same letter, 'that this resolution of the Scottish spirit, its disappearance finally into a larger spiritual group, to which it would inevitably contribute much, may be a consummation to be hoped for.' For my own part, I think that it does matter and mainly for two reasons.

The first of these reasons is the value of diversity for its own sake. Nowadays we are concerned about the survival of species of plant and animal life, and rightly because a species once lost can never be recovered. I think that a variety of the human spirit, a culture or a national identity, whatever you want to call it, is at least as important. In this matter, I find myself on the same side as Sir Walter Scott and T. S. Eliot. The threat of a dull and sterile uniformity was much less obvious in Sir Walter Scott's time and he was probably the first to recognise the danger and write about it, particularly in *The Letters of Malachi Malagrowther* of 1826. 'For God's sake, Sir, let us remain as Nature made us, Englishmen, Irishmen, and Scotchmen, with something like the impress of our several countries upon each! We would not become better subjects, or more valuable members of the common empire, if we all resembled each other like so many smooth shillings.' I do not know if T. S. Eliot had read this passage, but more than 100 years later he wrote something remarkably similar in his *Notes Towards the Definition of Culture* of 1948: 'It is to the advantage of England that the Welsh should continue to be Welsh, the Scots Scots and the Irish Irish … if the other cultures of the British Isles were wholly superseded by English culture, English culture would disappear too'. This is an aspect of a world-wide problem because diversity is everywhere under threat from uniformity imposed from the outside.

The second reason why I think it important that the Scottish identity should survive, is quite simply that it has contributed so much that is valuable to our common civilisation. For some mysterious reason, this small country on the edge of Europe has been remarkably fruitful in invention and good ideas. The American, Harold Orel, was stating a simple fact when he wrote: 'No nation of its size has contributed as much to world culture'. If you want a rival, you would have to look to Ancient Greece, the Jews or the Florence of the Renaissance. Our social attitudes, with our instincts for equality and fairness, are valuable and so also are our intellectual habits with our combination of realism and imagination, our open reception of ideas from wherever they come, our distrust of superficial show, our addiction to effort and our polymathic approach. Of course, we have defects and failings like anybody else, but I do not think that there can be any doubt that there is enough that is desirable in the Scottish

approach to life to make it worth a struggle to cherish and
enhance it.

There is, of course, also a third reason. We want to remain Scots
just because that is what we prefer to be.

Have we advanced or retreated since Muir wrote to James Whyte
in 1931? At that time, I was at school in Edinburgh. Since then, I have
been much abroad with the army and the diplomatic service, although
I came back to Scotland nearly every year for at least a week or two
and I settled back in Edinburgh in 1980. I have therefore been able
to see what has been going on with both detachment and involvement.
When I think back to the 1930s, I have no doubt that there has been
some further erosion of the Scottish identity. Spoken Scots in accent,
vocabulary and idiom has retreated, under the influence, as much as
anything, of television. Where there used to be individual Scottish
shops, there are now impersonal shopping centres run by English
multiples. English social habits have crept in as well. Christmas was
not a holiday for shops and factories in the Thirties. Now it is
universal. It would never have occurred to us to celebrate Guy Fawkes
on 5 November because that was about something which happened
in the English Parliament at a time when we still had our own. That
distinction has now been obscured under the pressure from advertising
and the media to regard everything English as the norm.

These are comparatively trivial matters. In some more important
respects, there have been solid improvements. Scottish self-government
is no longer only an aspiration of a few bold spirits, but of three-
quarters of the population and of all the political parties except one
which is in a small and declining minority. The mere existence of the
SNP focuses attention on Scottish questions and on the case for
independence. Scottish literature, publishing, historiography, the
theatre, painting and the other arts are all flourishing. We are now
equipped with the research, the books, the ideas and the facts as never
before. We are in a better position both intellectually to understand
the Scottish approach to life and politically to assert it. The Scottish
identity can only be safe when we reassume responsibility for our
own affairs. In opinion polls for decades and very clearly in the last
three general elections, the Scottish people have shown that this is
what they want. No government that professes to be democratic,
even if elected by a different electorate, can continue to ignore this
demand indefinitely. I think that we can look forward with confidence.

*See George Bruce and Paul H. Scott (1986) A Scottish Postbag pp 225-26.

The Need for Independence

(*Glasgow Herald*, 6 June 1987)

In some strange way, Scotland has been left aside by one of the great tendencies of the twentieth century, the movement towards self-determination. Two world wars have been fought in defence of this principle. After the first, several European states emerged from the dissolution of the Austro-Hungarian Empire. The second was followed by the massive movement of decolonisation. From the former British Empire alone, 39 countries with a combined population of over 900 million obtained their independence. There has been a steady increase in the number of independent countries. The old League of Nations was founded in 1920 with 41 member countries. When the United Nations was founded in 1945 it had 51 members; it now has 159. The principle of self-determination was embodied in the Charter of the United Nations. It was reaffirmed in 1975 in the Final Act of the Helsinki Conference where it was defined in these terms:

> By virtue of the principle of equal rights and self-determination of peoples, all peoples always have the right, in full freedom, to determine, when and as they wish, their internal and external political status, without external interference, and to pursue as they wish their political, economic, social and cultural development.

The United Kingdom and all other countries of Europe, as well as Canada and the United States, were signatories of that Final Act. They included countries as small as Liechtenstein, Luxemburg, Malta and Monaco, but not Scotland. For the Scottish people are clearly not free, at present, 'to pursue as they wish their political, economic, social and cultural development'. That, I think, is the basic cause of our present malaise. We need self-determination as much as any other people, and have no less right to it.

Many of the countries which have become independent in the last forty years are smaller than Scotland and poorer in natural resources. Most of them had no previous experience of self-government and were critically short of personnel educated for administration or the professions. Scotland, on the other hand, has been exporting trained administrators, teachers, doctors, bankers and engineers for centuries. We have a long history of independent government and can, indeed, claim to have invented the idea of self-determination with the Declaration of Arbroath of 1320. We successfully defended our independence for over 300 years in the longest war in European history. It is therefore very strange that, in the general movement towards self-determination and decolonisation, Scotland of all places should be left behind as a sort of relic of colonialism. In the heyday of the British Empire, when it was the strongest and richest of world powers, Scotland was a partner in the management. We paid a price for this in the neglect of our own affairs and in a disproportionate tribute of blood to the army. In the past, the Empire provided an opportunity for individual Scots to make careers for themselves overseas. Now we have declined into a subordinate position without any compensating advantage. We have less autonomy than the Isle of Man or the Channel Islands. As Secretary of State for Scotland, Malcolm Rifkind is quite right to describe himself as a colonial Governor-General.

Some of the newly independent countries have suffered natural or man-made misfortunes of various kinds, but none of them doubt that they have benefited from independence. None would be willing to give it up. Independence has brought self-respect, the release of creative energy, increased prosperity, new opportunities and an enhanced quality of life. Scotland, with its resources and its educated and skilled population, would benefit even more dramatically.

Control over our own affairs would not automatically mean the solution of our problems, but at least it would give us a chance to begin to tackle them. At present, without a Parliament, we do not even have a mechanism to identify, discuss and face up to the problems. Policy is controlled remotely from London under the direction of a political party which, as in the last two General Elections, may have been overwhelmingly rejected by the Scottish electorate. The Westminster Parliament has little time for Scottish affairs, little knowledge and little interest. There is a devolved administration in the Scottish Office, but it is very limited in its functions and it is not subject to democratic control, other than of this indirect and unrepresentative kind. It would be difficult to imagine a more unsatisfactory constitutional arrangement, or one more calculated to bring about hopelessness, despair and contempt for the political process.

The tendency of the present arrangement is to impose upon Scotland policies which may seem reasonable from an English perspective but are disastrous for Scotland. It may seem advantageous to London to concentrate steel production in the south and therefore to close Gartcosh and run down Ravenscraig. The south-east of England has everything to gain in drawing away control over industry and finance, and the jobs and wealth which they involve, from what they see as the periphery to what they see as the centre. From this point of view, it makes good sense to centralise control over the TSB in London and use the funds accumulated by generations of depositors in Scotland, to expand their business in the south. A Government in London, elected preponderantly by English votes, can be content to preside over a process which relentlessly transfers control and wealth to the south and treats Scotland as a source of oil and a base for nuclear submarines. A Scottish Government, elected by the Socottish electorate, would have a very different set of priorities.

One of the reasons for the concentration of wealth around London, is quite simply that it is the seat of government. This means that the politicians and government departments have to congregate there, but so do all the other organisations that want to be close to the centre of power. This includes the head offices of important companies and the banks, newspapers and broadcasting, the embassies and the representatives of the foreign press and foreign institutions of all kinds. With them come all the services, the shops, restaurants and theatres that make the town more attractive and agreeable for both resident and visitor. All of this has a strong multiplier effect, with the congregation of talented and well-paid people creating congenial company and spreading wealth. Any real capital has these advantages. It was beginning to happen in Edinburgh in the seventies when there was a general expectation that a Scottish Assembly or Parliament was about to be established. Foreign banks and the foreign press started to take an interest. The BBC bought a site for a substantial head-quarters, but it abandoned the idea when the Scotland Act was repealed.

One of the powerful advantages of independence is the stimulus of responsibility, for dependence on the decisions of others is always demoralising. George Malcolm Thomson made the point in a book written as long ago as 1928:

> To be set on her own feet, in the necessity of standing or falling by her own exertions, to have the brutal facts of her national life extricated from their comfortable confusion with English conditions, to have no one but herself to blame and no one but herself to accept responsibility – these are heavy items on the credit side of Home Rule.

Decisions would be taken in Scotland by people who know and care about conditions in Scotland because that is where they live. They have more direct knowledge, a closer involvement with the people effected, a stronger incentive to achieve results. Scotland would become the principal concern of a legislature, not an occasional and grudging sideline. The whole country would be reinvigorated by a sense of common effort. We should have the opportunity to tackle our problems in accordance with our own views and preferences.

These views and preferences which make up the distinctive Scottish approach have made valuable contributions to our common civilisation. The distinctive characteristics of all countries are of value as part of the creative diversity of human life. The loss of any is an impoverishment to the world at large, and particularly of one which has been so prolific in invention, ideas and qualities. Our egalitarianism and compassion, our democratic intellect and respect for learning, our rejection of artificiality and pretention, our internationalism, our whole mixture of characteristics, have produced notable results in the past and can do so again. They are only likely to flourish if they can develop freely and are not suppressed by an imposed uniformity.

At present, the pressures towards imposed uniformity are intense. This is, of course, a world-wide phenomenon, but without a government of our own, we are particularly vulnerable. In spite of recent improvements, our education is still dominated by an Anglocentric view of the world, another relic of imperialism. It is still possible to go through the whole of our educational system and learn almost nothing about Scottish history, languages and literature. This gives the false impression that we have achieved little and that everything that matters happens somewhere else; it is a recipe for breeding an inferiority complex, alienation and despair. Broadcasting and especially television, largely controlled by London, contributes to the same result. Since the 1930s, when the modern renaissance began to gather pace, we have made progress in spite of these impediments. Scottish writing and publishing, the theatre and historical studies have all developed strongly; but any revival must remain fragile as long as we lack the coherent centre for our national life which only our own Parliament and Government can provide. As Donald Dewar once wrote, 'there is a real connection between political power and the survival of a culture'.

The extension of self-determination in the post-war world has been accompanied by the development of international co-operation through organisations such as the United Nations and its agencies and the EEC. Self-determination and international co-operation depend on each other because the component parts of the organisations are the independent status and therefore cannot participate in any direct and identifiable way. This is unfortunate because Scotland could contribute and benefit substantially. We have a great deal to offer in our accumulated skill, experience and habits of thought. Scotland has never been insular but cosmopolitan in outlook and is well disposed to benefit, as in the past, from direct contact with other countries.

The international organisations which have developed since 1945 have been of particular benefit to the smaller countries because they are all based on the principle that all countries should be treated equally and have an equal voice. The first article of the Charter of the UN, for instance, refers to equal rights as well as the self-determination of peoples as fundamental principles. Of course, the Super Powers may still attempt to abuse their military and financial strength. Even so, when these organisations take decisions, all member countries, no matter how small, have votes of equal value. The views and interests of even the smallest have therefore to be taken into account. Until Scotland has asserted its right to self-determination, it has no claim to these equal rights. Within the European Community there is an arrangement for weighted voting on the implementation of agreed policies, but even here the allocation of votes is such that no decision can be made without the assent of at least some of the smaller countries.

Before the United Kingdom joined the EEC, an argument which was used against self-government was that it would deprive Scotland of the advantages of a larger market. Even then, this argument, like others, was more trumped up than real. The distinguished economist, E. F. Schumacher, discussed the question in his book *Small is Beautiful*, first published in 1973:

> What about the absolute necessity of having a large internal market? This again is an optical illusion if the meaning of 'large' is conceived in terms of political boundaries. Needless to say, a prosperous market is better than a poor one, but whether that market is outside the political boundaries or inside, makes on the whole very little difference. I am not aware, for instance, that Germany, in order to export a large number of Volkswagens to the United States, a very prosperous market, could only do so after annexing the United States. But it does make a lot of difference if a poor community or province finds itself politically tied to, or ruled by, a rich community or province. Why? Because in a mobile, footloose society the law of disequilibrium is infinitely stronger than the so-called law of equilibrium. Nothing succeeds like success, and nothing stagnates like stagnation. The successful province drains the life out of the unsuccessful, and without protection against the strong, the weak have no chance; either they remain weak or they must migrate and join the strong; they cannot effectively help themselves.

We need our own government precisely to provide a defence against this sort of drain to the south.

Membership of the EEC has radically changed the nature of the market. An independent Scotland, as a member country with full rights, would continue to operate in the same market as at present, but it would no longer be defenceless against protecting its interests. The EEC provides a large market which is increasingly harmonising trade regulations and removing barriers to the free circulation of goods. It therefore demolishes completely any argument that there might be about the size of the market in which an independent Scotland would find itself. This makes it much easier to achieve independence because it would not disturb present market relationships. It also makes independence more necessary and more urgent because the Council of Ministers of the EEC is increasingly the body responsible for policies which vitally affect our interests. This applies especially to agriculture and fishing, where Scottish interests are different from the English. UK ministers are bound to give priority to English interests and sacrifice those of Scotland whenever there is a conflict. It is essential for Scotland to have her own seat at the Council of Ministers and that means that Scotland has to be as independent as Denmark or any other member of the EEC. Otherwise, we are even further removed from the centre of power than we were before the EEC was established, defenceless at two removes, a periphery of a periphery.

Independent membership of the EEC would strengthen our position immeasurably. Take, for instance, the question of steel. The EEC has a policy of responding to the problem of over-production, but this is intended to preserve the industry of each member country, not to destroy it. The destruction of the Scottish steel industry becomes a real possibility when Britain is the unit and the British company decides to concentrate in the south. Member states have equal rights and the EEC will always respect and advance them. Dependent territories within member states have no direct voice and can be disregarded.

The European Parliament has, so far, little power, but the number of seats allocated to Scotland and to the independent countries of a comparable size, is a good barometer of their relative importance in the eyes of the Community. Scotland, with a population of about 5 million, has 8 seats; Denmark, with about 4 million, has 16.

For all these reasons, I am convinced that Scotland needs independence, a return to normality, like so many other countries in the modern world. Independence is the only course which would give us direct and equal contact with the other countries of the world and the voice which we urgently need in Brussels. In an interdependent world, independence is, of course, a relative term. By it, I mean the same rights and responsibilities of self-government, within a framework of freely negotiated international agreements, as enjoyed by Denmark or any other member of the EEC, no more and no less. There is no good reason why Scotland should be less free than any other country to make her own decisions about all aspects of government, including foreign affairs and defence. This is not 'separatism'. On the contrary, it is the present system, with London interposed between us and the rest of the world, which is the real separatism. With our own government, we could develop a much fairer and more satisfactory relationship with England and other countries, to the mutual benefit of us all.

Scotland, England, the Union and Europe

(*Glasgow Herald*, December 1990)

In a recent article in the *Glasgow Herald* (10 September 1990) Allan Massie said that he thought that I underestimated the English influence on Scottish culture. This surprised me because my view of English influence on Scotland is that it has long been excessive, is increasing and ought to be diminished. This is not because English influence is always bad. On the contrary, there are many admirable things about the English, although usually not the things on which they generally pride themselves. They have a great literature, for example, but their vaunted form of parliamentary democracy is a sham and an absurdity. The most objectionable thing about English influence is quite simply that it is forced on us whether we like it or not. External influence on any country can be very beneficial and stimulating, but generally the essential condition for that to happen is that it is voluntary. Something which we choose because we like the look of it is quite another matter from something imposed, regardless of our own wishes, tastes or interests. In his famous book *Small is Beautiful*, E. F. Schumacher remarked that it is not necessary to be annexed by a country before you can trade with it. The same is true of cultural influence. We could take what we may happen to like from the English example without being subject to their political control.

Of course, the reason why England is in a position to impose itself on us is partly because we share an island in which they are ten times more numerous; but it is mainly because of the strange arrangements which were made in the Treaty of Union of 1707. The Treaty purported to abolish the Parliaments of both Scotland and England and create a new entity, the Parliament of Great Britain. This is a fact which the English prefer to forget as they have always behaved as though the English Parliament simply carried on without change, other than the absorption of a few Scottish members and the extension of its authority over Scotland. They were encouraged in this view by two factors: the absence of any machinery to safeguard Scottish interests and the fact that Scottish membership of the two Houses of Parliament was so small that it could be ignored. Scotland had forty-five members in the Commons, which was about the same as Cornwall. The fifteen representative Scottish Peers in the House of Lords were outnumbered by English bishops alone.

Historians have long had great difficulty in explaining how it was that Scotland came to accept such a poor bargain. This was especially remarkable of a country which was probably the first to evolve the idea of national self-determination and which had defended its national independence against heavy odds for more than 300 years. Historians in the nineteenth century thought that they had found an explanation in trade. They suggested that the Scottish ruling class, against the wishes of the great majority of the people, had deliberately exchanged Scottish independence for access of Scottish trade to England and the colonies. This theory, which is highly implausible when you think about it, still lingers on as the established wisdom on the matter. In fact, a study of the contemporary evidence shows that considerations of trade played a very small part. The Scottish trading interests were opposed to the Union because they saw that they would suffer great damage from the imposition of duties and regulations designed for English conditions, and the unrestrained flood of English goods into the Scottish market. They were right. The Scottish economy was devastated and only recovered, through Scottish efforts alone, towards the end of the eighteenth century.

For a long time, historians clung to their trade theory, with a sort of historical prudery, because it was more palatable than the sordid facts of bribery and military intimidation which did no credit to either side. Now that the Union is no longer a sacred cow and it is probable that it will soon either be abolished or radically changed, there is no need for this polite evasion. The distinguished English historian Christopher Hill, admitted recently that 'Scotland was bribed and swindled into Union with England'. It is now widely accepted that, apart from the bribery and the swindling, the Scottish ruling class surrendered independence largely because the alternative was invasion by Marlborough's army and the imposition of worse terms.

In fact, the Union settlement could have been much worse. Scotland lost her Parliament, and therefore any capacity to legislate for her own needs and in accordance with her own wishes; but virtually everything else was left intact and even guaranteed under the Treaty or in an entrenched Act associated with it. This applied to the Church, the Universities, the legal system and local government. All of these affected the daily lives of the people far more than Parliament and Government did at that time. Schools and welfare provisions, for instance, were mainly in the hands of the Church. The Government only started to intervene, slowly at first and then with increasing momentum, from early in the nineteenth century. Scotland, after centuries of independence, followed by this semi-independence, has developed strong and distinctive traditions. They are not dead yet in spite of all the anglocentralising efforts of the Thatcher administration.

In the early part of this century two distinguished constitutional historians, one English and one Scottish, A. V. Dicey and R. S. Rait, jointly wrote one of the most substantial books ever written on this subject, *Thoughts on the Union between England and Scotland*. They both took the then conventional, and now widely discredited, view that the Union was an act of wise and enlightened statesmanship. Even so, their final conclusion was that the 'supreme glory' of the Union was that 'while creating political unity it kept alive the nationalism both of England and of Scotland'. It is simply untrue, as unionist politicians argue when it suits them, that Britain is a unitary state. It is, and has been since 1707, a clumsy and unsatisfactory association between two nations, in which one of them, Scotland, is in a particularly vulnerable position. The English doctrine of Parliamentary Sovereignty, according to which Parliament can do whatever it pleases, allows Westminster to disregard both the safeguards of the Treaty and the evident wishes of the Scottish people. Our history since 1707 is full of examples.

Of course, much has changed since Dicey and Rait wrote their book. The factors which made the Union more or less tolerable in the nineteenth century have all evaporated. Britain is no longer a model, as people used to believe, of freedom and parliamentary democracy. It is an increasingly intolerant state, riddled with secrecy, patronage and pompous absurdity, with a parliamentary system that allows a Prime Minister, usually elected on a minority vote, to assume virtually absolute power. It is no longer a Great Power with a vast Empire which provided jobs for the boys on a massive scale. It has an economy with endemic problems of inflation and a balance of trade which steadily declines in prosperity in comparison to the other countries of Western Europe.

At the same time, the European Community, to which so many of the English react with distrust and hostility, has many solid attractions for Scotland. The EC makes Scottish independence more necessary, because otherwise we are pushed further to the periphery. It also makes independence easier to achieve as it removes any worry about a small market and customs posts on the Tweed. All international organisations have special advantages for small nations. They curb the excesses and the bullying of larger countries and have a tendency to regard all member states as equal. Even the weighted voting system, which the EC uses for certain decisions, is so arranged that the larger countries cannot take a decision without the support of some of the smaller ones. In 1704 Andrew Fletcher of Saltoun, one of the leading opponents of the Union, looked forward to a Europe of small autonomous states co-operating to preserve peace and promote trade. Nearly 300 years later, such a European settlement is now emerging. Scottish membership of the European Community, 'Independence in Europe', would be a valuable contribution to this process. John Robertson, in a recent article in *Chapman* about Fletcher, reached the same conclusion: 'A separate Scottish presence within the EC, aligning itself with the smaller nations of the community, is thus desirable in its own right, representing a more constructive response to Franco-German predominance than Mrs Thatcher's little England obstructiveness'.

One of the worst effects of the Union was that it cut Scotland off from direct contact with the rest of the world. Before that, Scotland had for centuries been very closely involved in Europe. To this day, our law and our educational system are closer to the European norm than the insular self-sufficiency of England. In a very real sense, Scotland as a full and independent member of the EC would be returning to the associations which served us well in the past.

The pooling of aspects of sovereignty in Europe does not frighten us in Scotland because we should have infinitely more control over our own affairs than we have at present and a say in the evolution of common European policies. At present, we have internally a Government imposed on us, which we have repeatedly rejected at the polls, and no right to participate in European decision making. Luxemburg, with a population of about the same size as Edinburgh and no coastline, has more say in European fishing policy than Scotland which has most of the fish.

In the matter of cultural identity, Europe is much more likely to be supportive than threatening because this is something which all European countries value. European agencies, for example, are already taking a more constructive interest in lesser-used languages, such as Gaelic and Scots, than British Governments are ever likely to do. European influence is beneficial, partly because it is diverse. The same is true of the freedom of movement which allow nationals of any member state to take employment in any other.

On the other hand, the strongest threat to our cultural identity at present is the extraordinary extent to which the top posts in many areas of our national life have been virtually monopolised by immigrants from one country, England. This applies especially to posts which are particularly crucial for the way in which we see ourselves and are seen by others, the arts, the universities, local government, public bodies, even those which are responsible for presenting us to the tourist industry. Many of the people appointed to these jobs are new to Scotland and know very little about our history, literature, attitudes and traditions. They are likely to weaken and confuse our identity. What can be done about this, without curbing that freedom of movement which is desirable in itself and part of the ethos of Europeanism?

In 1988, the Advisory Council for the Arts in Scotland (AdCAS), suggested that the obvious course was to include among the essential qualifications, whenever such posts are advertised, a knowledge of the appropriate segment of Scottish life. You would expect, for example, the director of a major art gallery in Scotland to be familiar with Scottish painting, and the director of a theatre to know about the Scottish acting tradition, the corpus of Scottish plays and have an appreciation of spoken Scots. You would expect a director of tourism to have a deep knowledge and experience of the part of the country that he represents. Curiously enough, there is usually no such requirement. Often it seems that ignorance is preferred.

I think that the explanation lies in a deep-seated sense of inferiority which is a consequence of our historical position and is one of our major problems. In a recent interview, the playwright Chris Hannan, said: 'the Scots still believe in imported culture. They call their own culture parochial and that of others, the true culture'. I think that this is true of some people in Scotland and perhaps that includes many of those responsible for these curious appointments. It is an attitude fostered by our system of education and by most of the media, which concentrates on the English experience, as though everything important always happens there and nothing Scottish is of any consequence. This may not be designed to breed an inferiority complex, but that is certainly the effect. The less people know about our own history and literature, the more likely they are to succumb. In the final analysis it is a result of the fact that we have been deprived of the dignity of responsibility for our own government. A critic writing recently about Neil Gunn noted that he was conscious in Scotland of 'the absence of hope, and of the lacerating self-contempt which is a marked component in the psyche of colonised peoples'.

There is a risk that this is one of these chicken and egg questions. Perhaps we can only free ourselves from this debilitating sense of inferiority when we have the responsibility of independence. But can we have the spirit to achieve independence as long as we are plagued by ideas of inferiority, even if they are false and ill-founded? Fortunately, there are many signs that we are recovering the spirit. We have been remarkable for resilience in the past and we may be again.

References

In Bed with an Elephant

1. Henry Thomas Buckle (1970) *On Scotland and the Scotch Intellect* (Part of his *History of Civilisation in England* 1857 and 1861), ed. H. J. Hanham, p. 31.
2. James Anthony Froude (1873) *History of England from the Fall of Wolsey in the Defeat of the Spanish Armada,* Vol IV, p. 5.
3. *The Declaration of Arbroath* (1970), ed. Sir James Fergusson, p. 9.
4. Robert Burns in a letter to Dr John Moore of 2 Aug. 1787 in *The Letters of Robert Burns (1931)* J. De Lancy Ferguson, Vol I, p. 106.
5. John Hill Burton (1881) *The Scot Abroad,* pp. 364-65.
6. Dugald Steward (1884)*Collected Works,* ed. Sir William Hamilton, Vol I, p. 551.
7. Francis Jeffrey (1808) in his review of Scott's *Marmion* in the April *Edinburgh Review,* Vol XII.
8. John Grierson (1979) 'The Salt of the Earth' in *John Grierson's Scotland,* ed. Forsyth Hardy, p. 33.
9. T. B. Macaulay (1858) *History of England,* Vol IV, pp. 782-83.
10. Sir Walter Scott *Rob Roy,* Chapter 20.
11. John MacQueen (1982) *Progress and Poetry: The Enlightenment and Scottish Literature,* p. 5.
12. Quoted in R. L. Mackie (1958) *King James IV of Scotland,* p. 93.
13. This is discussed in my 1707: *The Union of Scotland and England* (1979), especially Chapter 7.
14. Edward Topham (1776, Facsimile Edition, 1971) *Letters from Edinburgh* 1774-5, p. 55.
15. John Ramsay of Ochtertyre *Scotland and Scotsmen in the Eighteenth Century* (1888), ed. A. A. Allardyce, Vol I, p. 9.
16. David Hume in a letter to Gilbert Elliot of Minto of 22 Sept. 1764 in *The Letters of David Hume* (1932), ed. J. Y. T. Greig, Vol I.
17. Ibid ,Vol I, p. 436, p. 121, Vol II, pp. 309-10, Vol I, p. 255.
18. Adam Smith (1776) *The Wealth of Nations,* Book V, Chapter 1-2, Everyman's Library Edition (1971), Vol II, pp. 247 and 291-294.
19. Adam Ferguson (1767) *An Essay on the History of Civil Society,* ed. Duncan Forbes (1966), p. 59.
20. John Gibson Lockhart (1819) *Peter's Letters to his Kinsfolk,* Vol II, Letter LV, p. 359.

21. Edwin Muir (1936) *Scott and Scotland: The Predicament of the Scottish Writer*, p. 137.
22. John Gibson Lockhart (1837-8) *Memoirs of Sir Walter Scott*, Chapter 15.
23. Sir Walter Scott in a letter to James Ballantyne of 26-27 Feb. 1826 in *The Letters of Sir Walter Scott* (1932-37), ed. H. J. C. Grierson, Vol IX, p. 437.
24. Sir Walter Scott (1826), *The Letters of Malachi Malagrowther* ed. P. H. Scott (1981). See also my *Walter Scott and Scotland* (1981), especially Chapter 7.
25. Ibid., p. 136.
26. Hugh MacDiarmid (1943) *Lucky Poet: A Self-study in Literature and Political ideas*, p. 203.
27. Alexander Murdoch (1980) *The People Above: Politics and Administration in Mid-Eighteenth Century Scotland*, p. 106.
28. As 24, pp. 9-10.
29. John Buchan (1932) *Sir Walter Scott*. Edition of 1961, pp. 209-10.
30. Henry Cockburn *Life of Francis Jeffrey*. Edition of 1872, pp. 151 and 153.
31. Ibid., p. 154.
32. Sir Walter Scott *Journal*. Entry for 24 March 1829. Edition of 1891, p. 570.
33. As 20, p. 356.
34. As 30, p. 153.
35. As 24, p. 4.
36. George Elder Davie (1961) *The Democratic Intellect: Scotland and her Universities in the Nineteenth Century*, p. 337.
37. William Power *My Scotland* (1934), p. 296. Since I wrote this pamphlet, William Donaldson in his book, *Popular Literature in Victorian Scotland* (1986) has produced evidence that the 'native tradition' was not lost but disappeared from books into the pages of the periodical press.
38. Sir Walter Scott in a letter to J. W. Croker of 19 March 1926. As 23, vol IX, p. 472.
39. Edward Gibbon (1932) *Autobiography*, Everyman's Library Edition. p. 81.
40. As 36, pp. 58 and 106.
41. C. P. Snow in a speech in Edinburgh to the International Federation of Library Associations on 4 Sept. 1961. (*Scotsman* 5 September, 1961.)
42. V. H. Galbraith in a speech to the Historical Association of Scotland on 1 March 1944 (*Scotsman* 2 March 1944).
43. James Grant (1880) *Old and New Edinburgh*, p. 110.
44. Henry Brougham in a speech in Edinburgh on 5 April 1825. (*Scotsman* 6 April 1825).
45. Elizabeth Hay (1981) *Sambo Sabib*, p. 111.
46. Edwin Muir (1935) *Scottish Journey*. Edition of 1979, pp. 3-4.
47. Henry Cockburn (1874) *Journal*, Vol II, pp. 31-32.
48. As 21, p. 144.
49. Michael Hechter (1975) *Internal Colonialism: The Celtic Fringe in British National Development*, pp. 64, 73, 80, 81.

50. R. L. Stevenson: 'The Foreigner at Home' in *Memories and Portraits* (1887).
51. As 49, p. 117.
52. As 24, p. 143.
53. T. S. Elliot (1948) *Notes Towards the Definition of Culture*, p. 57.
54. Harold Orel (1981) *The Scottish World: History and Culture of Scotland*, p. 12.
55. H. W. Thompson (1931) *Henry Mackenzie: A Scottish Man of Feeling*, p. 1.
56. J. K. Galbraith in a BBC television programme in 1977.
57. Christopher Harvie (1977) *Scotland and Nationalism: Scottish Society and Politics, 1707-1977*, p. 18.
58. J. A. Froude quoted by Professor Gordon Donaldson in his Inaugural Lecture in the University of Edinburgh, 1964.
59. As 1, p. 395.
60. Eric Linklater (1935) *The Lion and the Unicorn*, p. 130.
61. As 36, p. xvi.
62. C. J. Watson in *Literature of the North* (1983), ed. David Hewitt and Michael Spiller, p. 140.
63. Philip Mairet (1957) *Pioneer of Sociology: The Life and Letters of Patrick Geddes*, p. 68.
64. Tom Scott (1970) in his Introduction to *The Penguin Book of Scottish Verse*, p. 50.
65. Donald Dewar in *The Scottish Debate* (1970), ed. Neil MacCormick, p. 77.
66. As 60, pp. 26-27.
67. *Scottish Resources in Schools*, a Discussion Paper published by the Dundee College of Education for the Consultative Committee on the Curriculum, 1985.
68. James Campbell (1984) *Invisible Country: A Journey Through Scotland*, p. 83.
69. Andrew Dewar Gibb (1950) *Scotland Resurgent*, p. 203.

The Scottish Enlightenment

1. Wm Smellie (1800) *Literary and Characteristical Lives of Gregory, Kames, Hume, and Smith*, pp. 161-62.
2. Harold W. Thompson, (1931) *Henry Mackenzie: A Scottish Man of Feeling*, p.1.
3. Dugald Stewart *Collected Works*, ed. Sir William Hamilton, Vol I, pp. 550-1.
4. T. B. Macauley *History of England*, Vol IV, pp. 782-3.

The Royal Society of Edinburgh

1. Neil Campbell and R. Martin S. Smellie, with a Foreword by Lord Cameron (1983) *The Royal Society of Edinburgh*.

The Malachi Episode

1. R. Coupland (1954) *Welsh and Scottish Nationalism*, H. J. Hanham (1969) *Scottish Nationalism*.
2. This sentence has been quoted inaccurately by Professor Trevor-Roper in *The Times* (28th April 1976) to suggest that it showed that Scott was opposed to Scottish independence. It is obvious to anyone who reads the whole paragraph that it was violence, not independence, which Scott was rejecting.

John Buchan: 'A Decent Man in the Wrong Party'

1. William Buchan (1982) *John Buchan: A Memoir*.
2. There is a photocopy in the National Library of Scotland (Acc 6542; Box 2).